EPITAPHES, EPIGRAMS, SONGS AND SONETS (1567) and EPITAPHES AND SONNETTES (1576)

By George Turberville

FACSIMILE REPRODUCTIONS
WITH AN INTRODUCTION BY

Richard J. Panofsky

SCHOLARS' FACSIMILES & REPRINTS
DELMAR, NEW YORK, 1977

Published by
Scholars' Facsimiles & Reprints, Inc.
Delmar, New York 12054

Printed in the United States of America

Library of Congress Cataloging in Publication Data

Turberville, George, 1540?-1610?
Epitaphes, epigrams, songs, and sonets
and Epitaphes and sonnettes.

Reprint of the 1567 ed.
of Epitaphes, epigrams, songs, and sonets,
published by H. Denham, London;
and of the 1587 ed.
of Epitaphes and sonnettes,
first published about 1575.
I. Turberville, George, 1540?-1610?
Epitaphes and sonnettes. 1977.
II Title.
PR2384.T5E6   1977   821'.3   77-16311
ISBN 0-8201-1303-4

INTRODUCTION

In 1557 Richard Tottel dedicated his influential collection of short poems in English, the *Songes and Sonettes*, "to the honor of the Englishe tong, and for profit of the studious of Englishe eloquence." Like his contemporaries who wrote short verses between 1557 and 1580,* George Turbervile worked to fulfill Tottel's desire for a learned, aristocratic English short poetry. His school training in language and rhetoric armed him for the task. It gave him a method of applying rhetorical devices and literary models to produce the amatory and complimentary verses which were then newly fashionable in high society. Although we must make allowances for clumsy language, distracting meter, and tiresome amplification, we can still find Turbervile an interesting minor poet who is sometimes refreshingly frank and who takes pleasure in the verbal delights and delicate devices of the new Elizabethan poetry.

Turbervile was born probably in 1544 (although some biographical accounts assign different dates), a lesser member of an ancient and noble family, the colorful D'Urbervilles of Thomas Hardy's *Tess*. As was common for gentlemen of slender means who did not wish a church career, Turbervile sought patronage and employment through his talents; his father left him no property, only an annuity of thirteen pounds. He was educated at Winchester College and then New College, Oxford. Like Googe, Gascoigne, and Kendall, in 1562 (see p. 120) Turbervile left the university without taking a degree. He entered one of the inns of court, where he cultivated social graces and made social contacts. There

*Among others, Richard Edwards, Barnabe Googe, Thomas Proctor, Thomas Howell, Isabella Whitney, Hugh Plat, H. D. *(Forrest of Fancy)*, J. C. (ed., *A Poore Knight his Pallace*), Timothe Kendall, Humfrey Gifford, James Yates, and Matthew Grove. George Gascoigne and his imitators George Whetstone and the young Nicholas Breton are transitional and not entirely representative of the earlier poets.

he joined a literary circle which included Edwards, Googe, Arthur Broke, Thomas Twynne, Roger Baynes, and Gascoigne.

Turbervile took his place among these authors as a translator and occasional poet, publishing in 1567 his *Heroides* of Ovid and Mantuan's *Eclogues*.* The *Epitaphes, Epigrams, Songs and Sonets* appeared the same year, a collection of short verses which may have been first published or presented in manuscript a year or two before. In 1568 Turbervile translated the didactic *Plaine Path to perfect Vertue* of Mancinus. He next published, probably in 1574 or 1576, the *Tragical Tales* (surviving in the edition of 1587), verse versions of moral tales from Boccaccio and others which reflected the current interest in Italian *novelle*. To this volume he appended his later collection of occasional verses, the *Epitaphes and Sonnettes*.

The works of Mantuan and Mancinus which Turbervile translated (like Googe's of Palingenius, Naogeorgus, Heresbachius, and Mendoza) were not masterpieces of continental or classical *belles lettres*. They were tracts or humanistic imitations popular (especially Mantuan and Palingenius) in the schools. Translations of such works were aimed at the improvement of middle-class readers who knew no Latin, as part of a program to spread learning beyond the schoolroom. Even the *Heroides* could be used for instructive purposes: mythological, tragic, and epistolary, they present literary subjects with studied rhetorical dignity, and were not considered light poetry.

Although also consciously literary, the short poems of the *Epitaphes, Epigrams, Songs and Sonets* are frankly occasional and social, the *nugae* of a young literary gentleman with court connections. Here are found poems addressed to friends or "answers" to poems by friends, epitaphs, and epigrams; and in the many amatory poems are recorded—though artifically—daily emergencies in a lover's life. "The Authors excuse for writing these and other fancies," which closes the *Epitaphes and Sonnettes*, is

---

*Reprinted in 1937 by Scholars' Facsimiles & Reprints.

valuable for its glimpses into a social world in which love poetry is a necessary ritual. At the same time, it tellingly distinguishes Turbervile's conceptions from the courtly idealism of Castiglione or Sidney. For Turbervile, love is a social game at which even the disinterested must play; love's practitioners desire social reputation, sexual conquest, or other gains; the poet often exaggerates or lies outright. Love is a wordly vanity more than an expression of aulic sensibility. Turbervile portrays himself during these years as studious and retiring, a literary but not an actual lover and a reluctant participant in the court's vanities (see pp. 119-39, 455-58).

In 1568 Turbervile was appointed secretary to Lord Thomas Randolph, and so found himself in the English diplomatic mission to Russia led by Lord Randolph in 1568-69, which successfully negotiated favorable trade privileges. The *Epitaphes and Sonnettes* refers repeatedly to this adventure, which supplied the occasion for many poems to friends and ladies. Typical is a poem which uses the severe Moscow winter as a poignant contrast to the lover's freezing and burning (p. 355). The account of the mission in Hakluyt's *Voyages* (1589) includes three verse epistles from Russia which Turbervile had published in the *Epitaphes and Sonnettes* (pp. 424-444), although the poet's descriptions of Russian homosexuality (p. 425) were deleted. Part of a contemplated longer series on Russian geography, politics, and customs, these interesting, detailed poems make successful journalism out of the conventions of the familiar verse epistle.

Information on the rest of Turbervile's life is sketchy. We find him no longer employed by Lord Randolph after returning to England, and continuing with his literary productions. In 1573 he suffered an attack on his life which left him ill for many months (the "time of troubles" referred to on the title page and in the prefatory poems to the *Tragicall Tales*). We learn from a poem in the *Epitaphes and Sonnettes* (p. 445), first published in 1574 or 1576, that he had just married. The union brought him some prosperity, for our next account shows him a landholder at Shapwick, Dorchestershire. His elder brother was murdered in 1579/80

by a brother-in-law, who was hanged; the case inspired some
ballads and was cited in Anthony Munday's *View of sundry
Examples* (1580). Tubervile occupied his remaining years in
minor services to the state. A late account of him shows that
he knew Arthur Gorges, Spenser's Alcyon in *Colin Clout*. He
may have been that poem's "good Harpalus"; however, the
Spencer addressed in *Epitaphes and Sonnettes* (pp. 358,
364, 429) was almost certainly not the celebrated younger
poet. As for his literary activities, Turbervile was silent
after 1575, when his *Book of Hauking* and *Booke of Hunting*
appeared—although his authorship of the latter is contested.
The date of his death, like his birthdate, is in question, but
1597 (considerably earlier than the 1610 of the *DNB*) appears
probable.

Turbervile was the first English poet to present amatory
poems in a lengthy narrative series, in the *Epitaphes, Epi-
grams, Songs and Sonets*. "The Argument to the whole dis-
course" (pp. 35-36) introduces a sequence of poems which
follow the course of the courting of Pyndara (often "P."
and once "Pandora") by Tymetes. Curiously, however,
these poems do not appear in proper narrative order in the
1567 and 1570 editions that we know, although they can
readily be rearranged to fit the story promised by "The
Argument." They may have been properly ordered in the
presumed prior version of 1565 or 1566. The different moral
verses, the epitaphs, and the epigrams may also have been
grouped together (as the ∉| marks indicating epitaphs in
"The Table" suggest); generic grouping was a common prac-
tice in neo-Latin collections, which Turbervile's title re-
calls. His reasons for removing such an ordering, so that the
collection became in effect a miscellany, are obscure.

Turbervile's story of Pyndara and Tymetes reenacts the
courting of Creseyde by Troilus, their plighted troth, and
the inevitable betrayal. The lovers are often seen as victims
of fortune, while the many poems of their time of plighted
troth become "test cases" for truthfulness and amity. Such
a story is tragic, pathetic, and ultimately moral. It is the
prototypal early Elizabethan love story. Turbervile's note
"To the Reader" (pp. 9-13) interprets these amatory poems
as providing moralistic instances: the poems warn against

love "by meere fiction of these Fantasies," showing what
youthful readers should avoid. It is questionable, however,
whether his note describes a developed theory of a "moral"
amatory lyric, for as we shall see, Turbervile's love poetry
seems primarily a vehicle for literary display.

The best starting point into Turbervile's poetry is through
his practice of literary imitation, which is characteristically
loose and literalistic at the same time. John Erskine Hankins
has shown the great extent to which Turbervile found
models for the amatory poems in *Tottel's Miscellany*, turning
to it instead of to Italian originals. A passage which imitates
Surrey's famous translation of Petrarch's *sonnetto in morte*
42 will indicate the process:

> The hart hath hong his olde hed on the pale:
> The buck in brake his winter cote he flinges:
> The fishes flote with newe repaired scale:
> The adder all her sloughe awaye she slinges.

Turbervile's poem (see p. 249) makes Surrey's pathetic
springtime details into general attributes used in a formal
"proof." Surrey's passage provided materials by which
Turbervile could expand an "original" poem. Another poem
borrows and reworks *Troilus and Creseyde* 5. 547-53 (Turber-
vile used this poem frequently but slighted Chaucer's other
works). Chaucer's natural dialogue becomes in Turbervile
(pp. 158-59) formal and consciously literary; and the missing-
ruby comparison is extended cleverly. Another important
source of passages for reworking was Ovid, Turbervile's
favorite classical poet. Often a passage in Ovid or in *Tottel*
provided the entire structure for a new poem, or suggested
a "plot" for a somewhat different development (see the poem
on pp. 140-41, which uses "Nature that taught my silly dog"
in *Tottel*, and one on pp. 169-71, which reworks Ovid, *Tris-
tia* 4. 6. 1-18). In using a source, Turbervile felt at liberty to
add and to take away and to shift direction and emphasis;
at the same time, he used many specific details literally.
These literary imitations can be variously described: as
shortcuts providing "instant poems" for all occasions, as
opportunities for the exercise of skill with language and
verse mechanics, as literalistic ways of naturalizing a tra-
dition. It is clear that Turbervile's amatory poems do not

make a close study of Italian originals, and they misunder-
stand the ways in which Surrey's and Wyatt's translations
of Petrarch and Seraphino do. In these poems Turbervile's
primary motive, beyond the social, is to show "the queintnes
of [his] quil" (p. 458). This is how he saw Surrey's lighter
works (probably thinking of all of *Tottel* as Surrey's):

> Reproue him not for fansies that he wrought,
> For Fame thereby and nothing else he sought.
> What though his verse with pleasant toyes are fright?
> Yet was his honours life a Lampe of light. [p. 49]

It was easy (and even necessary, given his view of love's
vanity) for Turbervile to appreciate poetic skill while ig-
noring a poem's content. Here he reflects his own view of
Ovid, whose fictions, though often immoral, yet excell in
"pleasant wit" (p. 138), "lincked tales and filed stuff," and
"Noble stile" (pp. 121-22).

The modern reader is likely to find the many epigrams
which appear in little clusters throughout the *Epitaphes,
Epigrams, Songs and Sonets* odd but appealing. These are
the first translated epigrams to appear in quantity in English
poetry, inspiring the fuller collection made by Timothe
Kendall, *Flowers of Epigrammes* (1577), which used directly
some of Turbervile's versions. The epigrams come either
from the *Greek Anthology* or from Latin imitations of it by
Renaissance humanists; Turbervile worked from a Latin
collection made by Janus Cornarius (1529). They are what
Professor Hoyt Hudson in *The Epigram in the English Renais-
sance* (1947), calls epigrams "a la Grecque": they present
some paradoxical happenstance or a brief and stylish com-
ment, usually without direct moralizing. Like the love poems,
the epigrams show Turbervile's interest in popularizing an
exotic mode for English readers. Yet there are ambiguities
in his conception of the type, as moralism and clumsy lan-
guage often obscure the original's effect.

Other instances of modish innovation appear in the col-
lections. The second book uses, again for the first time in so
developed a manner, brief posies which glance backward,
commenting upon the poems they append. Both collections
present poems to various friends, some specific replies to
poems they had written. (The fashion for this, as for much

else in Turbervile, was set by Googe's *Eglogs Epytaphes, and Sonettes* of 1563,* in which can be found all of Googe's poems for which Turbervile wrote replies.) These give the reader a sense of participation in the polite recreations of young literary gentlemen. They display a literary wit based on rhetorical and formal variation in a social context of play. Like the poems paired to replies are other fashionable poetic epistles, mostly giving serious (but see pp. 364-67) advice on moral themes. They resemble sample letters for secretaries, revealing the polite forms of upper-class discourse and a fashionable rhetoric. Again, they only loosely imitate classical examples: the reader might compare Turbervile's poem on the country life (pp. 188-89) to its "source" in *Tottel,* Wyatt's "Myne owne Iohn Poyns," a Horatian satire imitated from Alamanni.

In all of these verses, Turbervile prizes his ability to take off from, expand upon, or condense any text, to gloss any idea, to compose for any occasion. Behind such skills lie school-room exercises in language and rhetoric. Grammar school and lower division university students daily wrote themes and epigrams, imitated literary set-pieces, and paraphrased authors or each other. (These school activities are described in well-known studies by Foster Watson and T. W. Baldwin.) Many exercises involved competition as students vied in the different expression of an idea or argued opposite sides of an issue. An episode in Gascoigne's *Glasse of Gouernement* (1575) shows such an exercise in actual schoolroom use (see 2. 1; 3. 4, 6). The master Gnomaticus assigns a list of precepts on duty to be versified in different ways. One student presents them "adding neither dilatations, allegories, nor examples," while another has "some what more dilated and enlarged everie point." A moral generalization was often assigned for exposition, and this practice is seen in many poems of the period; such are Turbervile's poems on luck (pp. 139-40), death and disease (p. 166), use (pp. 233-35), virtue (pp. 358-59), and moderation (pp. 377-78). Behind all these activities lies schoolroom instruction in *paraphrase* (see Quintilian 10.5 and Erasmus *De*

*Reprinted in 1968 by Scholars' Facsimiles & Reprints.

Copia 1. 9), which trained students in rhetoric and language through the writing of many versions of a given text.

These activities profoundly influenced Turbervile's conception of poetic style. They led him to write with different degrees of amplification and compression. His style is now expansive, piling on words and ideas, and now more brief. Thus his poem on "use" (pp. 233-35) dilates details and arguments in a tiresome manner which Turbervile found eloquent; in contrast, his treatment of "virtue" (pp. 358-59) presents a denser texture. That poems like the latter may appeal to the modern reader while the former do not has led critics to distinguish a "plain" from an "ornate" style in the period's verse. But both kinds result from the same literary theory, one which values rhetorical exercises as means of producing poems.

Also in school, Elizabethan poets learned that literature teaches morality by "praising" virtue and "blaming" vice through examples (see Joan Marie Lechner, *Renaissance Concepts of the Commonplaces* [1962]). This process called for copious citation of instances and sayings, such as the different *exempla* making up the "eleventh method" of Erasmus' *De Copia,* Book II. Turbervile uses them ostentatiously and with little consideration of tone, often in accord with a notion found in rhetorical treatise that a piling-together of rhetorical expressions ("heaping") expresses emotion and conviction ("vehemence") in a speaker:

> We encrease our cause by heapyng of wordes & sentences together, couchyng many reasons into one corner which before were scaterde abrode, to thentent that our talke might appere more vehement—

as it is put in a representative passage from Thomas Wilson's *Arte of Rhetorique* (1553).*

For the earlier Elizabethan poet, school practices thus led to a distinctive conception of poetic wit: to show a virtuoso skill in expressing an idea in different ways; to have a command of apposite rhetorical devices; to apply literary ideas on appropriate occasions. "Gascoignes Memories," five extempore poems each in different form and meter on five

---

*Reprinted in 1962 by Scholars' Facsimiles & Reprints.

different themes supplied by five friends, dramatically demonstrated such skills. A passage in Puttenham's *Art of English Poesie* (2. 10 [11]) claims "great arte," "promptnesse of wit," and a "notable memorie" for the poet who can compose successfully from any first line and in any metrical form, however unusual, which his friends choose to assign him. Also revealing is "a peece of hollydayes exercise" in which Gabriel Harvey's young brother composed short poems on assigned themes and texts, as reported in Harvey's *Three . . . Letters* (1580) to Spenser. In these instances, none far from Gnomaticus' school assignment in Gascogine's play, poetic variables are manipulated obtrusively, as rhetorical "gems" are applied and difficulties of verse mechanics are overcome. Sir Philip Sidney deplores such poets, who use "Art to shew Art, and not to hide Art"; were he a lady, their amatory verses "would neuer perswade mee they were in loue; so coldely they apply fiery speeches." The poets of the eighties and nineties worked to transcend their schooling.

Turbervile's preference for the strong iambics and long lines popular in earlier Elizabethan poetry calls for brief discussion. English long verses were modeled on long lines in Latin in an attempt to create a stately, regularized medium useful for line-for-line translation. Characteristically, Turbervile's units of half-line, line, couplet, and stanza (like Ovid's) are matched by units in his syntax; thus metrical form reinforces rhetoric and language. Turbervile's metronomic, unmodulated iambs also sought strong, regularized effects (see John Thompson, *The Founding of English Metre* [1961]).On the page Turbervile's printers broke his hexameters, fourteeners, and sixteeners at the caesura, beginning again near the left-hand margin without capitalizing the second half-line. (Here and there the printer of *Epitaphes and Sonnettes* erred in making these divisions.) These verses should be read as longer single lines, not as couplets.

Turbervile's short poetry did not remain popular in the 1580s and '90s, although his translations continued to be read to the end of the century (his *Heroides* came out in six printings and his Mantuan in five). In *Pierce's Supererogation* (1593) Gabriel Harvey grouped Turbervile with Elderton, Gascoigne, Drant, and Tarleton as old-fashioned now that "the winde is chaunged, & there is a busier pageant vpon the stage." An epitaph by Sir John Harington stressed Turbervile's contributions to an incipient English literature and his moral probity:

> When rimes were yet but rude, thy pen endeuored
> To pollish Barbarisme with purer stile:
> When times were grown most old, thy heart perseuered
> Sincere and just, vnstain'd with gifs or guile.

Turbervile himself did not claim to be a first-rate poet. In his preface to the *Tragical Tales* (pp. 334-44) he admitted his inability to translate the rhetorically difficult, elevated style of Lucan. "The Authors Epilogue" to the *Epitaphes and Sonnettes* (pp. 450-55) states that he wrote of "familiar stuffe," not "of former ancient deedes: / Or new deuice but lately wrought, that breatheth yet and bleedes," and that he hoped for acceptance by courtiers, not learned clerks.

Turbervile's lyrics can shed light on the more refined practices to come, if only by being more technically transparent. Spenser and Sidney brought in a more sophisticated dramatic verisimilitude and subtler literary imitation, and they sought a new aesthetic foundation for their art. The later age's fashions grew narrower, however, as sophisticated readers rejected anything too-immediately occasional, too-directly didactic. Increasingly towards the end of the century, schoolmaster and courtier, country gentleman and citizen became separated, isolated; and the same poetry could no longer inculcate morality and also amuse high society. Thus, aesthetic considerations and a higher art and learning created new perfections that could be appreciated only by limited audiences.

The *Epitaphes, Epigrams, Songs and Sonets* are reprinted here from the 1567 edition, the earliest surviving. A later edition (1570) differs only in orthography. The 1570 edition has been reprinted by Alexander Chalmers, *The Works of the British Poets* (London, 1810), vol. 2, and the 1567 by John Payne Collier, *Seven English Poetical Miscellanies* (London, 1867 [1866-1870]), vol. 1, both times inaccurately. The 1929 Yale University dissertation of John Erskine Hankins, "The Poems of George Turbervile" (Xerox University

Microfilms #3706 [1952]) appends a useful introduction and
notes to a modern edition. Much of its introduction appeared
in 1940 as *The Life and Works of George Turbervile* (Univer-
sity of Kansas Publications, Humanistic Series, 25). The
Epitaphes and Sonnettes are reprinted here from the only
surviving edition of 1587. Together with the *Tragicall Tales*
they have been reprinted by Collier (Edinburgh, 1837), and
the *Epitaphes and Sonnettes* are included in Hankins'
dissertation. Hankins' two works are valuable. The reader
should also consult L. G. Black, "Some Renaissance Chil-
dren's Verse," *Review of English Studies* 24 (1973); William
E. Sheidley, "George Turbervile and the Problem of Passion,"
Journal of English and Germanic Philology 69 (1970), and
"George Turbervile's Epigrams from the Greek Anthology,"
Studies in English Literature, 1500-1900 12 (1972); Lloyd
E. Berry, "Hakluyt and Turbervile," *Papers of the Biblio-
graphical Society of America* 61 (1967); and G. K. Hunter,
"Drab and Golden Lyrics of the Renaissance," *Forms of
Lyric: Selected Papers from the English Institute*, ed. Reuben
A. Brower (New York, 1970). I am indebted to these works
for this study.

I am also indebted to the Bodleian Library, Oxford, for per-
mission to reprint from copies of Turbervile's two works in
its collection (shelfmarks Malone 357 and 358). A few sub-
stitutions of poor or missing pages have been made from
the copy of *Epitaphes, Epigrams, Songs and Sonets* in The
Huntington Library, San Marino, California. The Bodleian
copies were formerly in the library of the eighteenth-century
editor and scholar Edmond Malone. In his note on the fly-
leaf of the *Epitaphes, Epigrams, Songs and Sonets*, Malone
has confused the poet with his elder brother, Nicholas (to
whom Turbervile dedicated the *Tragical Tales*), who was
murdered in 1579/80.

RICHARD J. PANOFSKY

New Mexico Highlands University
Las Vegas, New Mexico
July, 1977

I dittie of M. Turbervile murthered, and
the Morgan that murthered him, with a
letter of the sayd Morgan to his mother
and another to his sister Turbervile;
entred on the Stat.rs Books in 1579 by
R. Jones.

This book was reprinted in
1570 with the same title.

The authour G. Turbervile
was killed by his servant.
see above.

In 1587 was entred on the
Stationers Books "Tragical
Tales by Turbervile in
time of his troubles out of
sundrie Italians" with the
argument and L'envoye to
eche tale." [They were published in
1576]

I suspect he also published some
comick tales; for Harrington men=
tions the Tale of Geneura "a prettie
comical matter, written in English verse some
yeares past, learnedly and with good grace
by Mr George Turbervile." Ita v. Ariosto, 1591.
Turbervile also translated Mantuan's. 1567.

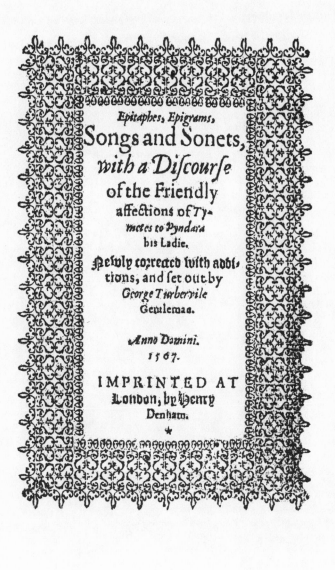

Epitaphes, Epigrams,
Songs and Sonets,
with a Discourse
of the Friendly
affections of Ty-
metes to Pyndara
his Ladie.

Newly corrected with addi-
tions, and set out by
George Turbervile
Gentleman.

Anno Domini.
1567.

IMPRINTED AT
London, by Henry
Denham.

*

2 Cook

Essonia!

¶ To the Right Noble and his
singular good Lady, Lady Anne,
Countesse Warwick. &c. George
Turberuile wisheth increase of
Honor with all good
Happes.

S AT WHAT
time (Madame)
I first published this
fond & slender trea-
tise of Sonets, I made bolde with you
in dedication of so vnworthy a booke
to so worthie a Ladie: so haue I now
also rubde my browe and wiped a-
way all shame in this respect, aduen-
turing not to cease, but to increase
my former follie, in adding moe So-
nets to those I wrote before. So much

*.2.   the

the more abuſing in mine owne con-
ceite your Ladiſhippes patience, in
that I had pardon before of my raſh
attempt. But ſee (Madame) what
preſumption raignes in retchleſſe
youth. You accepted that my firſt of-
fer of honorable and meere curteſie,
and I thereby encouraged, bluſh not
to procede in the like trade of follie,
alwayes hoping for the lyke accep-
tance at your hands, which if ſhould
faile me (as I hope it ſhal not faile)
then ſhould I hereafter not once ſo
much as dare as to ſet pen to paper
for feare of controlment and check,
which howe grieuous it is to a yong
man

man nowe (as it were) but taſting
with his lippe the brim of learnings
fountaine, and ſaluting the Muſes
at the doore and threſholl, neyther
is your Ladiſhip ignorant, and I
my ſelfe preſume to know. Wherfore
as I haue (Madame) by a little in-
larging this Booke, inlarged not a
little my follie : ſo is my humble
ſute to you a little to inlarge your
bounteous curteſie, J meane in well
accepting the increaſe of theſe my
follies, proceding not ſo much vpon
any light affection, as deſire to ac-
knowledge a greater dutie. It ſhall
not be long (I hope) but that my

hande ſhall ſeeke in ſome part the
requitall of your bountie by ſome
better deuiſe, though not more lear-
ned treatiſe. But what ſhoulde I
ſtande vpon termes of ſkill? know-
ing that it is not the worke that your
Ladiſhip doth ſo much regarde as
the Writer, neyther the worthineſſe
of the thing, as the good will and
meaning of the Deuiſer therof, of-
fering his dutie in ſuch wiſe as beſt
aunſweres his abilitie and power.
For as if ſubiectes ſhoulde haue re-
ſpect more to the vnworthineſſe of
ſuch things as they giue their Prin-
ces, than regard the worthie mindes
and

and good natures of their Souereig-
nes in well accepting ſuch ſlender
trifles at their vaſſels handes, they
ſhould quyte be diſcouraged from e-
uer offering the like and ſlender gif-
tes : ſo if I ſhould caſt an eie rather
to the baſeneſſe of my Booke, than
account of your Noble nature and
accuſtomed curteſie in well recey-
uing the ſame: neither ſhould I here-
tofore enboldned my ſelfe ſo farre as
to haue offred you this trifling trea-
tiſe, nor now haue the hart to aduē-
ture anew, although ſomewhat pur-
ged of his former faults and ſcapes.
I cannot leaue to moleſt your noble

eies with ſuruey of my raſhe compi-
led toyes. It may pleaſe your Lady-
ſhip to wey my well meaning hart,
at what time occaſion miniſters you
the peruſing of my booke, and this to
deeme, that deſire alone to manifeſt
my dutie to you, was the onely cauſe
of this my enterpriſe. Which done, I
haue at this time no more to trouble
your Ladyſhip, but ending my Epi-
ſtle, to craue the Gods your happie
preſeruation of preſent Honor, and
luckie increaſe of bleſſed happes in
all your life.

Your Ladiſhips daily Orator
George Turberuile.

HERE HAVE I (Gentle Reader) according to promiſe in my Tranſlation, giuen thee a fewe Sonets, the vnripe ſeedes of my barraine braine, to pleaſure and recreate thy wearye mind and troubled hed withal. Truſting that thou wylte not loth the beſtowing thy time at vacant houres in pervſing the ſame. Waying that for thy ſolace alone (the bounden dutie which I owed the noble *Cownteſſe* reſerued) I vndertoke this

ſlender

slender toyle, and not for anye pleasure I did my selfe in penning thereof. As I deeme thou canst not, so do I hope thou wilt not mislike it at all. But if there be any thing herein that maye offend thee, refuse it, reade and pervse the reast with pacience. Let not the misliking of one member procure thee rashlye to condemne the whole. I stand to thy iudgement, I expect thy æquitie. Reade the good, and reiect the euill: yea rather condemne it to perpetuall silence. For so woulde I wyshe thee to

deale

deale wyth vnworthye Boo-
kes : But aſſuredlye there is
nothing in thys whole ſlender
Volume that was ment amiſſe
of me the Writer, howſoeuer
the Letter goe in thy iudge-
ment that arte the Reader.
Whatſoeuer I haue penned, I
write not to this purpoſe, that
any youthlie head ſhoulde fo-
low or purſue ſuch fraile affec-
tions, or taſte of amorous bait:
but by meere fiction of theſe
Fantaſies, I woulde warne (if I
myghte) all tender age to flee
that fonde and filthie affection
of

of poyſoned & vnlawful loue.
Let this be a Glaſſe & Myrror
for them to gaze vpon : the ſo-
ner may I (I truſt) preuayle in
my perſwaſiō, for that my ſelfe
am of their yeares and diſpoſi-
tion. And as I am not the firſt
that in this ſort hath written &
imployde his time : ſo ſhall I
not be the laſt, that without de-
ſarte (perhaps) ſhalbe miſdee-
med for attempting the ſame.
But let thoſe curious Knightes
caſt an eye to home, and looke
well about whether they them
ſelues are blameleſſe, or as well
worthie

To the Reader.
worthie reproche as others.
This done and my intent con-
sidered, hoping of thy courtesie
I ende, alwayes readie to plea-
sure thee by my pains, wishing
vnto thee, that arte the patient
Reader, as to my self the Wri-
ter and thy very Friend.

George Turberuile.

14

To the rayling Route of
Sycophants.

IF he that once encountred with his Foes
In open field at sound of blasted Trumpe,
Doe dare to yéelde his hewed head to bloes,
And go again to heare ỹ Canons thumpe:
With dreadlesse hart and vnappalled brest
Not fearing till he be by Foes opprest:

If such as earst in cutting of the Surge
By passing to the straunge and forraine lande
Bode bitter blast and scornefull Neptunes scurge,
Dreade not to take the lyke attempt in hande,
But rashly runne like sturdie ventrous Wights
Not fearing wind nor waue when Borias fights:

If these (I say) doe nothing doubt at all
But valiantly giue fresh assault anew,
Not dreading daunger that is like to fall,
As they long earst by proufe and practise knew:
Then why should I of yore that haue assayde
The foxe of Zoylls mouth be ought dismayde ?

Then why should I, like one that fearde to fight
Or neuer crusht his head with Helmets hest,
Now shew my selfe a weake and coward Wight
As long as life or lym vncut is left ?
For Ouid earst did I attempt the like,
And for my selfe now shall I sticke to strike ?

No,

No, no, I march gainst Momus once againe,
My courage is not quailde by cruell Fo,
Though Zoyll did his best my Flag to gaine,
Twas not his hap to haue the Conquest so :
And since it was my luck to scape his might,
I here assaile the Beast with nouell sight.

Thou Sycophant, vnsheath thy shamefull blade
Pluck out that bloudie Fawchon (Dastard thou)
Wherewith thou hast full many a skirmish made
And scotcht the braines of many a learned brow.
Now doe thy worst, I force not of thy stroke,
Thou shalt not bring my neck to seruage yoke.

Though thou affirme with rash & railing iawes
That I inuita haue Minerua made
My other Booke, I gaue thee no such cause
By any dæde of mine to drawe thy blade :
But since thou hast shot out that shamelesse worde,
I here gainst thee vncote my cruell sworde.

I know thou wilt eche worde and sentence wrest
That in this slender Booke of me is writte,
And wilt the same vnto thy sense applie
Hoping for soue thereby to bræde dispite :
And toke what I amisse did neuer meane,
Thou wilt mistake and eke misconster cleane.

Thou wilt the wylie braine that ought is bent
To fowle surprt and spot of fell distrust,
Perswade that here something of him was ment,
And iealous Coales into his bosome thrust,

Thinkng

Thincking thereby thy purpose to aspire
In setting of his boyling breast a fire.
   But as thou art in all thy other dædes
Deseruing no beliefe or trust at all :
Likewise what so from thy bile Iawes procædes,
Is lothsome lie, fowle fitton, bitter Gall.
Beleue him not but reade the Treatise through,
He sowes debate with helpe of hatefull Plough.

   The modest mind that meanes but vertues trade
And shunnes the shamefull shop of bawdie sect,
This spitefull Beast will (if he may) perswade
That these are Toyes: for that he should reiect
And not peruse the meaning of the same,
Thus Zoyll sækes but blot of black defame.

   But thou that vewste this stile with staid brow,
Marke erie worde, vnioint eche Verse of mine,
Thy iudgement I and censure will allow,
Nor once will sæme for rancour to repine :
Thou art the man whose sentence I expect,
I scorne the scoffes of Zoylls shamefull sect.

FINIS.

A.j.   **The**

         Turber-

The Table. 19

A.ij.

The

A.iij.   The

The Table.

To

The

¶ An

The Table.

FINIS.

67

The Lyon ſtout, whome neuer earſt
coulde any beaſt ſubdue :
Here (Madame as you ſe) doth yeelde
both to your Beare and you.

In prayse of the Renowmed Ladie *Anne*, *Ladie Cown-* teſſe Warwicke.

1

WHen Nature firſt in hande did take
The Clay to frame this Cownteſſe corſe
The Earth a while ſhée did forſake,
And was compelde of verie force
With mowlde in hande to flée to Skies,
To ende the worke ſhée did deuiſe.

The Gods that tho in counſell ſate,
Were halfe amaзde (againſt their kinde)
To ſée ſo nére the ſtoole of ſtate
Dame Nature ſtande, that was aſſignde
Among hir worldly Impes to wonne,
As ſhée vntill that day had donne.

First Ioue began : what (Daughter déere)
Hath made thée ſcorne thy Fathers will?
Why doe I ſée thée (Nature) hére,
That oughtſt of dutie to fulfill
Thy vnder taken charge at home:
What makes thée thus abroade to rome?

Diſdainefull Dame, how didſt thou dare
So retchleſſe to depart the grownde,
That is alotted to thy ſhare?
(And therewithall his Godhead frownde.)
I will (quoth Nature) out of hande
Declare the cauſe I fled the lande.

I

I vndertooke of late a péece
Of Claye a featurde face to frame,
To match the courtly Dames of Gréece
That for their beautie beare the name :
But (Oh good Father) now I sée
This worke of mine it will not bée.

Vicegerent since you mée assignde
Belowe in Earth, and gaue mée lawes
On mortall Wightes, and willde that kinde
Should make and marre, as shée sawe cause:
Of right (I think) I may appeale
And craue your helpe in this to deale.

When Ioue sawe how the case did stande
And that the worke was well begonne,
Hée prayde to haue the helping hande
Of other Gods till hée had donne :
With willing mindes they all agrée de
And set vpon the Clay with spée de.

First Ioue ethe limme doth well dispose
And makes a Creature of the Clay :
Next Ladie Venus she bestowes
Hir gallant gifts as best shée may,
From face to foote, from top to toe
Shée let no whit vntoucht to goe.

When Venus had donne what she coulde
In making of hir (carcas) braue
Then Pallas thought shée might be bolde
Among the reast a share to haue,

A pal

A paſſing wyt ſhée did conuaye
Into this paſſing péece of claye.

Of Bacchus ſhée no member had
Saue fingars fine and feate to ſée,
Hir head with Heare Apollo clad
That Gods had thought it golde to bée:
So gliſtring was the treſſe in ſight
Of this newe formde and featurde Wight,

Diana helde hir peace a ſpace
Untill thoſe other Gods had donne:
At laſt (quoth ſhée) in Dians chaſe
Wyth Bowe in hande this Nymph ſhall ronné,
And chiefe of all my Noble traine
I will this Virgin entertaine.

Then ioyfull Iuno came and ſayde
Since yóu to hir ſo friendly are,
I doe appoint this Noble Mayde
To match with Mars his péere for warre:
She ſhall the Cownteſſe Warwick bée,
And yéelde Dianas Bowe to mée.

When to ſo good effect it came
And euery member had hys grace,
There wanted nothing but a name:
By hap was Mercurie then in place,
That ſayde: pray you all agrée
Pandora graunt hir name to bée.

For ſince your Godheads forged haue
With one aſſent this Noble Dame,

B.j.   And

And eche to hir a vertue gaue,
This terme agrǽth to the same:
The Gods that heard Mercurius tell
This tale, did lyke it passing well.

   Report was sommonde then in hast
And willde to bring his Trumpe in hande
To blowe therewith a sownding blast
That might be heard through Brutus lande:
Pandora streight the Trumpet blewe
That eche this Cowntesse Warwicke knewe.

   O sielie Nature borne to paine,
O wofull wretched kinde (J say)
That to forsake the soyle were faine
To make this Cowntesse out of Claye :
But oh most friendly Gods that woulde
Uouchsafe to set your handes to mowlde.

¶The

¶ The Argument to the whole discourse and
Treatise following

BY soddaine sight of vnacquainted shape
Tymetes fell in loue with Pyndara,
Whose beautie farre excelde Sir Paris rape,
That Poets cleape the famous Helena.

His flame at first he durst not to displaye,
For feare he should offended Pyndara.
But couert kept his torments many a daye,
As Paris did from worthie Helena.

At length the coale so fierie redde became,
Of him that so did fansie Pyndara
That fuming smoke did wrie the hidden flame
To hir that farre exceeded Helena.

Which when shee saw, shee seemde with friendly eie
To like with him that lyked Pyndara :
And made as though shee would eftsoone applie
To him, as to hir guest did Helena.

Tymetes (loouing man) then hoped well,
And mooude his sute to Ladie Pyndara :
He plide his Penne and to his writing fell
And sude as did the man to Helena.

Within a while dispayring wretched Wight
He found his Loue (the Ladie Pyndara)
So straunge and coye, as though she tooke delight
To paine hir Friend, as did faire Helena.

B.ij.

Another.

The Argument.

Another time hir cheere was such to see,
That poore Tymetes *hoapte that* Pyndara
*W**oulde yeelde him grace : But long it woulde not bee,*
She kept aloofe as did Dame Helena.

Thus twixt dispaire and hope the doubtfull man
Long space did liue that loued Pyndara,
In wofull plight : At last the Nymph began
To quite his loue as did faire Helena.

Then ioyed he, and cheresull ditties made
In praise of his atchiued Pyndara :
But sone (God wote) his pleasure went to glade,
Another tooke too wife this Helena.

Thus euer as Tymetes *had the cause*
Of ioy or smart, of comfort or refuse :
He glad or griesull woxe, and euer drawes
His present state with Pen as here ensues.

To

To a late acquainted
Friende.

IF Vulcan durſt preſume
　　that was a Gnuffe to ſee,
　　And ſtrake with Hammer on the Stithe
　　a cunning Smith to bæ,
Whoſe chiefe and whole delight
　　was aye to frie at Forge,
And liſten to that melodie
　　Smithes ſorrowes to diſgorge :
If Vulcan durſt (I ſaye)
　　Dame Venus to aſſaile
That was the worthyſte Wight of all,
　　if witneſſe may preuaile :
Then may you muſe the leſſe,
　　though fanſie force me wright
To you a ſecond Venus (Friende)
　　and Helen in my ſight.
For what he ſaw in hir
　　a Goddeſſe by hir kinde,
That I in you (my choſen Friende)
　　and ſomewhat elſe doe finde.
And as that ſielie Smith
　　by Cupid was procurde
To fawne on hir, to whome in fine
　　hæ firmely twas aſſurde :
　　　　　　　　　　B.iy.　　　　　　So

So by none other meanes
   my Senses are in thrall,
But by procurement of the God
   that conquers Gods and all.
Tis hée that makes mée bolde,
   tis hée that willes me sue
To thée (my late acquainted Friende)
   loues torment to eschue.
Not too this day was séene
   that any durst rebell
Or kicke at Cupid Prince of Loue,
   as learned Poets tell:
But rather would with frée
   and vncoacted minde
Applie to please in any case
   what so the God assignde.
What néede I here displaye
   the spoyles by Cupid wonne?
Not I, but you (my Friende) woulde faint
   ere halfe the tale were dónne.
His Banner doth declare
   what harts haue béene subdude:
Where they are all in Sabels set
   with blood and gore imbrude.
Not mightie Mars alone,
   nor Hercules the stoute:
But other Gods of greater state,
   there standing in a route.

                           Then

There may you plainely sée
  how Ioue was once a Swanne,
To lure faire Leda to his lust
  when raging Loue beganne.
Some other when a Bull,
  some other time a showre
Of golden drops : as when he coyde
  the closed Nunne in towre.
Appollos Loue appeares
  and euer will be knowne,
As long as Lawrell leaues shall last,
  and Daphnes brute be blowne.
May brainsick Bacchus brag
  or boast himselfe as frée :
Not I, but Aryadnas Crowne
  shewes him in loue to bée.
Since these and other mo
  that Gods were made by kinde
Might not auoyde that guilefull God
  that winged is and blinde :
Should I haue hope to scape
  by force, or else by flight,
That in respect of those his thralls
  am of so slender might :
As they did yélde to Loue
  for feare of Cupids pre :
Euen so am I become his thrall
  by force of flaming fyre.

         A.iij.   What

What time I first displayde
  mine eies vpon thy face,
(That doth allure eche lokers hart)
  I did the P. imbrace.
And since that time I feele
  within my breast such ioye,
As Paris neuer felt the like
  when Helen was at Troye.
How coulde so barraine soyle
  bring forth so good a Graffe,
To whome the reast that seeme good Corne
  are in respect but Chaffe?
(O God) that Cupid woulde
  vpon thy breast bestowe
His golden shaft, that thou the force
  of lyking loue mightst knowe.
Then should I stande in hope
  and well assured bir,
That thou wouldst be as friendly (P.)
  as I am now to thee.
Whome (till thy friendship sayle,
  and plighted hest doe swerue)
I daunt and bowe by mightie loue
  with hart and hande to serue.
My Senses all take heede,
  and yee my wits beware
That you attentiue be on hir
  and for none other care.

You

You eies that woonted were
  light louing lookes to cast,
I giue conmaundment on hir hue
  that yée be ankred fast.
Mine eares admit no sounde
  ne Womans woords at all:
Be shut against such Syrens Songs
  repleate with lurking gall.
Tongue sée that thou be tyde,
  and vse no wanton stile :
By lawe of Loue I thée consure
  such topes to crile.
Legges looke that yée be lame
  when you should reache a place
To take the vewe of Venus Nymphes
  Pees beautie to deface.
For such a one is shée
  whome I would will you serue,
As to be plaste for Pallas péere
  for wisedome may deserue.
So constant are hir lookes
  and cake as chaste a face :
As if that Lucrece liuing were
  shée Lucrece would disgrace.
So modest is hir mirth
  in erie time and tyde,
As they that prick most nearsse of all
  their shiuerde shafts are wyde.

                              Pause

Pause Pen a while therefore,
  and vse thy wonted meane:
For Boccas braine, and Chaucers Quill
  in this were foyled cleane.
Of both might neither boast
  if they did liue againe:
For P. would put them to their shifts
  to Pen hir vertues plaine.
Yet one thing will I vaunt
  and after make an ende,
That Momus can not for his lyfe
  deuise one iote to mende.
Thus to conclude at length,
  se thou (my Friend) peruse
This slender Verse, till leysure serue
  abrode to bring my Muse.
For then you shall perceiue
  by that which you shall se,
That you haue made your choise as well
  as I by choosing P.

The Louer extolleth the singular
beautie of his Ladie.

Let Myron muse at Natures passing might,
  And quite resigne his pieuish Painters right:
For sure he can not frame hir featurde shape
That for hir face excels the Greekish rape.

Let

Let Zeuxis Grapes not make him proude at all,
Though Fowles for them did skyr against a wall:
For if hœ should assay my Loue to paint,
His Art would fayle, his cunning fist would faint.

Let Praxitell presume with Pensill rude
Base things to blaze the people to delude:
Hir featurde limmes to drawe let him not dare
That with the fayre Diana may compare.

Though Venus forme Apelles made so well,
As Greece did iudge the Painter to excell:
Yet let not that enbolde the Greeke to graue
Hir shape, that beauties praise deserues to haue.

For Nature when she made hir, did entende
To paint a pæce that no man might amende:
A paterne for the reast that after shoulde
Be made by hande, or cast in cunning moulde.

The Louer declareth how first he was ta-
ken and enamoured by the sight
of his Ladie.

Hauing neuer earst
the craft of Cupid tride,
Ne yet the wylie wanton wayes
of Ladie Venus spide,
But spent my time in sporte
as youth is wont by kinde,
Not forcing fansies pinching powre
that other Wights did blinde:

By

By fortune founde a face
　　that lykte my hart so well,
As by the sodaine vewe thereof
　　to fansies frame I fell.
No sooner had mine eies
　　vpon hir beautie stayde,
But Wit and Will without respect
　　were altogither wayde.
Vnwarely so was none
　　in such a snare before :
The more I gazde vpon hir face,
　　I lykte my Loue the more.
Forthwith I thought my hart
　　out of his roome was rapt :
And wits (that woonted were to wayte
　　on Reason) were intrapt,
Downe by mine eies the stroke
　　descended to the hart :
Which Cupid neuer crazde before
　　by force of golden dart.
My bloud that thought it bounde
　　his Maisters part to take,
No longer durst abide abroade,
　　but outwarde limmes forsake.
Which hauing bæne in brest
　　and frostie colde dismayde :
It hasted from the hart againe
　　externall partes to ayde.

　　　　　　　　　　　　　And

And brought with it such heate
    as did enflame the face,
Distayning it with Scarlet redde
    by rashnesse of the race.
And since that time I feele
    such pangues and inwarde fits,
As now with hope, and then with feare
    encombred are my wits.
Thus must I Miser liue
    till shee by friendly ruth
Doe pittie mee hir louing Thrall
    whose deedes shall trie his truth.
Thrise luckie was the day,
    thrise happie cake the place,
And yee (mine eies) thrise blessed were
    that lighted on hir face.
If I in fine may force
    hir pittie by my plaint :
I shall in cunningst verse I may
    hir worthie prayse depaint.
Thereis one thing makes me ioy
    and bids me think the best :
That cruell rigor can not lodge
    where beautie is possest.
And sure vnlesse she salue
    and heale this cankred wounde
By yeelding grace, it must in time
    of force my corps confounde.

                        For

For long it may not last
    that in such anguish lies :
Extreames in no case can endure
    as Sages did deuise.
No Tyger gaue hir Teate,
    she is no Lyons whelpe :
Ne was she bred of cruell rocks,
    nor will renounce to helpe
Such as she paines with loue,
    and doth procure to wo :
She is not of the Currish kinde,
    hir nature is not so.

Maister Googe his Sonet of the paines of Loue.

Two lynes shall tell the griefe
    that I by Loue sustaine :
    I burne, I flame, I faint, I freeze,
    of Hell I feele the paine.

Turberuiles aunswere and distich to the same.

Two lynes shall teach you how
    to purchase ease anewe :
    Let Reason rule where Loue did raigne,
    and ydle thoughts eschewe.

¶ An

¶An Epitaphe on the death of Dame
Elyzabeth Arhundle.

Ere graued is a good and Godly Wight,
That yeelded hath hir cynders to the soyle,
Who ran hir race in vertues tylt aright
    And neuer had at Fortunes hand the foyle:
The guide was God whome shee did aye ensue,
And Vertue was the marke whereat she thrue.

Descending of a house of worthie fame
Shee linckt at length with one of egall state,
Who though did chaunge hir first & former name,
Did not enforce hir vertues to rebate:
For Dannat shee Dame Arhundle was hight,
Whose Feere was knowne to be a worthy Knight.

Hir beautie I not blaze ne brute at all,
(Though with the best she might therein compare)
For that it was to age and fortune thrall:
Hir thewes I touch which were so passing rare,
As being earthde and reaft hir vitall breath,
Hir chiefest part doth liue and conquer death.

Let Spite not spare to speake of hir the wurst,
Let Enuie feede vpon hir godly life,
Let Rancour rage, let Hatreds bellie burst,
Let Zoill now vnsheath his cutting knife:
For death hath closde hir corse in Marble graue,
Hir soule is fled in Skies his seate to haue.

                                        Let

Let Leyster laugh that such a Mirrour bred :
Let Matrons mourne for losse of their renowne,
Let Cornewall crie since Dannat now is ded,
Let Vertue eke doe on hir mourning gowne :
For she is reft that was at Vertues beck
Whome Fortune had no powre to giue the check.

To Piero of Pride.

FRiend Piero, Pride infects a friendly minde,
The haughtie are pursude with deadly hate :
   Wherfore eschue the proude ꝧ Peacocks kinde.
That grædie are to sit on stole of state :
The lowly hart doth winne the loue of all,
But Pride at last is sure of shamefull fall.

Piero to Turberuile.

GOod is the counsell (Turberuile) you giue,
It is a vertue rare well to aduise,
   But if your selfe in Peacoks sort doe liue
Men d rmen may you are not perfite wise :
Whose chiefest point in act consisteth aye,
Well doing farre excelleth well to saye.

Verse in prayse of Lorde Henrye Howarde Earle of Surrey.

WHat should I speake in prayse of Surreys skill
   Unlesse I had a thousand tongues at will?
No one is able to depaint at full,
The flowing fountaine of his sacred Skull.

                         Wholl

Whose Pen approude what wit he had in mue
Where such a skill in making Sonets grue.
Eche worde in place with such a sleight is coucht,
Eche thing whereof he treates so firmely toucht,
As Pallas seemde within his Noble breast
To haue soiournde, and bene a daylie guest.
Our mother tongue by him hath got such light,
As ruder speach thereby is banisht quight :
Reproue him not for fansies that he wrought,
For Fame thereby and nothing else he sought.
What though his verse with pleasant toyes are fright ?
Yet was his honours life a Lampe of light.
A Mirrour he the simple sort to traine,
That euer beate his brayne for Britans gaine.
By him the Nobles had their vertues blazde,
When spitefull death their honors liues had razde.
Eche that in life had well deserued aught,
By Surreys meanes an endles fame hath caught.
To quite his bone and aye well meaning minde,
Whereby he did his Sequell seeme to binde :
Though want of skill to silence me procures,
I write of him whose fame for aye endures,
A worthie Wight, a Noble for his race,
A learned Lorde that had an Earles place.

Of Ialousie.

A Straunge disease, a griefe exceeding great,
A man to haue his hart in flame inrolde,

In sort that he can neuer chose but sweate,
And fæle his fœte benumde with frosty colde.
No doubt if he continue in this heate,
He will become a Cœke hereafter olde,
Of such diseases such is the effect,
And this in him we may full well suspect.

To his Ladie, that by hap when he kissed
hir and made hir lip bleed, controld
him and tooke disdaine.

Ischarge thy dole,
Thou subtile soule,
It standes in little stæde
To cursse the kisse
That causer is
Thy chirrie lip doth blæde.
Thy bloud ascends
To make amends
For domage thou hast donne :
For by the same
I felt a flame
More scorching than the Sunne.
Thou restst my harte
By secret Arte,
My sprites were quite subdude:
My Senses fled
And I was ded,
Thy lippes were scarce imbrude.

The

The kiſſe was thine,
The hurt was mine,
My hart felt all the paine:
Twas it that bled
And lookte ſo red,
I tell thee once againe.
But if you long
To wreake your wrong
Upon your friendly ſo;
Come kiſſe againe
And put to paine
The man that hurt you ſo.

Mayſter Googe his Sonet.

ACcuſe not God if fanſie fonde
doe moue thy fooliſh braine
To wayle for loue, for thou thy ſelfe
art cauſe of all the paine.

Turberuiles aunſwere.

NOt God (friend Googe) ỹ Louer blames
as worker of his woes:
But Cupid that his fierie flames
ſo frantickly beſtowes.

A compariſon of the Louers eſtate
with the Souldiars paine-
full lyfe.

IF Souldiers may for ſeruice done,
and labours long ſuſtainde,

C.iij. Foi

For wearie watch, and perils past,
　and armes with armour painde :
For push of Pike, for Holbers stroke,
　for standing in the frunt,
If they expect rewarde (I say)
　for byding battayles brunt :
Then what shall Cupids Captaines craue,
　what recompence desire,
That warde the day, and wake the night
　consumde with fretting fire :
No roome of rest, no time of truce,
　no pleading for a peace :
When Cupid sounds his warlike Trumpe,
　the fight will neuer cease.
First shall you see the shiuering shafts
　and bewe the thirled darts
Which from their eies they cast by course
　to pierce their enmies harts.
But if the Foe doe stande aloose,
　(as is the Louers guise)
Then Canons with their cruell cracks
　as thick as thunder flies.
Sweete wordes in place of powder stande
　by force which think to win,
That louing lookes of late had lost
　when fight did first begin.
But on the breast to beare the brunt
　and keepe them from the hart,

A

A sure and priuie cote is worne
  repelling pellats smart.
They stop their eares against the sound,
  which is the surest shielde
Against the dreadfull shot of wordes
  that thousandes had beguilde.
But when Cupidians flatly see
  nor gunne, nor Bowe preuaile,
They then begin their friendly foes
  with other fight tassaile.
Then set the daskardes dreade aside,
  and to the walles they run,
As though they woulde subdue the Forte
  or ere the fight begun.
Forthwith the scaling Ladders come,
  and to the walles are set,
Then sighes and sobs begin to clime,
  but they are quickly met.
Thus Cupid and his Souldiers all
  the sharpe repulse sustaine :
Whome Beauty batters from the walles
  whose Captaine is Disdaine.
When all are gone and yeeld it lost,
  comes Hope and whote Desire,
To see where they can haue the hap
  to set the Forte afire.
But nought preuailes their lingring fight,
  they can not Beautie win :

                       C.H.   Yet

Yet doe they skirmish still behinde
   in hope to enter in.
At length when Beautie doth perceyue
   those Souldiers are so true,
That they will neuer from the walles
   till they the holde subdue:
She calles to Pittie for the keyes
   and bids hir let them in:
In hope they will be true to hir
   as they to Loue had bin.
The gates no sooner are vnlockt,
   but souldiers all retire:
And enter into Beauties Forte
   with Hope and hote Desire.
Now iudge by this that I haue saide
   of these two fightes aright,
Which is the greatest toyle of both
   when warlike Tents are pight.
For Mars his men sometime haue ease,
   and from their battaile blin:
But Cupids souldiers euer serue
   till they Dame Beautie win.

The Louer against one that compared his Mistresse with his Ladie.

A Madnesse to compare
   the Pipler with the Pine,

Whereof

Whereof the Mariner makes his Mast,
  and hanges it all with line.
A follie to preferre
  a Lampe before the Sunne,
Or brag that Balams lumpish Asse
  with Bucephall shall runne.
Then cease for shayne to vaunt,
  and crowe in craking wise
Of hir that least deserues to haue
  hir beauties fame arise.
Thou foolish Dame beware
  of haughtie Peacocks pride:
The fruite thereof in former age
  hath sundrie times bene tride.
Arachne can expresse
  how angrie Pallas was,
When she in needle worke would seeme
  the Heauenly Wight to passe.
The Spider shewes the spite
  that she (good wench) abid,
In token of hir pride shee hanges
  at roufe by rotten thrid.
No foode she hath allowde
  lesse Fortune sende the Flie:
The Cobweb is hir costly Couch
  appointed hir to lie.
With venim ranck and vile
  hir wombe is like to burst,

                    C.liij.   A

A token of hir inwarde hate
and hawtie minde at furst.
And thou that surely thinkst
thy Ladie to excell,
Example take of others harme
for iudgement that befell :
When Pan the Pastors prince,
and Rex of Rustick route,
To passe Apollo in his play
and Musick went aboute :
Mount Tmolus was the Iudge
that there the roome possest,
To giue his verdite for them both
which vttered Musick best.
First came the Rustick forth
with Pipe and puffed bag,
That made his eies to run like streames,
and both his lips to wag.
The noyse was somewhat rude
and ragged to the eare:
The simplest man aliue would gesse
that picuish Pan was there.
When Phœbus framde his frets,
and wrested all his pinnes,
And on his curious strings to strike
the skilfull God beginnes.
So passing was his play
as made the træs to daunce,

And

And ſtubborne Rocks in deepeſt vales
   for gladſome ioy to praunce.
Amphyon bluſht as red
   as any glowing flame :
And Orpheus durſt not ſhew his face,
   but hide his head for ſhame.
Ynough quoth Tmolus tho,
   my iudgement is that Pan
May pipe among the ruder ſort
   that little Muſick can.
Apollos playe doth paſſe
   of all that ere I hearde :
Wherefore (as reaſon is) of mee
   the Luter is preferde.
Meanewhile was Mydas preſt,
   not pointed Iudge in place :
But (lyke a dolt that went about
   Apollo to deface)
Tuſhe Tmolus, tuſhe quoth hee,
   Pan hath the better ſkill :
For hee the emptie bagge with winde
   and ſtrouting blaſt doth fill.
Apollo wagges his ioints
   and makes a iarring ſounde :
Lyke pleaſure is not in the Lute
   as in the Bagpipe founde.
No ſooner had hee ſpoke
   thoſe witleſſe wordes and ſed,

                       But

But Phœbus graft on Asses eares
   vpon his beastly hed.
In proofe of iudgement wrong
   that Mydas did maintaine,
Hee had a paire of sowsing eares
   to shilde him from the raine.
Wherefore (my Friende) take héede
   of afterclaps that fall :
And déeme not hir a Dearling that
   deserues no prayse at all.
Your iudgement is beguilde,
   your Senses suffer shame :
That so doe séeke to blaze hir armes,
   and to aduaunce hir fame.
Let hir go hide hir head
   in lothsome lurking mue,
For crabbed Crowsoote marres hir face
   and quite distaines hir hue.

The Louer to a Gentlewoman , that after great
   friendship without desart or cause of mis-
     lyking refused him.

Haue you not heard it long ago
   of cunning Fawkners tolde,
That Haukes which loue their kéepers call
   are woorth their weight in Golde :
And such as knowe the luring voice
   of him that féedes them still :

                              And

And neuer rangle farre abroade
  against the kéepers will,
Noe farre excéede the haggarde Hauke
  that stoepeth to no stale :
Nor forceth on the Lure awhit,
  but mounts with euery gale ?
Yes,yes, I know you know it well,
  and I by proufe haue tride,
That wylde and haggard Hawkes are worse
  than such as will abide.
Yet is there eke another kinde,
  farre worser than the rest :
And those are they that flie at check,
  and stoupe to erie gest.
They leaue the lawe that nature taught
  and shun their woonted kinde,
In flieing after erie Foule
  that mounteth with the winde.
You know what I doe meane by this,
  if not, giue eare a while :
And I shall shewe you my conceyte
  in plaine and simple stile.
You were sometime a gentle Hawke,
  and woont to féede on fist :
And knew my luring voice right well
  and would repaire at list.
I could no sooner make a beck
  or token with my hand,

                        But

But you would quickly iudge my will
   and how the case did stand.
But now you are become so wylde
   and rammage to be séene,
As though you were a haggard Hawke,
   your maners altred cléene.
You now refuse to come to fist,
   you shun my woonted call :
My luring lyketh not your care,
   you force mée not at all.
You flée with wings of often chaunge
   at random where you please :
But that in time will bréede in you
   some fowle and fell disease.
Liue like a haggard still therefore,
   and for no luring care :
For best (I sée) contents thy minde
   at wishe and will to fare.
So some perhaps will liue in hope
   at length to light on thée,
That carst reclaimde so gentle werts
   and louing birde to mée,
But if thou chaunce to fall to check,
   and force on erie fowle,
Thou shalt be worse detested then,
   than is the nightish Owle.
This counsell take of him that once
   did kéepe thée at his beck :

But now giues vp in open field
for feare of filthie check.

The Louer obtayning his wishe by all
likelyhode, yet not able to at-
taine his desire, compares
himself to *Tantalus.*

OF Tantalus plight
The Poets wright,
Complayning
And fayning
In sorowfull sownding songes:
Who feeles (they saye)
For Apples gaye
Such payning,
Not gayning
The fruite for which hæ longes:
For when hæ thinkes to feede therone,
The fickle flattring Tree is gone:
And all in vaine hæ hopes to haue
his famine to expell
The flitting fruite that lokes so braue
and likes his eie so well:
And thus his hunger doth increase,
And hæ can neuer finde release.
As want of Meate
Doth make him freate

With

With raging,
And gaging,
   To catch the fruite that flées:
Euen so for drythe
The Miser crythe,
  Not swaging,
  But waging,
   For licour that hée sées:
For to his painefull partched mouth
The long desired water flouth,
  And when he gapes full grædilie
   vnthriftie thirst to slake,
  The riuer wasteth spædilie,
   and awaywarde goes the Lake:
  That all the licour from his lips
  And dryed chaps away it slips.
This kinde of pains
Doth he sustaine,
  Not ceasing,
  Increasing,
   His pittifull pining wo:
In plenties place,
Deuoide of grace,
  Releasing,
  Or ceasing
   The pangs that pinch him so:
Of all the fretting fits of Hell
This Tantals torment is most fell:

Foz that the reaſt can haue no hope
their frœdome to attaine,
And he hath graunted him ſuch ſcope
as makes the Myſer faine :
But all foz nought in fine it ſerues,
Foz he with dzyth and hunger ſterues.
Euen ſo fare I
That am as nie
My pleaſure,
My treaſure,
As I might wiſh to bœ :
And haue at will
My Ladie ſtill
At leaſure,
In meaſure,
As well it liketh mœ.
The amozous blincks flœ to and fro,
With ſugred wozds that make a ſhow
That fanſie is well pleaſde withall
and findes it ſelfe content :
Eche other friendly friend doth call
and eche of vs conſent :
And thus we ſœme foz to poſſeſſe
Eche others hart and haue redzeſſe.
We coll, we clip,
We kiſſe with lip,
Delighted,
Requighted,

                                        Aw

And merily ſpend the day :
The tales I tell
Are fanſide well,
  Recited,
  Not ſpited,
   Thus weares the time away.
Looke what I like ſhæ doth imbrace,
Shæ giues good eare vnto my caſe
  And yældes mæ lawfull libertie
   to frame my doloꝛus plaint,
  To quite hir Friend from ieopardie
  whome Cupid hath attaint :
  Reſpecting nought at all his welth
  But ſæking meane to woꝛke his helth.
I ſæme to haue
The thing I craue,
  Shæ barres not,
  Shæ iarres not,
   But with a verie good will
Shæ heares my ſute,
And foꝛ the frute
  Shæ warres not,
  But dares not
   To let me fæde my fill.
Shæ would (I know) with hart agræ,
The fault is neyther in hir noꝛ mæ,
  I dare auowe full willinglie
   ſhæ would conſent thereto,

                              And

And gladly would mée remedie
to baniſh away my wo :
Lo thus my wiſh I doe poſſeſſe,
And am a Tantal naytheleſſe.
For though I ſtande
And touch with handꝭ
    Allured,
    Procured,
        The Saint I doe deſire :
And may be bolde
For to enfolde,
    Aſſured,
    Indured,
        The Corps that I require :
Yet by no meanes may I attaine
To haue the fruite I would ſo faine
    To rid mée from extremitie
    and cruell oppreſſing care,
    Euen thus with Tantals penaltie
    my deſtnie may compare :
Who though endure exceſſiue paine,
Yet mine is not the leaſt of twaine.

    The Louer to the Thems of London
        to fauor his Ladie paſſing
            thereon.

Thou ſtately Streame ý with the ſwelling Tide
Gainſt London walles inceſſantly doſt beate,
                    D.i.   Thou

Thou Thems (I say) where barge & bote doth ride,
And snowhite Swans do fish for needefull meate:
　When so my Loue of force, or pleasure shall
Flit on thy floud as custome is to to:
Seeke not with dread hir courage to appall,
But calme thy tyde, and smoothly let it go:
As shee may ioy, arriue to siker shore
To passe the pleasant streame she did before.

　To weltre vp and surge in wrathfull wise,
(As did the floud where Helle drenched was,)
Would but procure defame of thee to rise:
Wherefore let all such ruthlesse rigor passe,
So wish I that thou mayst with bending side
Haue powre for aye in wonted goulfe to glide.

To his Ring giuen to his Ladie, wherein was grauen this Verse.

My hart is yours.

Though thou (my Ring) be small,
　and slender be thy price:
Yet hast thou in thy compasse coucht
　a Louers true deuice.
And though no Rubie red,
　ne Turkesse trim thy top,
Nor other Iuell that commends
　the golden Vulcans shop:
Yet mayst thou boldlye vaunt
　and make a true report

F ij

For me that am thy Mayster yet
  in such a semblant sort,
That aye (*my hart is hirs*)
  of thee I aske no more:
My Pen and I will shew the rest,
  which yet I kepe in store.
Be mindefull of thy charge,
  and of thy Maysters case:
Forget not that (*my hart is hirs*)
  though I be not in place.
When thou hast tolde thy tale
  which is but short and swete:
Then let my Loue contect the rest
  till she and I doe mete.
For as (*my hart is hirs*)
  so shall it be for aye:
My hart, my hand, my lyfe, my limmes
  are hirs till dying daye.
Yea when the spirite giues vp
  and bodie breathes his last,
Say naythelesse (*my hart is hirs*)
  when life and all is past.

Sit fast to hir finger,
But doe thou not wring her.

        S.ij.   The

The difpairing Louer craues eyther mer-
cie in time at his Ladies hands,
or cruell death.

Ike as the fearefull Foule
within the Falwcons fœts
Doth yælde himfelfe to die,
and fæs none other bœt:
Euen fo dread I (my Deare)
leaſt ruth in thæ will want,
To mæ that am thy thrall,
who fearing death doe pant.
So faſt I am in Gyue
within your beauties Gayle,
As thence to make a breach
no engin may preuaile.
The hart within my breaſt
with trembling feare doth quake:
And faue your loue (my Deare)
nought can my torment ſlake.
To ſlea a yælding pray
I iudge it not your kinde:
Your beautie bids mæ hope
more ruth in you to finde.
Where Nature hath pformde
fuch featurde ſhape to ſhowe,
There hath ſhe clofde in breaſt
a hart for grace to growe.

Where.

Wherefore my lingring paines
  redꝛesse with ruthfull hart :
And doe in time become
  Phisition to my smart.
Oh showe thy selfe a friende
  and Natures Impe to bee,
As thou a Woman art by kinde
  to womans kinde agrée.
But if you can not finde
  in hart my lyfe to saue,
But that you long to sée
  your thꝛall lye deade in graue:
Sende mée the fatall toole,
  and cruell cutting knife :
And thou shalt sée me rid
  my wretched limmes of life.
No lesse to like thy minde
  than to abꝛidge my smart :
Which were an yll rewarde
  foꝛ such a good desart.
Of both I count it least
  by cursed death to fall,
Than ruthlesse here to lyue
  and aye to be a thꝛall.

> To his Friende to be constant
>   after choise made.

What made Vlysses Wife
    so be renowmed so ?
                    D.ij.   What

What forced Fame hir endlesse bruts
   in blasting trumpe to blow ?
What Cleopatra causde
   to haue immortall prayse ?
What did procure Lucrecias laude
   to lasten to our dayes ?
Cause they their plighted hestes
   vnbroken aye reserude :
And planted Constance in their harts
   from whome they neuer swerude.
What makes the Marble stone
   and Diamond so deare ?
Haue that the longest last of all,
   and alwayes one appeare ?
What makes the waxen formes
   to be of slender prise ?
But cause with force of fire it melts
   and wasteth with a trice.
Then if thou long for prayse
   or blasted Fame to finde,
(My Friend) thou must not chaunge thy choyce
   or turne lyke Cock with winde.
Be constant in thy worde
   and stable in thy dæde :
This is the readiest way to win
   and purchase prayse with spæde.

Coun.

Counsell returned by *Pyndara*
to *Tymetes,* of con-
stancie.

What made the Troyan Duke
that wandring Prince to haue
Such yll report, and foule defame
as him Carthago gaue ?
What faythlesse Iason forcde
a Traytors name to gaine ?
When he to Colchos came, and did
the golden Floese attaine ?
What Theseus causde to bée
reported of so yll,
As yet record thereof remaynes
(I think) and euer wyll ?
Cause they their faithfull Friendes
that saude their doubtfull lyues
Forsooke at last, and did disdaine
to take them to their wyues.
They brake their vowed hestes,
by ship away they went :
And so betrayde those siely soules
that craft nor falsehood ment.
Wherefore if you (my Friend)
the like report will flée
Stand euer to the promise made,
and plighted troth to mée.

                 D.llf.   Those

Those Dames of whome you spake
    were constant (as you say)
But sure these Louers I alleage
    vnfaithfull parts did play.
More cause haue I to doubt
    of you (Tymetes) then,
For (as you sée) we Women are
    more trustie than you men.

The Louers must not dispaire
though their Ladies seeme
straunge.

Though Neptune in his rage
    the swelling Seas doe tosse,
    And crack the Cables in dispite
    to further shipmens losse :
Though Ancker holde doe fayle,
    and Myssion go to wrack,
Though Sayles with blustring blast be rent,
    and Keale begin to crack :
Yet those that are a borde
    and guide the ship with steare,
Although they sée such daungers prest
    and perils to appeare :
Yet hope to light at last
    vpon some harbour holde,
And finde a Porte where they to cast
    their Anckers may be bolde.

                          Though

Though Thæues be kept in Gayle
  faſt bound in ſureſt Gyues,
They lay not all good hope aſide
  foꝛ ſauing of their lyues.
They truſt at length to ſée
  ſuch mercie in the Iudge,
As they in open pꝛeſence quit
  may from the pꝛiſon trudge,
And thoſe foꝛ græedie gaine
  and hope of hidden Golde
In déxpeſt Mynes and Dungeon darck
  that byde the bitter colde;
In fine doe looke to light
  vpon ſome Golden baine,
VVhich may be thought a recompence
  foꝛ all their paſſed paine.
The Ploughman eke that toyles
  and turnes the ground foꝛ graine,
And ſowes his ſæde (perhaps to loſſe)
  yet ſtandes in hope of gaine.
He will not once diſpaire,
  but hope till Harueſt fall :
And then will looke aſſuredly
  to ſtuffe his Barnes withall.
Since theſe in perils point
  will neuer once diſpaire,
Then why ſhould Louers ſtand in dꝛead
  of ſtoꝛmes in weather faire?

                         Why

Why should they haue mistrust
   some better hap to finde,
Or think that Women will not chaunge
   as is their woonted kinde?
Though straunge they seeme a while
   and cruell for a space :
Yet see thou hope at length by hap
   to finde some better grace.
For Tygers will be tame,
   and Lyons that were woode,
In time their keepers learne to knowe
   and come to them for foode.
What though they scorne as now
   to listen to thy sute?
Yet thou in time when fortune serues
   shalt reape some better frute.
And though thy sighes they scorne
   and mock thy welling teares :
Yet hope (I say) for after stormes
   the shining Sunne appeares.
And neuer cease to sue,
   nor from lamenting stint :
For often drops of falling raine
   in time doe pierce the Flint.
Was neuer stone so strong
   nor womans hart so harde,
But thone with toole, and thother with teares
   in processe might be scarde.

A

A Letter sent by *Tymetes* to his Ladie
Pyndara at the time of his
departure.

OF Pennes I had good store,
   ne Paper did I want
When I began to write to thée:
   but Inck was somewhat scant.
Yet Loue deuisde a fetch,
   a friendly sleight at néede:
For I with pointed Pensill made
   my middle finger bléede.
From whence the bloud as from
   a clouen Conduite flue,
And these fewe rude and skillesse lines
   with quaking quill I drue.
Now Friend I must depart
   and leaue this lyked lande:
Now canckred Hap doth force me take
   a new founde toyle in hande.
Shée spites that I should liue,
   or leade a quiet life:
Aye séeking how to bréede my bale
   and make my sorrowes rife.
From whence I passe I knowe,
   a place of pleasant blisse,
But wither I shall I wote not well,
   I know not where it is.

                    Where

Where she by Sea or Lande
  me (cruell) will compell
To passe, or by the desatt Dales,
  were verie hard to tell.
But nédes I must away,
  the Westerne winde doth blowe
So full against my back that I
  of force from hence doè go.
Yet naythelesse in pawne
  (O Friend) I leaue with you
A faithfull hart, that lasting lyfe
  will shewe it selfe as true,
As louing earst it hath:
  and if mée trust you dare,
Fill vp the emptie place with yours,
  if you the same may spare.
Inclose it in my breast,
  in safetie shall it lie:
And thou shalt haue thy hart againe,
  if I doe chaunce to die.
Thus dubble is your gaine,
  a dubble hart to haue:
To purchase thée another hart,
  and eke thine owne to saus.
Liue mindefull of thy Friend,
  forget not promise past:
Be stoute against the stubborne strokes
  of frowarde Fortunes blast.

                    Penelope

Penelope be true
  to thy Vlyſſes ſtill;
Let no newe choſen Friend breake off
  the thzeed of our good will.
Though I on ſeas doe paſſe,
  the ſurge will haue no powze
To quench the flame that in my bzeaſt
  increaſeth day and howze.
And thus (*the heart that is
  your owne*) doth wiſh thee well,
With good increaſe of bleſſed haps
  ſiniſter chaunce to quell.
Adue my choſen Friend,
  if Fortune ſay Amen,
From hence I go thine owne, and will
  thine owne returne agen.

  Pyndara aunſwere to the Letter which
    Tymetes ſent hir at the time
      of his departure.

When firſt thy Letters came
    (O louing Friend) to mee,
    I leapt for ioy, in hope to haue
      receyude good newes of thee.
I neuer ſtayde vpon
  thoſe lines that were without :
But raſhly ript the Seale, to rid
  my minde from dzeadfull dout.

                              Which

Which done (Oh cruell griefe)
   I saw a mournefull sight :
This Verse (*of Pennes I had good store*)
   with Purple bloud ywright.
With flouds of flowing teares
   straight drowned were mine eies,
On eyther Cheeke they trickled fast
   and ranne in riuer wies.
My minde did yll abode,
   it yrkt to read the rest :
For when I saw the Inck was such,
   I thought I saw the best.
Long stode I in a dumpe,
   my hart began to ake :
My Liuer leapt within my bulck,
   my trembling hands did shake.
My Senses were bereft,
   my bowing knees did bende :
Out from my Nose the bloud it brake,
   much like the Letter pende,
Up start my staring Locks,
   I lay for dead a space :
And what with bloud and brine I all
   bedewde the drerie place,
From out my feeble fist
   fell Needle, cloth and all,
I knewe no Wight, I saw no Sunne,
   as deafe as stone in wall.

At

At laſt when ſtanders by
  had bʒought my Senſe againe,
And foʒce of life had conquerd griefe
  and baniſht deadly paine:
I thought the woʒſt was paſt,
  I dœmde I could abide
No greater toʒment than I had,
  vnleſſe I ſhould haue dide.
To vewing then againe
  of bloudie lynes I go:
And euer as I read the woʒds,
  mœ thought I ſaw the blo.
Which pointed Penſell gaue,
  from whence that dolefull Inck
As from a clouen Conduit flue:
  remembʒance make me ſhʒinck.
Oh Friend Tymetes why
  ſo cruell were thou than:
What didſt thou meane to hurt thy fleſh
  thou raſh and retchleſſe man?
What? didſt thou dœme that I
  could vew that goʒie ſcrole
Withouten anguiſh of the minde:
  oʒ think vpon the hole
Of that thy friendly fiſt
  and finger that did blœde:
No, no, I haue a Womans hart,
  I am no Tygers ſœde.

                        As

As great a griefe it was
   fo2 me to think in hart
Of thy mishap, as if my selfe
   had felt the p2esent smart.
O cruell cursed want
   of fitter Inck to w2ite:
God sayth that lycour was vnmæte
   such louing lines tindite.
But yet in some respect
   it fitted with the case:
Fo2 (out alas) I read therein
   that thou hast fled the place,
Where friendly we were wont
   like faithfull friends to bœ:
Where thou moughtst chat with me thy fill
   and I conferre with thœ.
Oh spitefull cruell Chaunce,
   oh cursed canckred Fate:
Art thou a Goddesse (Monster vile)
   deseruing stœle of State?
O blinde and muffled Dame,
   couldst thou not sæ to spare
Two faithfull harts, but reauing those
   must b2æde the others care?
No wonder tis that thou
   dost stande on whirling whæle:
Fo2 by thy dædes thou dost declare
   thou canst doe nought but rœle.

                                 Art

Art thou of Womans kinde
  and ruthfull Goddesse race,
And hast no more respect vnto
  a sielie womans case?
Auaunt thou froward Fiend,
  thou so my Friend dost driue
From shore well knowne to forraine coast
  our sugred ioyes to riue.
If so thy minde be bent
  that my Tymetes shall
Depart the presence of his Friend:
  Yet so doe guide the ball
As he at lande may liue
  not trying surge of seas:
Nor ship him from the Hauens mouth
  to breede him more vnease.
(Good Friend) aduenture not
  so rashly on the floud,
As earst thou didst in writing of
  this Letter with thy bloud.
Seeke not tincrease my cares
  or dubble griefe begon:
Think of Leanders bolde attempt
  the lyke distresse to shon.
What suretie is in ship?
  what trust in Oken plancks?
What credit doe the windes deserue
  at lande that play such pranks?

C.j.

If

If houses strongly built,
   and Towers battled hie,
By force of blast be ouerthrowne
   when Æols Impes doe flie:
In puffing windes the Pine
   and aged Oke doe teare,
And from the bodies rent the boughes
   and loftie lugges they beare :
Then why shouldst thou affie
   in Reale or Cable so,
Or hazard thus thy selfe vpon
   the tossing Seas to go?
Hast thou not heard of yore
   how good Vlysses was
With stormie tempest chased sore
   when he to Greece did passe?
A wearie trauaile hee
   for ten yeares space abid.
And all the while this noble Græke
   on waltring wallow slid.
Hast thou not read in Bookes
   of fell Charybdis Goulfe,
And Scyllas Dogs, whome ships doe dread
   as Lambes doe feare the Woulfe?
Nor of the raggie Rocks
   that vnderlurck the waue?
And rent the Barcks that Æols blasts
   into their bosome draue?

                           Not

Not of the Monsters huge
  that belch out frothie fleame,
And singing Sirens that doe drowne
  both man and ship in streame:
Alas the thought of Seas,
  and of thy passage paines
(If once thou gage thy selfe to surge)
  my hart and members straines.
The present fits of feare
  of afterclaps to cum.
Amaze my louing tender breast
  and Senses doe benum.
But needes thou must away,
  (oh Friend) what hap is this
That ere thou flie this friendly coast
  thy lips I can not kisse:
Nor with my folded armes
  im brace that neck of thine:
Nor clap vnto thy manly breast
  these louing Dugs of mine:
Not shed my trilling teares
  vpon thy moisted face:
Nor say to thee (Tymet adue)
  when thou departst the place:
O that I had thy forme
  in waxen table now,
To represent thy liuely lokes
  and friendly louing brow.

              E.I.   That

That mought perhaps abridge
　　some part of pinching paine :
And comfort me till better chaunce
　　did sende thée home againe.
Both winde and waue atonce
　　conspire to worke my wo,
Or else thou shouldst not so be forst
　　from me (thine owne) to go.
O waywarde Westerne blast
　　what didst thou meane so full
Against Tymetes back to blow,
　　and him from hence to pull ?
Hast thou bene counted earst
　　a gentle gale of winde,
And dost thou now at length bewray
　　thy fierce and frowarde kinde ?
I thought the Northren blast
　　from frostie Pole that came
Had bene the worst of all the windes
　　and most deserued blame.
But now I plainely sée
　　that Poets did but faine :
When they of Borias spake so yll
　　and of his cruell raigne.
For thou of Æols brats
　　thy selfe the worst dost showe :
And hauing no iust cause to rage
　　to sone beginst to blowe.

If

If needes thou wouldſt haue vſde
  thy foꝛce and fretting mœde,
Thou ſhouldſt haue bꝛoyld among the trées
  that in the Mountaines ſtœde:
And let vs friends alone
  that liude in perfite bliſſe.
But to requeſt the windes of ruth
  but laboꝛ loſt it is.
Well (Friend) though cruell hap
  and windes did both agrée,
That thou on ſodaine ſhouldſt foꝛgo
  both countrie coaſt and mée :
Yet haue I founde the pawne
  which thou didſt leaue behinde :
I meane thy louing faithfull hart,
  that neuer was vnkinde,
And foꝛ that firme beheſt
  and plighted truth of youre,
Wherein you vow that lous begon
  ſhall to the death endure :
To yœlde thée thy demaunde
  my wꝛitten lines pꝛoteſt,
Incloſe my hart within thy bulck
  as I will thine in bꝛeſt.
Shꝛine vp that little lumpe
  of friendly fleſh (my Friend)
And I will lodge in louing wiſe
  the gueſt that thou didſt ſend.
                         C.ſf.   I

I ioy at this exchaunge:
    for I assured stande,
Thy tender hart that I doe kéepe
    shall safelie lie at lande.
Nor doe I doubt at all
    but thou wilt haue regarde
Of that thy charge, and womans hart
    committed to thy warde.
Why dost thou write of death ?
    I trust thou shalt not die,
As long as in thy manly breast
    a womans hart doth lie.
To cruell were the case,
    the Sisters cake were shroes:
If they woulde séeke the death of vs,
    that are such friendly foes.
But if the worst shoulde fall,
    and that the cruell death
Doe stop the spindles of our life,
    and reaue vs both of breath:
Yet this doth make me ioy,
    that thou shalt be the graue
Unto my hart, and in my brest
    thy hart is Pierce shall haue.
For sure a sunder shall
    these members neuer go.
As long as life in lims doth lodge
    and breath in lungs bylow.

I

I mindefull liue of thée
and of my promise past :
I will not séeke to chaunge my choise,
my loue is fixed fast.
To my Tymetes I
as faithfull will be found :
As to Vlysses was his wife
whilst Troie was laide on ground.
As for new choise of Friends,
presume vpon thy P.
Thou knowst I haue thy hart in breast
and it will none but thée.
Abandon all distrust
and dread of mistie minde :
For to the hart (*that is mine owne*)
I will not be vnkinde.
Adue my chosen Friend,
Adue to thée agen :
Remaine my loue, but pray the write
no more with bloudie Pen.

Thine owne in life, thine owne in death,
Thine owne whilst lungs shall lende me breath :
Thine owne whilst I on earth doe wonne
Thine owne whilst eie shall see the Sonne.

To

To his abſent Friend the Louer
writes of his vnquiet and
reſtleſſe ſtate.

Hough curious ſkill I want to wel endite,
And I of ſacred Nymphes and Muſes nine
Was neuer taught w Poets pen to write,
Nor barrain braine to learning did incline
To purchaſe prayſe, or with the beſt to ſhine:
Yet cauſe my Friend ſhall finde no want of will,
I write, let hir accuſe the lack of ſkill.

No leſſe deſerues the Lambe to be imbraſt
Of lowring Ioue at ſacred Altar ſlaine,
If with good zeale it offred be at laſt
By Irus, that doe Cræsus Bullocks twaine:
For no reſpect is to be had of gaine
In ſuch affayres, but to the giuers hart
And his good will our Senſes muſt conuart.

Wherfore to thée (my Friend) theſe lines I ſend
As perfite proufe of no diſſembling minde,
But of a hart that truely doth intend.
To ſhew it ſelfe as louing and as kinde,
As woman woulde hir Louer wiſh to finde :
And more than this my Paper can declare,
I loue thée (Friend) and wiſhe thée well to fare.

I would thou wiſt the torment I ſuſtaine
For lack of hir that ſhould my wo redreſſe,
And that you knew ſome parcel of my paine,
Which

Which none may well by deeming iudgemēt gesse,
Nor I with quill haue cunning to expresse:
I know thou couldst but rue my wofull chaunce,
That by thy meanes was brought into this traunce

    The day doth breede my doole, and ranckling rage
Of secret smart in wounded breast doth boyle,
No pleasant pangue my sorrowes may asswage,
Nor giue an ende vnto my wofull toyle:
The golden Sunne that glads the earthly soyle,
And erie other thing that breedes delight
Of kinde, to mœ are forgers of my spite.

    I long for Phœbus glade and going downe,
My drearie teares more couertly to shed:
But when the night with vglie face doth frowne,
And that I am yplaste in quiet bed,
In hope to be with wished pleasure fed:
A greater griefe, a worser paine ensues.
My vaporde eies their hoped sleepe refues.

    Then rowle I in my deepe dispayring brest
The sweete disdaines, and pleasant anger past,
The louely strifes: when Stars doe counsell rest
Incroching cares renue my griefe as faste,
And thus desired night in wo I waste:
And to expresse the harts excessiue paine,
Mine eies their deawie teares distill amaine.

    no reason why they should be moysted so,
Is for they bred my hart this bitter bale:
They were the onely cause of cruell wo

                   Vnto

Unto the hart, they were the guilefull skale.
Thus day and night ytost with churlish Gale
Of sighes in Sea of surging bryne I bide
Not knowing how to scape the scowring Tide.

At last the shining Rayes of Hope to finde
Your friendship firme, these cloudy thoughts repels
And calmed Skie returnes to mistie minde:
Which dæpe dispaire againe eftsœne compels
To fade, and case by Dolours drift expels:
That Gods themselues (I iudge) lament my fate,
And doe repine to sæ my wofull state.

Wherefore to purchace prayse, and glozse gaine,
Do ease your Friend that liues in wretched plight,
Doe not to death a louing hart constraine,
But sæke with loue his seruice to requight,
Doe not exchaunge a Fawcon for a Kite:
Refuse him not for any friendship nue
A worse may chaunce, but none more iust and true.

Let Cressed myrror bæ that did forgo
Hir former faythfull friend king Priams Sonne,
And Diomed the Græke imbraced so,
And left the loue so well that was begonne:
But when hir Cards were tolde and twist yspönne
She found hir Troian Friend the best of both
For he renounst hir not, but kept his oth.

This don, my griping griefs will söwhat swage
And sorrow cease to grow in pensiue breast,
Which otherwise will neuer blin to rage

                                        And

And crush the hart within his carefull Cheast
Of both for you and meé it were the best,
To saue my life and win immortall fame,
And thus my Muse shall blase your noble name
For ruine on my wofull case.

The aunswere of a woman to hir **Louer,**
supposing his complaint to be
but fayned.

You want no skill to paint
   or shew your pangues with Pen,
It is a worlde to seé the craft
   that is in subtile men.
You seéme to write of woes
   and wayle for deadly smart,
As though there were no griefe, but that
   which gripes your faythlesse hart.
Though we but Women are
   and weake by lawe of kinde,
Yet well we can discerne a Friende,
   we winke, but are not blinde.
Not euery thing that giues
   a gleame and glittering showe,
Is to be counted Gold in deéde
   this prouerb well you knowe:
Nor euery man that beares
   a faire and fawning cheére,

Is

Is to be taken for a Friend
   or chosen for a Feere:
Not euerie teare declares
   the troubles of the hart,
For some doe wéepe that féele no wo
   some crie that taste no smart.
The more you séeme to me
   in wofull wise to playne,
The sooner I perswade my selfe
   that you doe nought but fayne.
The Crocodile by kinde
   a floud of teares doth shed
Yet hath no cause of cruell crie
   by craft, this Fiend is led.
For when the sicly soule
   that ment no hurt at all
Approcheth néere, the slipper ground
   doth giue the beast a fall,
Which is no sooner done
   but straight the monster byle,
For sorow that did wéepe so sore
   for ioy beginnes to smyle :
Euen so you men are woont
   by fraude your friends to traine
And make in wise you could not sléepe
   in carefull Couch for paine:
When you in déede doe nought
   but take your nightly nap,

                                  Mj

Or hauing slept doe set your snare
  and tylle your guilefull trap.
your braynes as busie bée
  'n thinking how to snare
Us women, as your pillowes soft
  and bowlsters pleasant are.
As for your dayes delights
  our selues can witnesse well
Tó sundrie women sundrie tales
  of sundrie iestes you tell:
And all to win their loues:
  which when you doe attaine
Within a while you shew your kindes
  and giue them vp in plaine.
A Fawcon is full hard
  amongst you men to finde,
For all your maners more agrée
  vnto the Kytish kinde:
For gentle is the one
  and loues his kéepers hande,
But thother Busserolske doth scorne
  on Fawckners fist to stande.
For one good turne the one
  a thousand will requite,
But vse the other nere so well
  he shewth himselfe a Kite.
If Cresyd did amisse
  the Troian to forsake

                              Then

Then Dyomedes did not well
  that did the Ladie take.
Was neuer woman false,
  but man as false as shée
And commonly the men doe make
  that women slipper bée.
Wherefore leaue off your plaints
  and take the shéete of shame
To throwde your cloking harts from colde
  and fayning browes from blame.
Yf she that reades this rime,
  bé wise as I coulde wishe,
She will auoyde the bayted hooke
  that takes the biting fishe,
And shoon the lymed twig
  the flying Foule that tyes
Tis good to feare of erie bush
  where thréed of thraldome lyes.

The Louer exhorteth his **Ladie**
to take time, while
time is.

Though braue your Beautie be
  And feature passing faire,
Such as Apelles to depaint
  might vtterly dispaire:
Yet drowsie drouping Age.
  incroching on apace,

Kn iiij

With pensiue Plough will raze your hue
  and Beauties beames deface.
Wherefore in tender yeares
  how crooked Age doth haste
Reuoke to minde, so shall you not
  your minde consume in waste.
Whilst that you may, and youth
  in you is fresh and grœne,
Delight your selfe: for yeares to flit
  as fickle flouds are sœne.
For water slipped by
  may not be callde againe:
And to reuoke forepassed howres
  were labour lost in vaine.
Take time whilst time applies
  with nimble foote it goes:
Nor to compare with passed Prime
  thy after age suppoes.
The holtes that now are hoare,
  both bud and bloume I sawe:
I ware a Garlande of the Bryer
  that puts me now in awe.
The time will be when thou
  that doste thy Friends defie,
A colde and crooked Beldam shalt
  in lothsome Cabbin lie:
Nor with such nightlie brawles
  thy posterne Gate shall sounde,

Nor Roses strawde asront thy dore
   in dawning shall be founde.
How soone are Corpses (Lorde)
   with filthie furrowes fild?
How quickly Beautie, braue of late,
   and seemely shape is spild?
Euen thou that from thy youth
   to haue bene so, wilt sweare:
With turne of hand in all thy head
   shalt haue graye powdred heare.
The Snakes with shifted skinnes
   their lothsome age doowap:
The Buck doth hang is head on pale
   to liue a longer day.
Your good without recure
   doth passe, receiue the flowre:
Which if you pluck not from the stalke
   will fall within this howre.

The Louer wisheth to be conioyned and fast linckt with his Ladie neuer to sunder.

I Reade how Salmacis sometime with sight
  On sodaine lowde Cyllenus Sonne, and sought
Forthwith with all hir powre and forced might
To bring to passe hir close conceyued thought:
Whome as by hap she saw in open mead
She sude vnto, in hope to haue bene spead.

                          With

With sugred words she woo't sparde no speach,
But bourded him with many a pleasant tale,
Requesting him of ruth to be hir Leach
For whome she had abid such bitter bale:
But hee repleate with pride and scornefull cheare
Disdainde hir earnest sute and songs to heare.

A way shee went a wofull wretched Wight,
And shrowded hir not farre from thence a space:
When that at length the stripling saw in sight
No creature there, but all were out of place,
Hee shifts his robes and to the riuer ran,
And there to bath him bare the Boy began.

The Nymph in hope as then to haue attainde
Hir long desired Loue, retirde to flood
And in hir armes the naked Boye strainde:
Whereat the Boy began to striue a good,
But strugling nought auailed in that plight
For why the Nymph surpast the Boy in might.

O Gods (quoth tho the Girle) this gift I craue
This Boy and I may neuer part againe,
But so our corpses may conioyned haue
As one we may appeare, not bodies twaine:
The Gods agreed, the water so it wrought,
As both were one, thy selfe would so haue thought.

As from a tree we sundrie times espie.
A twistell grow by Natures subtile might,
And being two, for cause they grow so nie
For one are tane, and so appeare in sight.

F.j.   So

Ho was the Nymph and Morie ioynde yfere,
As two no more but one selfe thing they were.

   O Ladie mine, howe might we séeme ybest?
How friendly mought we Gods account to bée?
In semblant sort if they woulde bréede my rest
By lincking of my carkasse vnto thée?
So that we might no more a sunder go,
But limmes to limmes, & corse to carkasse grow?

   O, where is now become that blessed Lake
Wherein those two did bath to both their ioy?
How might we doe, or such prouision make
To haue the hap as had the Maiden Boy?
To alter forme and shape of either kinde,
And yet in proufe of both a share to finde?

   Then should our limmes wt louely linck be tide,
And harts of hate no taste sustaine at all,
But both for aye in perfite league abide
And eche to other liue as friendly thrall:
That thone might féele the pangues the other had
And partner be of ought that made him glad.

   O blessed Nymph, O Salmacys I saye,
Would thy good luck vnto hir lot would light
Whome I imbrace, and louen shall for aye,
By force of God to chaunge hir nature quight:
And that I might haue hap as had the Boy
To neuer part from hir that is my Ioy.

   I would not striue, I would not stirre awhit,
(As did Cyllenus Sunne that stately Wight:)

                        But

But well content to be Hermaphrodit,
Would cling as close to thee as ere I might,
And laugh to thinke my hap so good to bee,
As in such sort fast to be linckt with thee.

The Louer hoping assuredly of attaining his
purpose, after long sute, begins to
ioy renouncing dolors.

BE farre from mee you wofull wonted cries,
Adue Dispaire, that madste my hart agries:
Ye sobbing sighes farewel & pensiue plaint,
Resigne your roomes to ioy, ý long restraint
    Without desart endurde.
Reiect those ruthfull Rymes ý (quaking Quill)
Which both declarde my wo and want of skill:
(Mine eies) that long haue had my Loue in chase,
With teares no more imbrue your Mystresse face
    But to your Springs retyre.
And thou (my Hart) that long for lack of Grace
Forepinde hast bene and in a doolefull case,
Lament no more, let all such gripings go
As bred thy bale, and nurst thy cankred wo
    With milke of mournefull Dug.
To Venus doe your due (you Senses all)
And to hir Sonne to whome you are in thrall:
To Cupid bend thy knee and thankes repay
That after lingred sute, and long delay
    Hath brought thy ship to shore.
      F.Y.   Let

Let crabbed Fortune now expreſſe hir might,
And doe thy worſt to mée thou ſtinging ſpite:
My hart is well defenſt againſt your force,
For ſhe hath bowde on mée to haue remorce
     Whome I haue loude ſo long.
Henceforth exchaunge thy chére and wofu'l voice
That haſt yfounde ſuch matter to reioice :
With mirrie quill and pen of pleaſant plight
Thy bliſſull haps and fortune to endight
     Enforce thy barraine Skull.

   The Louer to his carefull bed decla-
     ring his reſtleſſe ſtate.

Thou that wert earſt a reſtfull place
    doſt now renue my ſmart,
  And woonted cake to ſalue my ſore
    that now increaſeſt two,
Unto my carefull Corſe an eaſe,
  a torment to my hart,
Once quieter of minde perdie,
  now an vnquiet fo:
The place ſometime of ſlumbring ſléepe
  wherein I may but wake,
Drenched in Sea of ſaltiſh brine
  (O bed) I thée forſake.
No Iſe of Apenynus top
  my flaming fire may quent,

                  Ne

Ne heate of brightest Phœbus beames
  may bate my chillic colde,
Nought is of stately strength ynough
  my sorrowes to relent,
But (such is hap) renewed cares
  are added to the olde :
Such furious fits and fonde affects
  in mæ my fansies make,
That bathed all in trickling teares
  (O bed) I thæ forsake.

❧The dreames that daunt my dazed-hed
  are pleasant for a space,
Whilst yet I lie in slumbring slæpe
  my carkasse fœles no wo,
For cause I sæme with clasped armes
  my Louer to imbrace :
But when I wake, and finde away
  that did delight me so,
Then in comes care to pleasures place
  that makes my limmes to quake,
That all besprent with brackish bryne
  (O bed) I thæ forsake.

❧No sooner stirres Auroras Starre,
  the lightest Lampe of all,
But they that rousted were in rest
  not fraught with fearefull dreames,
Do pack apace to labours left
  and to their taske doe fall :

        F.iij.   When

When I awaking all inragde
   doe baine my breast with streames,
And make my smokie sighes to Skies
   their vpwarde way to take,
Thus with a surge of teares bedewde
   (O bed) I thee forsake.

¶ Thus hurlde from hungrie Hope by Hap
   I die, yet am aliue,
From pangues of plaint to fits of fume
   my restlesse minde doth runne,
With rage and fansie Reason fights,
   they altogither striue,
Resistaunce vayleth naught at all,
   for I am quickly wunne:
Thus seeking rest no ruth I finde
   that gladsome ioy may make,
Wherefore consumde with flowing teares
   (O bed) I thee forsake.

¶ An Epitaph and wofull verse of the death
of sir *Iohn Tregonwell* Knight, and learned
Doctor of both Lawes

ANd can you cease from plaint,
   or keepe your Conduits drie?
May saltish brine within your breasts
   in such a tempest lie?
Where are your scalding sighes
   the fittest foode of paine?

And

And where are now thy welling teares
  I aske thée once againe?
Hast thou not heard of late
  The losse that hath befell?
If not, my selfe (vnhappie Wight)
  will now begin to tell:
(Though griefe perhaps will grutch,
  and stay my foltring tongue)
From whence this ragged roote of ruth
  and mourning moode is sprong.
Was dwelling in this shéere
  a man of worthie fame:
A Iustieer for his desart,
  Tregonwell was his name.
A Doctor at the Lawes,
  a Knight among the mo:
A Cato for good counsell callde
  as he in yeares did grow.
A Patrone to the poore,
  a Rampire to the rest:
As léefe vnto the simple sorte
  as friendly to the best.
No blinde affect his eie
  in iudgement blearde at all:
Whose rightous verdit and decrée
  was quite deuoyde of gall.
If he in hatefull hartes
  (where roote of rancour grew)

           F.iiij.   Of

Of faythfull friendship sedes might sow,
  no paines he would eschew.
Minerua thought of like
  and Nature did consent,
To proue in him by skilfull Arte
  what eyther could inuent.
A plot of such a price
  was neuer framde before:
To show their powre the Heauens had
  Tregonwell kept in store.
The Prince did him imbrace,
  and sought him to aduaunce,
And better former state of birth
  by furthering of his chaunce.
He still was readie bent
  his seruice to bestowe,
Thereby vnto his natiue soyle
  if gratefull gaine might growe.
If sage aduise were scarce
  and wholesome counsell scant,
Then should you see Tregonwels helpe
  ne wisedome would not want.
When Legats came from farre
  (as is there woonted guise)
To treate of truce, or talke of warre
  as matters did arise:
Tregonwell then was callde
  his verdit to expresse:

                                          Who

Who for the most part in the case
  of fruitfull things could gesse.
Or if hiinselfe were sent
  (which hap Tregonwell had)
Into a farre and forraine lande,
  then was Tregonwell glad.
For so he might procure
  wealepublick by his paine :
It was no corsie to this Knight
  long trauaile to sustaine.
But what? vndaunted death
  that seekes to conquer all,
And Atropos that Goddesse sterne
  at length haue spit their gall :
And reft vs such a one
  as was a Phœnix true,
Haue that now of his cindrie Corse
  there riseth not a nue.
Where may you see his match?
  where shall you find his læke?
None, though you from the farthest East
  vnto the Ocean seeke.
O house without thy head,
  O ship without a steare :
Thy Palynurus now is dead
  as shortly will appeare.
In daunger of distresse
  this Knight was euer wont

                        To

To yéelde himſelfe to perils preſt,
  and bide the greateſt brwnt.
No tumults tempeſt could
  ſubdue his conſtant hart :
Ne would the man by any meanes
  once from his countrie ſtart.
But (oh) it naught auailes,
  for death doth ſtrike the ſtroke
In things humaine, no worldly wealth
  his friendſhip may prouoke.
Let Trojans now leaue off
  by mourning to lament
The loſſe of Priam and his towne,
  when ten yeares warre was ſpent.
Pée Romaines lay your Hoods
  and black attire away :
Bewaile no more your Fabians fall
  nor that ſiniſter day
That reſt a Noble race
  which might haue floriſht long :
For neither loſſe is like to this
  our not deſerued wrong.
Now Cornewall thou mayſt crake,
  and Dorſet thou mayſt erie :
For thone hath bred, and thother loſt
  Tregonwell ſodainelie.
Whoſe corps though earthed bée
  in lothſome lumps of ſoyle,

                                          His

His peerelesse prayse by vertue won
　shall neuer feare the foyle.
Who so therefore shalt sée
　this Marble where he lies:
With that Tregonwels soule may finde
　a place aboue the Skies,
And reach a rowme of rest
　appointed for the nones:
For in this Toinbe interred is
　but flesh and bared bones.

The Louer confesseth himselfe to be
in Loue and enamored of
Mistresse. P.

IF banisht sléepe, and watchfull care,
　If minde affright with dreadfull dreames:
　If torments rife, and pleasure rare,
　If face besmearde with often streames:
If chaunge of cheare from ioy to smart,
If altred hue from pale to red:
If foltring tongue with trembling hart,
If sobbing sighes with furie fed:
If sodaine hope by feare opprest,
If feare by hope supprest againe,
Be proues that loue within the brest
Hath bound the hart with fansies chaine:
　Then I of force no longer may
In couert kéepe my piersing flame,
　　　　　　　　　　　　Which

Which euer doth it selfe betwray
But yéelde my selfe to fansies frame.
And now in sure to be a thrall
To hir that hath my hart in Gyue,
Shée may enforce me rise or fall
Till Death my limmes of life depriue.
P. with hir beautie hath bereft
My fréedome from my thralled minde,
And with hir louing lookes yeleft
My reason through both Barke and Rinde.
Yet well therewith I am content
In minde to take it paciently,
Since sure I am she will relent
And not enforce hir Friende to die.

So I in recompence may haue
Naught but a faithfull hart againe:
Then other friendship nill I craue,
But think my loue plent to gaine.

> That all things haue release of paine saue
> the Louer, that hoping and dreading
> neuer taketh ease.

What so the Golden Sunne
beholdes with blazing light,
When paine is past hath time to take
his comfort and delight.
The Ore with lumpish pace
and leasure that doth drawe,

Hath

Hath respite after toyle is past
  to fill his emptie mawe.
The lolearde Asse that beares
  the burden on his back,
His dutie done to stable plods,
  and reacheth to the rack.
The Deere hath woonted soyle
  his feruent heate to swage :
When woorke hath ende to respite runnes
  the Peasant and the Page.
The Owle that hates the day
  and loues to flee by night,
Hath queachie bushes to defende
  him from Apollos sight.
Eche Cunnie hath a Caue,
  eche little Foule a Nest
To shrowde them in at nædefull times
  to take their nædefull rest.
Thus vewing course of kinde
  it is not on the grounde,
That at some time doth not resort
  where is his comfort founde :
Saue me (O cursed man)
  whome neither Sunne ne shade
Doth serue the burthen of my breast
  and sorrowes to vnlade.
Eche sport porcures my smart,
  eche sæmely sight annoy :

                        Eche

Eche pleasant tune tormentes mine ease
　　and reaues my hoped ioy.
No Musick soundes so swæte
　　as doth the dolefull Drum,
For somewhat neare vnto my smart
　　that mournefull sounde doth cum.
A Gally slaue I seeme
　　vnto my selfe to bæ :
The Mayster that doth guide the ship
　　hath neare an eie to sæ:
You know where such a one
　　as Cupid is doth steare,
Amid the Goulfe of dæpe dispaire
　　great perill must appeare.
In steade of streaming sayles
　　bæ Wisshes hanges aloft :
Which if in tempest chaunce to teare
　　the Barck will come to nought.
For winde are scalding sighes
　　and secret sobbings prest :
Mixt with a cloude of stormie teares
　　to baine the Louers brest.
Though Cupid neare so well
　　his beaten Barck doe guie,
By slyding flats and sinking sandes
　　that in the wallow lie :
Yet those that are a borde
　　must euer stande in awe,

F o3

For cause a Buſſard is their guide
  not forcing any flawe:
That followes none aduice,
  but bluntly runnes on hed,
As proude as Peacock ouer thoſe
  that in his chaine or led.
Thus may you plainely ſée
  that eche thing hath releaſe
Of penſiue paine, ſaue Cupids thralls
  whoſe torments aye increaſe.

A poore Ploughman to a Gentleman,
   for whome he had taken a lit-
    tle paines.

Y Our Culter cuts the ſoyle that erſt was ſowne
  Your Harueſt was forereaped long agoe,
Your Sickle ſheares the Medowe ẏ was mowne,
Ere you the toyle of Tilmans trade did knowe:
God ſayth you are beholding to the man
That ſo for you your husbandrie began.
  Hée craues of you no Siluer for his Séde,
Ne doth demaunde a penny for his Graine,
But if you ſtande at any time in néede,
(God Maiſter) he as bolde with him againe.
You can not dóe a greater pleaſure than
To chooſe you ſuch a one to be your man.

To his Friende : P : of courting, tra
uailing, Dyſing, and Tenys.

TO liue in Court among the Crue is care,
Is nothing there but dayly diligence,
Nor Cap nor Knée, nor money muſt thou ſpare,
The Prince his Haule is place of great expence.

In rotten ribbed Barck to paſſe the Seas
The forraine landes and ſtraungie ſites to ſée,
Doth daunger dwell : the paſſage brédes vneaſe,
Not ſafe the ſoyle, the men vnfriendly bæ.

Admit thou ſée the ſtraungeſt things of all :
When eie is turnde the pleaſant ſight is gone :
The treaſure then of trauaile is but ſmall,
Wherefore (Friende P.) let all ſuch toyes alone.

To ſhake the bones, and cog the craftie Dice,
To Carde in care of ſodaine loſſe of Pence,
Vnſéemely is, and taken for a vice :
Vnlawfull play can haue no good pretence.

To band the Ball doth cauſe ý Coine to waſt,
It melts as Butter doth againſt the Sunne,
Naught ſaue thy paine, whé play doth ceaſe, ý haſt:
To ſtudie then is beſt when all is donne.
For ſtudie ſtayes and brings a pleaſaut gayne,
When play doth paſſe as glare wt guſhing raine.

The

The Louer declares that vnlesse he vtter his sorrowes by sute, of force he dyeth.

Lyke as the Gunne that hath to great a charge,
  And Pellet to the Powder ramde so sore,
As neyther of both hath powre to go at large,
Till shiuerd flawes in sounding Skies doe rore:
  Euen so my carefull breast that fraughted is
  With Cupids ware, & cloide with lurcking Loue,
  Vnlesse I shoulde disclose my drerinis,
  And out of hande my troubled thoughts remoue:
  A sunder woulde my cumbred Carcasse flee.
  The hart would breake the ouercharged Chace
  Of pensiue breast, and you (my Loue) shoulde see
  Your faythfull Friende in lamentable case.
  Wherefore doe what you may in gentle wyes
  The Gunner to assist in time of næde,
  And when you see the Pellet pierce the Skyes,
  And Powder make a proufe of woden glæde:
  Rue on his case, and seeke to quite his wo,
  Least in short time his Gunne too pæces go.

The Louer to a Friende that wrote him this sentence.

Yours assured to the death.

O faithfull Friend thrise happy was the fitt
  In so few wordes to such effect that wrought:
            G.i.   D

Of friendly hart a thousand folde yblist
That hath conceiude so iust and ioyful thought,
As not till death from pawned loue to bende
But Friend at first and Frind to be at ende.

Wherfore to counteruaile those words of thine,
And quit thy loue with faithfull hart againe,
I vow that I will neuer once decline
A foote from that I am for losse or gaine:
If thou be mine *till death,* I the assure
To be thy Friend *as long as life shall dure.*

Of certaine Flowers sent him by
his Loue vpon suspicion
of chaunge

YOur Flowers for their hue
    were fresh and faire to see:
Yet was your meaning not so true
    as you it thought to bee.
In that you sent me Bane,
    I iudge you ment thereby,
That cleane extinct was all my flame
    from whence no sparckes old flie.
Your Fenell did declare
    (as simple men can show)
That flattrie in my breast I bare
    where friendship ought to grow.
A Daysie doth expresse
    great follie to remaine,

I

I speake it not by roate oʒ geſſe,
  your meaning was ſo plaine.
Roſemarie put in minde
  that Bayes weare out of thought :
And Loueinpole came behinde
  foʒ Loue that long was ſought.
Pour Cowſlips did poʒtende
  that care was layde away :
And Eglantyne did make an ende
  where ſweete with ſower lay :
As though the leaues at furſt
  were ſwæte when Loue began :
But now in pʒoofe the pʒicks were curſt,
  and hurtfull to the Man.

           The Aunſwere to the ſame.

Erdie I næde no Bame
    ne foʒced heate by charme,
    To ſet my burning bʒeaſt in flame
      whom Cupids gleames doe warme,
On Bayes is my delight ,
  Remembʒance is not paſt :
Though Dayſie hit the nayle aright,
  my Friendſhip aye ſhall laſt.
Though Loue in pole bæ ,
  yet will I not foʒgoe
Ne caſt off care as you ſhall ſæ,
  and time the trouth ſhall ſhowe .
              G.y.   Sꝛ

So I may taste the swéete,:
  I force not on the sowre
The more is ioy when Friends doe méete,
  that Fortune earst did lowre.
Your Fenell failed quight
  where such good fayth is ment:
For Bayes are onely my delight
  though I for Bayes be shent.

Of a Foxe that wo ulde eate
no Grapes.

By fortune came a Foxe,
    where grue a loftie Uine,
  I will no Grapes (quoth hée)
    this yarde is none of mine :
The Foxe would none bicause that hée
Perceiude the highnesse of the Trée.
¶ So men that Forlie are,
  and long their lust to haue,
But cannot come thereby,
  make wise they would not craue :
Those subtill Marchants will no Wine
Bicause they cannot reach the Uine.

Of the straunge countenaunce of an
aged Gentlewoman.

It makes me laugh a good to sée thée lowre,
  and long to looken sad:

For

For when thy crabbed countnance is so sowre,
  thou art to seeming glad,
I blame not thee but nature in his case,
That might bestowde on thee a better grace.

To the Rouing Pyrat.

Thou winste thy wealth by warre
  vngodly way to gaine:
And in an houre thy ship is sunck
  goods drownde, the Pirat slaine.
The Gunne is all thy trust,
  it serues thy cruell fo
Then brag not on thy Canon shot
  As thought there were no mo.

Of one that had little Wit.

I Thee aduise   'Tis rare to get
  If thou be wise   And farre to set,
To keepe thy wit   'Twas euer yit
  Though it be small : Dearste wars of all.

In commendation of Wit.

Wit farre exceedeth wealth,
  Wit Princely pompe excels,
  Wit better is than Beauties beames
Where Pride and Daunger dwels.
Wit matcheth Kingly Crowne,
  Wit maisters Witlesse rage :
                    C.iij.   Wit

Wit rules the fonde affects of youth,
  Wit guides the steps of Age.
Wit wants no Reasons skill
  a faithfull Friend to know :
Wit wotes full well the way to voide
  the smooth and flæring fo.
Wit knowes what best becommes
  and what vnsæmely showes :
Wit hath a wile to ware the worst,
  Wit all good fashion knowes :
Since Wit by wisedome can
  doe this and all the rest,
That I imploy my painefull head
  to come by Wit is best.
Whome if I might attaine,
  then Wit and I were one :
But till time Wit and I doe cope,
  I shall be post alone.

An aunswere in dispraise of Wit

The Wit you so commend
    with wealth cannot compare :
  For wealth is able Wit to win
    when Wit is waxen barre.
Wit hath no Beauties braines,
  to Kingly crowne it yældes :
Wit subiect is to wilfull rage,
  Rage Wit and Reason wældes.

                              Wit

Wit rules not witlesse youth,
noz aged steps doth guide :
Wit knowes not how to win a friende,
Wit is so full of pzide.

Wit wots not how to flie
the smooth and flattering gest :
Wit cannot well discerne the thing
that doth become it best.

Wit hath no wyle to ware
mishap befoze it fall,
Wit knowes not what good fashion meanes,
Wit can doe naught at all.

Since Wit by wisdome can
doe nothing as you wéene,
If you doe toyle to come by Wit,
then are you ouer séene.

Whome when you doe attaine,
though Wit and you séeme one :
Yet Wit will to another when
your back is turnde and gone.

The Louer to *Cupid* for mercie, declaring
how first he became his thrall, with
the occasion of his defiyng Loue,
and now at last what caused
him to conuert.

O Mightie Lozde of Loue
Dame Venus onely ioy,

              G.iiij.   Whose

Whose Princely powre doth farre surmount
  all other heauenly Roy:
I that haue swarude thy lawes
  and wandred farre astray:
Haue now retyrde to thée againe
  thy statutes to obay.

And so thou wouldst vouchsafe
  to let me pleade for grace:
I would before thy Barre declare
  a sielie Louers case.

I would depaint at full
  how first I was thy man:
And show to that what was the cause
  that I from Cupid ran.

And how I haue since that
  yspent my wéerie time:
As I shall tell, so thou shalt here
  declarde in dwlefull rime.

In gréene and tender age
  (my Lorde) till .xviij. yeares,
I spent my time as fitted youth
  in Schole among my Féeares

As then no Bearde at all
  was growne vpon my Chin,
Which well approude that mans estate
  I was not entred in.

I néede not tell the names
  of Authors which I read,

Of

Of Proes and Verse we had inough
    to fine the dullest head.
But I was chiefly bent
    to Poets famous Art,
To them with all my deuor I
    my studie did conuert.
Where when I had with ioy
    yspent my time a while:
The reast refusde, I gaue me whole
    to Nasos Noble stile.
Whose volumes when I saw
    with pleasant stories fright:
In him (I say) aboue the rest
    I laide my whole delight.
What should I here reherse
    with base and barraine Pen,
The lincked tales and filed stuffe
    that I pervsed then :
In fine it was my loare
    vpon that part to light
Wherein he teacheth youth to loue,
    and women win by slight
Which Treatise when I had
    with iudging esc. suruayde:
At last I found thy Godly kynde
    and Princely powre displayde.
Of Cupid all that Booke
    and of his raigne did ring,

                      The

The Poet there of Venus did
  in sugred Dittie sing.
There read I of thy shafts
  and of thy golden Bow,
Thy shafts which by their diuers heads
  their diuers kindes did show.
I saw how by thy force
  thou madest men to stope:
And grisely Gods by secret flight
  and Deuilish Imps to drope.
There were depainted plaine
  thy quick and quiuer wings,
And what so else doth touch thy powre
  there Ouid swetely sings.
There I thy Conquests sawe
  and many a noble spoile:
With names annexed to the same
  of such as had the foile.
There Matrones marcht along
  and Maydens in their Roe,
Both Faunes and Satyrs there I saw
  with Neptuns troupe also.
With other thousands else
  which Naso there doth write,
But not my Pen or barraine Skull
  is able to recite.
O mightie Prince (quoth I)
  of such a fearefull forD,

                     How

How blest were I, so thou of mée
  wouldst daine to take remorce:
And choose mée for thy thrall
  among the rest to bée,
That liue in hope and serue in trust
  as waged men to thée:
With that (thy Godhead knowes)
  thou gauste a freindly looke:
And (though vnworthie such a place)
  mée to thy seruice tooke.
In token I was thine
  I had a badge of Blue
With Sabels set, and charge withall
  that I should aye be true.
Thou badste me follow Hope
  who tho thy Ensigne bare.
And so I might not doe amisse,
  thus didst thy selfe declare.
Then who reioyst but I:
  who thought himselfe yblist:
That was in Cupids seruice plaste
  as brauely as the best:
And thus in lustie youth
  I grue to be your thrall,
And was (I witnesse of thy Dame)
  right well content withall.
But now I minde to shewe
  (as promisse was to doe)

                          How

How firſt I fled thy Tents, and why
   thy campe I did forgoe.
When I had bene retainde
   well nigh a yeare or more,
And ſerude in place of wage and méede
   as is the Souldiars lore :
I chaunſt by hap to caſt
   my floting eies awrie,
And ſo a Dame of paſſing ſhape
   my fortune was to ſpie.
On whome Dame Nature thought
   ſuch beautie to beſtowe,
As ſhe had neuer framde before
   as proufe did plainely ſhowe.
On hir I gazde a while
   till vſe of ſenſe was fled :
And colour Paper white before
   was woren Scarlet red.
I felt the kindled ſparkes
   to flaſhing flames to growe :
And ſo on ſodaine I did loue
   the Wight I did not knowe.
Then to thy Pallace I
   with frowarde fote did run,
And what I ſaide, I mynde it yet ,
   for thus my tale begun.
O Noble Sir (quoth I)
   is this your frée aſſent

I

I should purſue a Game vnknowne
   within your ſtately Tent:
If ſo (quoth I) thou wilt,
   and giuſte the ſame in charge:
I mynde of all my brydled luſt
   to let the Raynes at large.
Then (Hope) did prick mǽ forth
   and bad mǽ be of chǽre:
Who ſaid I ſhould within a while
   ſubdue my Noble Fǽre.
He counſelde mǽ to ſhun
   no dreadfull daungers place,
But follow him who Banner bore
   vnto your Noble grace.
He would maintaine my right
   and further aye my cauſe,
And banniſh all diſpaire that grewe
   by frowarde fortunes flawes.
Tis Cupids will (quoth hǽ)
   our Maiſter and our Lorde
That thou with manly hart and hand
   ſhouldſt lay the Barck aborde.
She ſhall not chooſe but yǽlde
   the fruite for paſſed paines:
For ſhǽ is one of Cupids thralls,
   and bound in Venus Chaines.
Thinkſt thou our maiſter will
   his ſeruant liue in woe:

                        No

No not foz all his golden Darts
ne yet his crooked Bowe.
Wherefoze with luckie Mart
giue charge vnto the Wight :
Take Speare in hande, and Targe on arme,
and doe with courage fight.
With that, I armde me well
as fits a warring man,
And to the place of friendly fight
with lustie foote I ran.
My Foe was there befoze
I came vnto the fielde,
I thought Bellona had bene there
oz Pallas with hir shielde.
So well shæ was beset
with plate and pziuie Maile,
As foz my life my limber Launce
might not a whit pzeuaile.
Yet naythelesse with Speare
and Shielde, we fought a space :
But last of all we tooke our Bowes
and Arrowes from the case.
Then Dartes we gan to fling
in wide and weightlesse Skies :
And then the fiercest fight of all
and combat did arise.
In stead of shiuering shafts,
light louing lookes we cast,

And

And there I founde my selfe too weake
    hir Arrowes went so fast.
But one aboue the reast
    did cleaue my breast so farre,
As downe it went, where lay my hart,
    and there it gaue a farre.
So cruell was the stroke,
    so sodaine eke the wounde,
As by the fearefull force I fell
    into a senselesse sounde.
Thus hauing no refuge
    to quite my selfe from death:
I made a bowe to loue hir well
    whilst Lungs should lende me breath.
And since that time I haue
    endeuorde with my might
To win hir loue, but nought preuailes
    shee wayes it not a Mite.
Shee scornes my yelding hart,
    not forcing on my Hest:
But by disdaine of cloudy browe
    doth further my vnrest.
Yet ruthlesse though shee were,
    and farsed full of yre:
I loude hir well as hart coulde think,
    or woman might desire.
I sought to frame my speach
    and countnance in such sort,

                              As

As shée my couert hart mpght sée
　by shewe of outwarde port.
To Troilus halfe so true
　vnto his Creside was
As I to hir, who for hir face
　did Troiane Creside passe.
At length, when Reason saw
　mée sotted so in loue
As I ne would, ne might at all
　my fansie thence remoue :
Shée causde hir Trumpe be blowne
　to cyte hir seruants all
Into the place, by whose aduise
　I might be rid from thrall.
Then Plato first appearde
　with sage and solemne sawes :
And in his hand a golden booke
　of good and grékish lawes
Whose honnie mouth such wise
　and weightie wordes did tell:
Gainst thée and all thy troupe at once
　as Reason likte it well.
When Platoes tale was done,
　then Tullie prest in place :
Whose filed tongue with sugred talke
　would good a simple case.
With open mouth I heard
　and Iawes ystrecht awyde,

　　　　　　　　　　　How

How he gainſt Venus dearlings all
  and Cupids captiues cryde.
Then Plutarch gan to preach
  and by cramples proue,
That thouſand miſchiefes were procurde
  by meane of guilefull loue.
Whole Cities brought to ſpoyle,
  and Realmes to ſhamefull ſack:
Where Kings and Rulers god aduice
  by meane of Loue did lack?
Next Plutarch, Senec came
  ſeuere in all his ſawes:
Who cleane defide your wanton tricks,
  and ſcornde your childiſh lawes.
I nede not name the reaſt
  that ſtode as then in place:
But thouſandes more there were that ſought
  your Godhead to deface.
When all the Hall was huſht,
  and Sages all had donne:
Then Reaſon that in iudgement ſate
  hir ſkilfull talke begonne.
Gramercie Friends (quoth ſhœ)
  your counſell lykes me well:
But now lend eare to Reaſons wordes
  and liſten what I tell.
What madneſſe may be more
  than ſuch a Lorde to haue,

                  H.J.   Who

Who makes the chieftaine of his bande
  a ruke and raskall slaue ?
Who woonted is to yoelde
  in recompence of paine,
A ragged recompence God wote
  that turnes to moere disdaine ?
Who gladly would ensue
  a Conduct that is blinde ?
Or thrall himselfe to such a one
  as shewes himselfe vnkinde ?
What Ploughman would be glad
  to sowe his seede for gaine,
And reape when Haruest time comes on
  but trauaile for his paine ?
What madman might endure
  to watch and warde for nought ?
To ride, to runne, and last to loose
  the recompence he sought ?
To waste the day in wo,
  and restlesse night in care,
And haue in stead of better foode
  but sobbing for his fare ?
To bleare his eies with brine
  and salted teares yshead;
To force his fainting flesh to fade,
  his colour pale and dead ?
And to foredoe with carke
  his wretched witherde hart ?

                       And

And so to bꝛæde his bitter bale
  and hatch his deadly smart ?
I speake it to this fine,
  that plainly might appere
Cupidos craft and guilefull guise
  to him that standeth here.
Whose eies with fansies mist
  and errors cloudes are dim,
By meane that hæ in Venus Lake
  and Cupids goulfe doth swim.
And hath by sodaine sight
  of vnacquainted shape
So firt his hart, as hope is past
  for euer to escape.
Vnlesse to these my woꝛdes
  a listning care hæ lende :
Which oft art wont the Louers mindes
  and fansie to offende.
But he that would his health
  sowꝛe Sirops must assay :
Foꝛ erie griefe hath cure againe
  by cleane repugnaunt way.
And who so mindes to quite
  and rid himselfe from wo,
Must sæke in time foꝛ to remoue
  the thing that hurtes him so.
Foꝛ longer that it lastes
  it frets the farder in

        H. H.   Vntill

Untill it growe to cureleſſe maine
   by paſſing fell and ſkin.
The Pyne that beares his head
   vp to the haughtie Skie,
Would well haue bæne remooude at firſt
   as daylie pꝛoofe doth trie :
Which now no foꝛce of man
   noꝛ engine may ſubuart :
So wyde the cræping rootes are run
   by Natures ſubtile Art :
So Loue by ſlender ſleight
   and little paine at furſt
Would haue bæne ſtopt, but hardly now
   though thou wouldſt doe thy wurſt,
The woonted ſaw is true,
   ſhun Loue, and Loue will flæ,
But follow Loue and ſpite thy noſe
   then Loue will follow thæ.
And though ſuch graffed thoughts
   on ſodaine may not die,
Ne be foꝛgone : yet pꝛoceſſe ſhall
   their farther grouth deſtrie.
No Giaunt foꝛ his lyfe
   can cleaue a knarrie Oke,
Though h e would ſæke to doe his wurſt
   and vtmoſt at a ſtroke :
But let the meaneſt man
   haue ſpace to fell him downe,

                      And

And he will make him bende his head
  and b2ing his boughes to grownde.
No fo2ce of falling showze
  can pierce the Marble stone,
As will the often d2ops of raine
  that from the gutters gone.
Wherefo2e thou retchlesse man
  my counsell with the mo
Is, that thou péecemeale doe expell
  the loue that paines thée so.
Renounce the place where shée
  doth make soiourne and stay :
Fo2ce not hir trayning truthlesse eies,
  but turne thy face away.
Thinke that the hurtfull hooke
  is couerde with such baite :
And that in such a pleasant plot
  the Serpent lurcks in waite.
Waie well hir sco2nefull chére,
  and think shée sékes thy spoile :
And though thy conquest were atchiude
  may not acquite thy toile :
Not ydle sé thou bée,
  take aye some charge in hande :
And quickly shalt thou quench the flame
  of carelesse Cupids b2ande.
Fo2 what (I p2ay you) b2ed
  Ægisthus fowle desame ?

            H.iij.   And

And made him spoken of so yll :
  what put him to the shame :
What forcde the Foole to loue.
  his beastly ydle lyfe
Was cause that he besotted was
  of Agamemnons Wyfe.
If he had fought in field
  encountring with his Foe,
On stately stæde, or else on foote
  with glaue had giuen the blœ :
If he that Lecher lewde
  had warlick walles assailde
With Cannon shot, or bownsing Raw
  his fenced enmies quailde :
He had not felt such force
  of vile and beastly sin,
Cupidos shafts had fallen short
  if he had busie bin.
What Myrrha made to loue,
  or Byblos to desire
To quench the heate of hungrie lust
  and flames of filthy fire :
What Canace enforcde
  to frie with frantick brands,
In sort as vp to yæld hir selfe
  vnto hir brothers hands :
And others thousand mo
  of whome the Poets wright :

                     Nought

Nought else (good fayth) but for they had
   in ydle thoughts delight.
They spent their youthfull yeares
   in foule and filthie trade,
They busied not their ydle braines
   but God of Pleasure made.
Wherefore if thou (I say)
   dost couet to auoyde
That bedlam Boyes deceitfull Bowe
   that others hath anoyde :
Eschewe the ydle lyfe,
   flee, flee from doing nought :
For neuer was there ydle braine
   but bred an ydle thought.
And when those stormes are past
   and cloudes remoude away :
I know thou wilt on (Reason) think
   and minde the words I say.
Which are : that Loue is roote
   and onely crop of care,   *Discomo-*
The bodies foe, the harts annoy,   *dities of*
   and cause of pleasures rare.   *Loue.*
The sicknesse of the minde,
   the Fountaine of vnrest :
The goulfe of guile, the pit of paine,
   of griefe the hollow Chest.
A fierie frost, a flame
   that frozen is with Ise,

A heauie burden light to beare,
   a Vertue fraught with Vice.
It is a Warlike peace,
   a safetie set in dred,
A deepe dispaire annext to hope,
   a famine that is fed.
Sweete poyson for his taste,
   a Porte Charybdis leeke,
A Scylla for his safetie thought,
   a Lyon that is meeke.
And (by my Crowne I sweare)
   the longer thou dost loue,
The longer shalt thou liue a Thrall
   as tract of time will proue.
Wherefore retire in haste
   and speede thee home againe,
And pardned shall thy trespasse bee,
   and thou exempt from paine.
Take Reason for thy guide
   as thou hast done of yore :
And spite of Loue thou shalt not loue
   ne be a thrall no more.
Repaire to Platos schole,
   and Tullies true aduice :
Let Plutarch be and Seneca
   thy teachers to be wise.
This long and learned tale
   had brosed so my braine;

                   As

As I forthwith to reason ran,
　and gaue thee vp in plaine.
Fie, fie on Loue quoth I,
　I now perceiue his craft :
For Reason hath declarde at large
　how hee my freedome raft,
I see his promise is
　farre fayzer than his paie :
I finde how Cupid blearde mine eies,
　and made me run astraie.
I wote how hungrie Hope
　hath led mee by the lip,
And made mee mooue an endlesse sute
　well worth an Oken chip.
Hee trainde mee all by trust,
　I farde as Hounde at hatch :
The lesser fruite I founde, the moze
　I was procurde to watch.
Thus (mightie Lozde) I left
　thy lawes and statutes strong
For rayling Reasons trifling talke,
　and offerd thee a wzong.
But now Dame Venus knowes,
　and thou hir sonne canst tell
That I within my couert hart
　doe loue thee passing well.
Now fully bent to be
　(so thou wilt cleane put out

　　　　　　　　　　　Of

Of mind my paſſed iniuries)
  thy man and Souldier ſtout:
Preſt to obey thy will
  and neuer ſwarue againe,
As long as Venus is of foꝛce
  and thou ſhalt kéepe thy Raigne.
I weigh not Tullies tale,
  ne pꝛating Platos talke:
Let Plutarch bouch what Plutarch can,
  let ſkuruey Senec walke.
Olde Ouid will I reade,
  whoſe pleaſant wit doth paſſe
The reaſt, as farre as ſtubboꝛne Stéele
  excells the bꝛittle Glaſſe.
In him thy déedes of Armes
  and manly Marts appéere,
In him thy ſtately ſpoyles are ſéene
  as in a Mirrour cléere.
Thy mothers pꝛayſe and thine
  in him are to be founde,
Foꝛ conqueſtes which you had in Heauen
  and here bylow on grounde.
Foꝛgiue my foꝛmer guilt,
  foꝛget my paſſed toyes:
And graunt I may aſpire againe
  bnto my woonted ioyes.
If euer man did loue
  oꝛ ſerue in better ſtéede,

                             Then

Then shape my wagesse to the same
  and doe restraine my mœde.
But so I fight in fielde
  as fiercely as the best :
I hope that then your Godhead will
  reward me with the rest.

After misaduentures come
good haps.

I Neuer thought but this that luck in fine
  Would to my will and fansie well incline.
For dayly prœfe doth make an open show
That commen course of things would haue it so.
When stormie clouds from darkned skyes are fled,
Then Phœbus shewes his gay and golden hed.
His princely pride appeares whē showres are past,
And after day the night ensues as fast.
When winter hath his trembling carkas showne,
And wt his frostie fote the spring downe throwne,
Then in leapes Æstas gay with gladsome gleames
That Haruest brings & dries vp winter streames.
The Barck that broylde in rough & churlish Seas
At length doth reach a Port and place of ease.
The wailefull warre in time doth yœlde to peace,
The Larums lowde & Trupets sound doth ceasse :
Thus may we sée that chaunce is full of chaunge.
And Fortune sœdes on fœte that is still straunge.
                                          Wherefore

Wherefore doe not dispaire thou louing Wight,
For Seas doe ebbe and flow by Natures might :
From worse to good our haps are chaunged oft,
And basest things sometimes are raysde aloft.
So Gods would haue, and Fortune doth agrée,
Which proufe appéeres and is expxest by mée.

To his Loue that controlde his Dogge for sawning on hir.

IN déede (my Deare) you wrong my Dog in this
And shew your selfe to be of crabbed kinde,
That will not let my fawning Whelp to kisse
Your fist, y̌ faine would shew his Maisters minde :
A Mastife were moxe fit for such a one,
That can not let hir Louers Dog alone.

He in his kinde for mée did séeme to sue,
That carst did stande so highly in your grace,
His Maisters minde the wittie Spanell knewe,
And thought his woonted Mistresse was in place :
But now at last (good faith) I plainly sée
That Dogs moxe wise than Women friendly bée.

Wherefore since you so cruelly entreate
My Whelp, not foxcing of his fawning chéere,
You shew your selfe with pxide to be repleate,
And to your Friend your Nature doth appéere :
The Pxouerbe olde is verifide in you,
Loue mée and loue my Dog, and so adue,

Both

Both I and he that sicly Beast sustaine
For louing well and bearing faithfull harts,
Despitous checks, and rigorous disdaine,
Where both haue well deserued for our parts,
For Friendship I, for offred seruice hée,
And yet thou neyther louste the Dog nor mée.

Vpon the death of the aforenamed Dame Elizabeth Arhundle of Cornewall.

What Tongue can tell the wo :
what Pen expresse the plaint :
Vnlesse the Muses helpe at néede
I féele my wits to faint.

Yée that frequent the hilles
and highest Holtes of all,
Assist mée with your skilfull Muses
and listen when I call.

And Phœbus, thou that sitst
amidst the learned route,
Do way thy Bowe, and reach thy Lute
and say to sounde it oute.

Helpe (learned Pallas) helpe
to write the fatall fall
Of hir, whose lyfe deserues to be
a Mirrour to vs all.

Whose Parents were of fame
as Leyster well can showe :

Where

Where they in worship long had liude,
   with yeares did worship growe.
Of worship was the house
   from whence shee tooke hir line:
And she a Dannat by discent
   to worship did incline.
What næde I pen the prayse
   of hir that liude so well.
That of it selfe doth yælde a founde,
   we næde not ring the Bell.
Whilst Dannat did ensue
   Diana in the race,
A truer Nymph than Dannat was
   was neuer earst in place.
With Beautie so adrest
   with Uertue so adornde :
Was none that more imbraste the good,
   nor at the wicked scornde.
When flæing Fame with Trumpe
   and blasted brute had brought
This Dannats thewes to courtlike eo
   (which Dannat neuer sought)
To Court she was procurde
   on Princesse to attende
A seruice fit for such a one
   hir flowring yeares to spende.
Where when she had remainde
   and serude the Princesse well,

                          Not

Not rashly but with good aduice
  to Iunos yoke she fell.
A Woulfe by hap espide
  this siclie Lambe in place,
And thought hir fittest for his pray:
  not gastly was his face,
Not Woulflike were his eies,
  ne harrish was his voice:
Nor such as Lambes might feare to heare
  but rather might reioice.
A hart not bent to hate
  or yoelding pray to spill:
Unto Licaon farre vnlike
  whose pleasure was to kill.
Arhundle was his name,
  his stock of great discent:
Whose predecessors all their liues
  in Uertues path had spent.
Hee not vnlike the rest
  behaude himselfe so well,
As he in fine became a Knight,
  so to his share it fell.
Thus was this Ladie fast
  consoynde in sacred knot:
Whose prime and tender yeares were spent
  deuoyde of slaunders blot.
The match no sooner made,
  when mariage rites were donne:

                              But

But Dannat ranne hir race as right
 as shæ hir course begonne.
And sooth it is, shæ liude
 in wiuely bond so well,
As she from Collatinus wife
 of Chastice boze the bell.
Vlysses wyfe did blush
 to heare of Dannats prayse:
Admetus Make (the good Alcest)
 did pælde vp all hir Kayes.
The Grækes might take in griefe
 of such a one to hære,
Who foz hir well deserued fame
 could haue no Grækish Pære.
Thus many yeares were spent
 with good and soothfast life,
Twirt Arhundle that wozthie Knight
 and his appzoued wife.
Of whome such Impes did spzing,
 such fruite began to growe.
Such issue did pzocæde as we
 them by their bzaunches knowe.
The Oke will pælde no Grapes,
 the Vine will beare no Hawes:
Ech thing must follow kindly course
 by Natures fixed lawes.
Euen so that wozthie Trœ
 such fruite is fæne to beare,

As

As yet commends the withꝛed ſtocks
  and them to Welkin reare.
Thus did they liue in ioy,
  till chaunce and ſpitefull death
Theſe louing Turtles did deuide
  and reſt the Cock his bꝛeath.
Then firſt the bale began,
  then black attyꝛe came on:
And Dannats dꝛẻrie doole was ſẻne
  with neuer ſtinting mone.
Nought might hir ſoꝛow ſwage,
  but ſtill ſhe did bewaile
The Cinders of hir ſeuerd Make
  with teares of none auaile.
Seauen yeares ſhe ſpent in wo
  refuſing other Make:
Foꝛ ſuch is Turtles kinde you know
  they will none other take.
I doubt where Dido felt
  the like toꝛmenting rage,
When that the guilefull Gueſt was gone
  that laid his fayth to gage,
This Dannats vertues were
  ſo rife and eke ſo rare,
As few with hir foꝛ honeſt life.
  and wiſdome might compare,
Minerua did ſoiourne
  within that wineiy bꝛeſt:
                        I.ſ.   Hir

Hir dœdes declarde that in hir head
  Dame Pallas was a guest.
But what we couet most
  oz chiefest holde in pzice,
With grœdie gripe of darting death
  is reaued with a trice.
The cruell Sisters thzœ
  were all in one agrœde,
To let the spindle run no moze
  but shzid the fatall thzœde.
And foztune, (to expzesse
  what swing and sway she bare)
Allowde them leaue to vse their foze
  vpon this Iewell rare.
Thus hath the Welkin woon,
  and we a losse sustainde :
Thus hath hir Cozse a Claute founde out,
  hir Spzite the Heauens gainde.
Since sobbing will not serue,
  ne shedding teares auaile
To bzing the soule to Cozps againe
  his olde and woonted Gaile :
Leaue off to bath hir stone
  with Niobs teares to long,
Foz thou shalt aide hir naught at all
  but put thy selfe to wzong.
With that hir soule may reach
  the place from whence it came :

                                        And

And she be guerdond for hir life
  with neuer dying fame.
For sure she well deserude
  to haue immortall prayse,
And lawde more light than clearest Sunne
  or Phœbus golden rayes.
If ought my slender skill
  or writing were of powre,
No processe of ingratefull time,
  hir vertues should deuoure.

Dispraise of Women that allure and loue not.

When so you vew in Uerse
  and Poets rimes report,
Of Lucrece, and Vlysses wife
  that lyues in honest sort.
When Hippo comnies by hap
  or good Alcest yseare,
And other some that by desert
  with fame renowmed were,
Then you with hastie doome
  and rashfull sentence straight,
Will vaunt that women more and lesse
  were all with vertue fraight.
And, for those fewe that liude
  in wiuely bonde so well,

                    I.H.   You

You will eſtǽme the reaſt by thoſe
   that onely bare the bell,
But follow ſound aduice,
   let eche receyue hir dœme,
As ech in vertue did ſurmount,
   oꝛ ſit in higheſt rœme.
So cleane was neuer ſǽde
   yſifted, but among
Foꝛ all their paynes were wœdes that grew
   to put the graine to wꝛong.
That troupe of honeſt Dames
   thoſe Griſels all are gone :
No Lucrece now is left aliue,
   ne Cleopatra none.
Thoſe dayes are all ypaſt,
   that date is flǽted by :
They myꝛꝛoꝛs were Dame Nature made
   hir ſkilfull hande to try.
Now courſe of kinde exchaungde
   doth yœldꝛ a woꝛſer graine,
And women in theſe latter yeares
   thoſe modeſt Matrones ſtaine.
Deceit in their delight,
   great fraude in friendly lœkes :
They ſpoyle the Fiſh foꝛ friendſhips ſake
   that houer on their Hœkes.
They buye the baite to deare
   that ſo their frǽdome loꝛe ;

                        And

And they the moze deceitfull are
  that so can craft and gloze.
With beautie to allure,
  and murder with disdaine :
What moze may be gainst womens kind
  where ruth of right should raigne
So Memphite Crocodile
  (as we in Poets fine)
Where Nylus with his seuenfold streame
  to Seaward doth incline
With ruthlesse trickling teares
  and lamentable sounde,
The siely Beast with pittie mounde
  doth cruelly confounde.
So Marmaydes in the flood
  and Syzens swéetly sing,
Till they the musing Mariner
  to spædie death doe bzing.
Now Helen foz hir traine
  with Dian may compare :
Such sundzie Helens now are found,
  and Dians Nymphes so rare.
Who if by craft espie
  thy Senses once to bende,
And bow by Cupids subtile bzeach
  that burning gleames doth sende:
Then will they sæke in haste
  by foxce of friendly blinck,

               J.stf.   And

And wzested looke into thy bzeast
   their beauties shape to sinck.
Which if be bzought to passe,
   then haue they their desire:
And standing farre doe smile to sée
   the flaming of the fire.
Then looke they on a loose,
   and neuer once repaire
To ende the strife that they haue stirrde
   twixt Louer and Dispaire.
As Shepheards when they sée
   the Ganders foe in snare
Reioyce, that from their soldes of late
   their siely cattle bare:
Oz Boy that knowes the Foule
   to be in pithole caught,
That woonted was to scale the scale
   and set the snare at naught:
So wily Women woont
   to laugh, when so they spie
The louing Wight ytraynde by trust
   in poynt and pinch to die.
But if such chaunce doe chaunce
   (as often chaunce we sée)
The fish that earst was hangde on Hooke
   by better chaunce be frée,
If he by happie hap
   doe cast off Cupids yoke,

Not

Not setting of their Loue a Lœke
  that gaue the cruell ſtroke :
Then are remœude the cloudes
  of hir diſdainfull bꝛow :
And friendſhips flœd that earſt was dꝛie
  afreſh begins to flow.
Then wꝛeſteth ſhœ hir grace,
  and makes a ſœming ſhow
As though ſhe ment no chaunge at all,
  ne would hir Heſtes foꝛgo.
Thus are they fright with wiles
  whome Nature made ſo plaine,
Thus Sinons ſhifts they put in bꝛe
  their purpoſe to attaine.
Wherefoꝛe let be our care
  Vlyſſes trade to trie :
And ſtop our eares againſt the ſounde
  of Syꝛens when they crie.
Think when thou ſœſt the baite
  whereon is thy delite,
That hidden Hœkes are hard at hande
  to bane thœ when thou bite.
Think well that poyſon lurckes
  in ſhape of Sugar ſwœte :
And where the freſheſt flowꝛes are ſœne
  there moſt beware thy fœte,
But chiefly Women ſhonne
  and follow mine aduiſe,
                F.iiij.   If

If not, thou mayst perhaps in proufe
   of folly beare the price.
To trust to rotten boughes
   the daunger well is seene :
To treade the tylled trap vnwares
   hath alwayes perill bœne.
Haue Medea still in minde,
   let Circe be in thought :
And Helen that to vtter sack,
   both Greece and Troie brought
Let Creside be in coumpt
   and number of the mo,
Who for hir lightnesse may presume
   with falsest on the row :
Else would she not haue left
   a Troian for a Grœke.
But what ? by kinde the Cat will hunt,
   hir Father did the like.
As wylie are their wits,
   so are their tongues vntrue :
Inconstant and aye fleeting mindes
   that most imbrace the nue.
When fixed is their fayth
   it restes on brittle sande :
And when thou drinste them surste of all
   they beare thœ but in hande.
Though Argus were aliue
   whose eies in number were

As

As many as the Peacock proude
  in painted plume doth beare:
Yet Women by their wyles
  and well acquainted dzifts,
Would soone deceiue his waking head,
  and put his eies to shifts.
Nought haue they neede at all
  Cyllenus Pipe to blow
To forge their fraude, their tongues will serue
  as learned wziters show.

> First trie and then tell
> Where I haue sayd well
> For without a triall
> There vailes no deniall.

Of a Phisition and a Soothsayer.

MARCKE felt himselfe diseasde,
  the Soothsayer sayd: There bee
Sire yet remainder daies of life,
  no mo (Friend Marcke) to thee
Then skilfull Alcon came,
  he felt the pulses beate:
And out of hande this Marcus dide,
  there Phisick wzought his feate.
This showes Phisition doth
  the Soothsayer farre erceede:
For thone can make a shozt dispatch,
  when thother makes no speede.

                         A con-

A controuersie of a conquest in
Loue twixt Fortune
and Venus.

Hilſt Fiſſher keſt his line
the houering fiſh to hœke:
By hap a rich mans daughter on
the Fiſſher keſt hir lœke.
Shœ frydc with frantick Loue,
they maride ekc at laſt:
Thus Fiſher was from lowe eſſate
in top of Treaſure plaſt.
Stœde Foztune by and ſmylde:
how ſay you (Dame) quoth ſhœ
To Venus? was this conqueſt yours,
oz is it duc to mœ?
Twas I (quoth Vulcans Wiſe)
with helpe of Cupids Bowe,
That made this wanton wench to rage,
and match hir ſelfe ſo lowe.
Not ſo: twas Foztune I
that bzought the Trull in place:
And Foztune was it that the man
ſtœde ſo in Maydens grace.
By Foztune fell their loue,
twas Foztune ſtrake the ſtroke:
Then detter is this man to mœ
that did the match pzouoke.

The

The Louer voweth how so euer
he be guerdoned to loue
faithfully.

Vnthankfull though she were
　　and had disdainefull browe,
Regarding nought my constant hart,
　　ne forcing of hir bowe:
Since sowen is the sæde
　　of faithfull friendships lore,
Vnconstant will J neuer be
　　ne breake my Hest therefore.
Let Fortune vse hir force
　　so Cupide stande mine ayde,
And Cyprid laugh with louely loke,
　　J will not be afrayde.
By mæ the Noble kinde
　　of man shall not be shamde,
Recorde through mæ shall neuer force
　　our sequell be defamde.
Albe that J consume
　　my græne and growing youth,
Yea age and all without rewarde
　　yet nill J swarue my truth.
Eche that shall after come,
　　and liue when J am dust,
This louing hart shall well deserie
　　the Key of perfite trust.

　　　　　　　　　　　Sir,

Hir, while my vitall breath
   these fainting limmes shall moue:
Yea, after death in hollow Vawte
   ytombed, will I loue.
Force shee my seruice true
   I force it not at all,
Rue she by ruth my dræsie life
   or it to mercy call :
In stay my Loue shall stand,
   I will not false my fayth,
Ne breake my former plighted hest
   or promise to the death.
Disdaine shall neuer force
   my friendship once awrie :
Ere that I craue immortall Gods
   that ye will let me die.
Let Dido still complaine
   Æneas broken Hest,
Of all that came to Carthage Coast
   the most vnfaythfull guest.
Vntrustie Theseus eke
   let Ariadne clæpe,
Escaping from his friendly Fæere
   yled in slumbring slæpe :
So let Medea blame
   the knight that woon the Flise,
That forced naught at all in fine
   hir cleapings and hir cries :

                          Haue

Haue thou the faythfull hart
  of thine affured Friend,
Ere he be of that retchleffe race
  the Sunne awzie fhall wende,
Where fo thou yœlde him grace
  oz as an outcaft fhœn :
Expect his former plighted Heft
  as thou tofoze haft dœn.
Loue will hæ neuer blame
  ne Venus lawes forgo,
Life fœner fhall than loue decreafe
  his faith is fired fo.

He forrowes the long abfence
      of his Ladie.P.

Now once againe (my Mufe) renue the woes
  Which earft thou haft in dœlefull dittie fong,
For greater caufe of fozrow not arofe
To mœ at all, than now of late is fpzong :
As you fhall heare in fad and folemne Werfe,
A wofull Wight his haplefſe hap rehearſe,
  Come (Clio) come with penſiue Pen in hande
And cauſe thy ſiſters chaunge their chœreful voice,
Ye furies fell that lurcke in Plutos lande,
Come ſkip to Skies, and raiſe a dœlefull noice :
Helpe to lament the Louers wofull chaunce,
And let Alecto leade the lothſome daunce.

                                    All

All ye that Ladies are of Lymbo Lake
With hissing haire, and Snakie bush bedect,
Your boddes of stile and dankish Dennes forsak
And Stix with stinking Sulpher all infect :
Doe what you may to ayde my carefull Quill,
And helpe to ring a Louers latter knill.

And time (I trow) sith she from hence is fled
Who was the guide and giuer of my breath,
By whome I was with wished pleasure fed
And haue escapte the ruthlesse hande of death :
Who was the Key and Cable of my life,
That made me scape Charybdis carefull clife.

A Starre whereby to steare my bodies Barck,
And ship of soule to shoare in safetie bring,
To quite my Corse from painesull pining cark,
And fierie force of craftie Cupids sting :
Euen she that me from Syllas shelfe did shroude,
That light is lost, that Lodestarre vnder cloude.

Whose absence breedes the tempest I sustaine,
And makes my thoughts so clousie black to bee,
And brackish teares from swolen eies to raine,
And churlish gale of surging sighes to flee :
That Ancor scarce ne harbour I may haue
From deepe dispaire my broken Ship to saue.

The Rubie from the Ring is reft I finde,
The foile appeeres that vnderneath was set :
The Saint is gone, the Shrine is left behinde,
The Fish is scapte, and here remaines the Net !

That

That other choise for me is none but this,
To waile the want of hir that is my blisse.

  I cursse the VVight that causde hir hence to go,
I hate the Horse that hence hir Corse conuaide,
The Bit, the Saddle all I cursse aroe,
And ought that else might this hir iourney staide:
I cursse the place where she doth now soiourne,
And that whereto she mindes to shape retourne.

  My mouth, that kist hir not before she went,
Mine eies, that did not seeke to see hir face,
My head, that it no matter did inuent,
My hande, that it in Paper did not place:
My foete, that they refusde to trauell tho,
My legges I cursse that were so loth to go.

  My tongue, that it to parle did then procure
To vtter all my close and couert minde,
To hir who long hath had my woundes in cure,
In whome such ruth and mercie I did finde:
My hart I cursse, that sought not to bewray
It selfe to hir or ere she went hir way.

  And last my selfe and erie thing beside,
My life, my limmes, my carrion Corse I cursse:
Saue hir for whome these torments I abide,
That of my lyfe is onely well and sourse:
I oue shroude hir salfe, and keepe hir from annoy,
And sende hir soone to make returne with ioy.

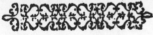

                                         To

To his Loue long ab-
fent,declaring his
torments.

LIngring Loue, O Friende
that abfent art fo long,
Where fo thou be,the Gods thée guide
and quit thy Corfe from wrong:
And fende thée harmeleffe health,
and fafely to reuart,
How foone your felfe may déeme full well
to faue a dying hart.
For fince your parture I
haue lead a lothfome ftate:
And faue the hope of your returne
nought might my woes abate.
And will you know the time
how I haue fpent away?
And doe you long in ruthfull rime
my torments to furuay?
Though but with wéeping eies
I may the fame recite:
Yet naytheleffe the truth herein
to thée (my Friend) I write.
When flickring Fame at firft
vnto mine eares had brought
That you to trauell were addreft,
and fired was your thought

In

In London long to lodge,
   and floe our friendly soile :
Then Dolour first in daunted Corps
   and wounded breast did boile.
I felt how griefe did giue
   the onset on my hart,
And sorow sware that pensiue pangues
   should neuer thence depart.
With clinching clawes there came,
   and talents sharply set,
A flock of græedie griping woes
   my grunting hart to fret.
The more I sought the meane
   by pleasaunt thought to ease
My growing griefe, the more I felt
   increase my new disease.
When other laught for ioy,
   it brought to minde my woe :
When Musick slakte their sorrowes, then
   my secret sore did growe.
When they at meate were set
   their daintie foode to taste,
In stead of Viands, hartie sighes
   I had for my repaste.
When Bacchus came to Boorde,
   and eche to other drincks :
My swolen floud of salted teares
   did ouerflow his brincks,

        R.J.   And

And out did gushe amaine
   of drinke to stande in stæde
To me, that of such monstrous meate
   as sorow was did fæde.
From borde to bed I go
   in hope to finde reliefe,
And by some pleasaunt nap to rid
   my troubled Ghost from griefe:
But slumbring slæpe is fled.
   and Morpheus shewes his spight:
That will not yælde on minuts reast
   in all a Winters night.
O Lorde, what sundrie kindes
   of care doe then begin
Assault my wearie waking head,
   and trembling hart within?
A thousande thoughts arise,
   eche thought his torment brings:
And thus the lothed night I spend
   and fæle how sorow springs.
And if in dawning chaunce
   some drouping slæpe to light
Upon the carefull Corse that thus
   hath spent the waking night:
It standes in little steade,
   so dreadfull are my dreames
As they by force of wo procure
   mine eies to runne with streames.

Then

Then bathe I bed with brine,
　and cloy my Couch with teares :
And mid my sleepe thy griesly Ghost
　in straungie sort appeares,
Not with such friendly face
　and brow of gladsome cheare
As earst thou hadst : those louely lokes
　and blincks are all areare.
More grimmer is your grace,
　more coye your countnance eake :
More lowring lokes than were of yore
　and Brow more bent to wreake.
In hande mee thinkes I see
　thee holde the hatefull knife
To slea thy Friend, and for god will
　to reaue deserued lyfe.
Wherewith I wake afright
　and straine my pillow fast,
To garde me from the cruell toole
　vntill your wrath be past.
At length I see it plaine
　that fansie did enforce
Vnto his vgly monstrous dreame
　my weake and slumbring Corse.
I vewe thy secret hart,
　and how it longs to bee
With him that for vnfayned loue
　impawnde his faith to thee.

　　　　　　　　　　D.H.　　　　　Fo

For mercie then I call
 of you that iudge so yll,
Whose pleasure is to garde your Friend,
 and not your Foe to kyll.
Of dreames a thousand such
 eche night I haue a share,
To bannish sleepe from pining Corse
 and nurse my canckred care.
Thus day and night I liue,
 thus night and day I die :
In death I feele no smart at all,
 in life great wo I trie.
Wherefore to rid my griefes
 and bannish all annoie :
Retire from Greece, and doe soiourne
 here with thy Friend in Troie.
Who longs to see thy face
 and witnesse of thy state :
no partner be of thy delights
This furious fits to bate.

To Browne of light beliefe.

BEware my Browne of light beliefe,
 trust not before you trie :
 For vnder cloke of great good will
 doth fained friendship lie.
As wylie Adder lurcks in leaues
 and greenest grasse of all,

 And

And ſtings the ſtalking Wight that thought
  no daunger would befall.
So is the plaine vnplayted man
  by ſubtile dealing guilde
And ſooneſt ſnarde by ſubtile ſhifts
  of him that ſmoothly ſmilde.
Wée neuer ſée the frowning Friend
  that frets to outwarde ſhowe,
Beguile or ſéeke to falſe his Friend,
  as doth the ſléering Foe :
The Maſtiſe Dog is voyded well
  that barcks or ere he bite :
But (oh) the Cur is cruell that
  doth neuer barck a whit.
Deale thou as Courtyers daylie doe,
  in wordes be franck and frée,
Speake fayre and make the weather cléere
  to him that gybes with thée.
For ſo thou ſhalt aſſured ſtande
  from hurt to be as farre,
As from the grounde of true good wſll
  thoſe gloſing marchaunts are.
A wiſedome to beware of Woulfes,
  and Foxes guilefull guiſe :
For tone is craftie by his kinde,
  the other paſſing wiſe.
So that it is a matter harde
  their double driſts to flée :

              T.H.   But

But yet thou shalt auoyde the wurst
if thou be rulde by mee.
(ꝓ)G. T.

That Death is not so much to be feared as daylie diseases are.

What : yst not follie for to dread
and stande of Death in feare,
That mother is of quiet reast,
and griefes away doth weare ?
That brings release to want of welth,
and poore oppressed Wightes ?
He comes but once to mortall men,
but once for all he smites.
Was neuer none that twise hath felt
of cruell Death the knife :
But other griefes and pining paines
doe linger on the life,
And oftentimes on selfe same Corse
with furious fits molest,
When Death by one dispatcht of life
doth bring the soule to rest.

The Epicures counsell, eate, drinke, and plaie.

My Friend, where as thou seest thy selfe
to be a man in deede,

Eate,

Eate, quaffe, and play, with present ioyes
  thy greedie fansie feede.
For I (thou seest) am dust become
  that earst so welthie was:
I haue that I aliue did eate,
  the rest away did passe.
What so I poore in pampred paunch
  and to my guts conuaide,
To gaping grounde with me I bore,
  the rest behinde is stayde.
My haughtie buildings huge to see,
  my Turrets and my traine,
My Horse, my Houndes, my costred Coine
  for others doe remaine.
Wherefore a Myrrour make of mee
  and drowne thee in delight:
For Death will sweepe away thy welth
  and reaue thy pleasures quight.

The Aunswere to the vile and canckred counsell of the outragious Epicure.

My Friend, for that I see my selfe
  to be a man in dede,
  Thy quaffing counsell I refuse,
    vnlesse to serue my neede.
I muse no whit that thou art dust,
  thy beastly lyuing heere

B.iiii.   was

Was meane to b?ing thée to thy bane,
  the ſooner fo? thy chére,
Thou thoughts to pamper vp thy paunch,
  but thou didſt féede ywis
The grædie Wo?mes that gnaw thy guts,
  fo? them a daintie diſh.
God reaſon that thou ſhouldſt fo?go
  and leaue thy gods behinde,
Fo? that a beaſt ſo lyke a beaſt
  didſt liue againſt thy kinde.
A man in name, no man in déede
  thou art that counſelſt mée
To liue as thou haſt liude, and die
  a Monſter like to thée.
Fo? ſince thy lyfe ſo lothſome twas,
  and ſhamefull eake thy death :
I will beware, and make a Glaſſe
  of thée whilſt I haue b?eath,
To ſhunne thy ſluttiſh ſinfull Seat,
  thy tipling and thy topes :
Fo? after death thoſe pleaſures paſſe
  as did thy ſickle ioyes.

Of Homer and his birth.

The Poet Homer Chius claimes,
  Colophon doth the léke :
And Smyrne ſweares that he is hirs
  that was the learned Greeke.

Of

Of Salamine some say he was,
  of Iō other some:
And diuers make report that he
  of Thessale line did come.
Thus sundred and deuided are
  the peoples mindes of thee,
(Thou Princely Poet) but my thought
  with neyther doth agree.
For I assuredly suppose
  and deeme the Heauenly Speare
Thy soyle, and Pallas lap the wombe
  that did thy body beare.
Hir breast (the Dug) that thou didst suck
  in Cradle when thou lapst:
With haughtie stile so much (thou Greeke)
  thy mazed head dismayst.

  That Time conquereth all things,
      saue the Louers paine.

WAs neuer Bull so fell
      with wrinckle fronted face,
    But Time would make him yéeld to yoke
      and toyle the ground apace.
The Horse ybred in Holte
  and fed in lustie Lease
In Time will champe the somse Bit
  his Riders will to please.

                              The

The Lions that are wode
  and raging in their kinde,
By trackt of Time their kæpers know
  in whome they friendship finde.
Those Beastes that come from Inde
  and farthest partes of all,
In Time doe swerue their sauage sect
  and to their dutie fall.
Time makes the Grape to growe
  and Uine to spreade at large,
So that the skin scarse able is
  to holde his inwarde charge :
So Ceres fruite doth sproute
  by force of growing Time,
Which makes the strength of hidden sæde
  into the stalke to clime.
Time makes the tender twig
  to bousteous Trée to grow:
It makes the Oke to ouerloke
  the slender shrubs bylow.
It frets the Culter kæne
  that cuts the froting soyle,
It forceth hardest Flint of all
  and Marble to recoyle.
Time wreakefull wrath subdues
  it breaketh angers gall,
And eche disease in Time hath helpe :
  thus Time doth conquer all.

                        Though

Though these and other like
  by processe are procurde,
Yet naythelesse my festred wounde
  can not in Time be curde.
For that which sendeth salue
  and comfort to the reast,
Doth cause my ranckling sore to rage
  and dubble in my breast.
As Sprigs that from a Mount
  doe take their downewarde sourse,
To whome there may no barre be founde
  to stop their headlong course:
So Lordlike Loue ystaulde
  and ceazde in yœlding minde
May not be dispossest againe,
  such is his stately kinde.

To his Friend riding to Londonwarde.

As Troylus did reioyce
    when Cresid yœlded grace,
  And dained him from seruice true
    so nœre hir hart to place:
So haue I ioyde (my Deare)
  for friendship which I founde,
And loue requited with the like
  which curde my carefull wounde.
And he full shrilly shright
  and dwlde his wofull chaunce,

On Gréekish Stéede from Troian towne
  when Cresid gan to praunce
And leaue the lyked soyle
  where did soiourne hir ioie,
I meane the worthy Troylus
  and louingst youth in Troie:
Euen so I waile at thy
  departure, would thou wist,
And out I crie a wretched Wight
  that thought himselfe yblist.
O London lothsome lodge
  why dost thou now procure
My Loue to leaue this pleasant soyle
  that hath my hart in cure?
Since néedes it must be so
  gainsend hir home in hast:
Let hir retire with harmelesse health
  that sicklesse hence is past.
Yéelde mée a good account
  of hir that is my ioie,
And send hir to hir Troylus
  that longs for hir in Troie.

Of the Raine and cloudy weather at the
time of his Friends departure
from Troie.

NO meruasle though the Sunne do hide his hed
  And vnder cloude do kéepe his lowring lokes,
                  No

No woonder that the Skie his teares doth shed
And with his streames increase the water brookes:
The cause is knowne, the proofe is passing plaine,
My Loue and I be sundred to our paine.

Now she is gone that did sustaine my breath
And saude my ship of bodie from the wrack,
By whome I scapte the cruell hande of Death
Which thought to bring my Corse to vtter sack:
The Welkin weepes and helpes me to bewaile
With gushing showres the losse of mine auaile.

Wherefore, O Heauenly states that Rulers bee
Of starrie Skies from whence these teares discende
And flush so fast as mortall Wights doe see:
Of ruth in needefull time my woes to ende,
Procure my Loue to make returne in post,
To gard from griefe hir Friends afflicted ghost.

If not, with flashing flame and Thunder dint
By Vulcan forgde and hammerd for the nones,
Consume to dust my flesh my wo to stint,
And with thy Mace (O Ioue) vnioint my bones:
That by such scath and losse of vitall breath
I may auoide a worse and straunger death.

For like the teene that now my hart sustaines
Was neuer felt nor such oppressing care:
Of force my life must yeelde to pinching paines
Of hasting Death, the fits so furious are:
Which though be so, when I am wrapt in Clay,
(My soule) to hir thou shalt repaire and say.

That

That whilſt the lyfe would ſuffer mee to wonne
With moꝛtall Wights, *my hart was hirs* at will,
And now my Spindle hath his courſe yronne
And twiſt is none pleſt, thou wilt fulfill
The dutie which thy Maiſter ought of right,
And which he would accompliſh if he might.

Of a couetous Niggard, and a needie Mouſe.

A Sclepiad that greedie Carle,
    by foꝛtune found a Mouſe
(As he about his lodgings lookte)
    within his niggiſh houſe.
The chiding Chuffe began to chauſe,
    and (ſparefull of his cheere)
Demaunded of the ſiely Beaſt
    and ſayde what makſte thou heere?
¶You neede not ſtand in feare (good Friend)
    the ſmiling Mouſe replide:
I come not to deuoure your Cates
    but in your houſe to hide.
¶No man this Miſer I accoũnt
    that chid this hurtleſſe Elfe:
No Mouſe the Mouſe, but wiſer than
    the Patch that owde the Pelfe.

A

A pretie Epigram of a Scholler, that
hauing read Vergils Æneidos,
maried a curſt Wyfe.

A Schollar ſkillde in Vergils Werſe
and reading of his booke
(Arma virumꝗ) that begins,
was caught in Cupids booke.
At length to mariage flat he fell,
when wedding day was don,
To play hir pꝛancks, and bob the Fole
the ſhꝛowiſh Wife begon.
The Husband daylie felt the fiſtes
and buffets of his Wife:
Untill at laſt he thus began
to plaine of painefull life.
(Oh Caitiffe mee) the Schollar cryde
well woꝛthy of this wo,
Foꝛ Arma I Virumꝗ read
in Vergill long ago:
Yet could not ſee to ſcape the plague
whereof the Poet ſpake.
No doubt that Noble Poet foꝛ
a Pꝛophet I will take.
Foꝛ Arma now Virumꝗ I
both day and night ſuſtaine
At home, I neede not runne to Schole,
to reade the Werſe againe.

Would

Would (Virum) were away, and then
  let (Arma) doe their wurst:
But when I matcht with such a shrew
  I think I was accurst.

To a yong Gentleman of ta-
king a Wyfe.

Long you with greedie minde to leade a lyfe,
  That pleasaunt is in deede, and voyde of care?
I neuer wishe you then to take a Wyfe
Nor set your foote in craftie Cupids snare,
A filthie Trull is yrkesome to the eie,
A gallant girle allures the lookers minde:
A wanton wench will haue the head to die,
An aged Trot to lyke is hard to finde.
A bearing Wyfe with brats will cloy thee sore,
A greater carcke than childrens care is none,
A barraine beast will greue thee ten times more,
No ioy remaines when hope of fruits is gone.
Wherefore let wyuing go, lyue single aye,
Apply the Booke and bande the Ball among?
A shrew (we see) is wedded in a day
But ere a man can shift his handes tys long.

The Aunswere for taking a Wyfe.

Long you with greedie minde to bleare mine eie
  And make mee thinke of marige thus amisse?

                          I

I cannot déeme so yll of wyuing I,
To loue and wed for loue is perfite blisse.
A filthy Trull (you say) is lothsome sight,
Put case she be not passing faire to vewe:
If she with vertue doe the want requight
Of comely shape thou hast no cause to rue.
A gallant girle allures the lookers minde,
What shall we say the womans is the shame?
Bicause the cléerest eies by course of kinde
Can not abide the Sunne, is hée to blame?
A wanton wench to die will haue the hed,
Canst thou not sée before thou wade so farre?
His be the hurt that lookes not ere he wed,
The Husband may the woman make or marre.
Put case an aged Trot be somewhat tough?
If coyne shée bring the care will be the lesse,
If shée haue store of muck and goods ynough
Thou néedste not force so much of handsomnesse.
A bearing Wyfe doth make the husband glad,
A greater ioye than Childrens may not bée:
A barraine wench sometime must néedes be had
There doth not fruite spring out of euery trée.
So that I finde no reason, none at all
In that thou wilst a man to single lyfe,
And quite to shun the comfort that may fall
And daylie doth to him that hath a Wyfe.
For sure though some be shrewes as some there be,
(As of the shéepe are some that beare no wull)

L.s.   Yet

Yet must we praise the match whereby we sée
The earth maintainde with men, and stored full.
But if you thinke so yll to take a Wyfe,
Let others wed, leave you the single lyfe.
(ꝙ) G. T.

Of a deafe Plaintife, a deafe Defendant, and a deafe Iudge.

By hap a man that could not heare
 but borne deafe by kinde,
Another cited to the Court,
 much like himselfe to finde,
Whose bearing Sense was quight bereft:
 the Iudge that of the Case
Should giue his verdit, was as deafe
 as deafest in the place.
To Court they came: the Plaintife prayde
 to haue the vnpaid rent.
Defendant saide, in grinding I
 this wearie night haue spent.
The Iudge behelde them both a while,
 is this at last (quoth hée)
Of all your stirred strife the cause:
 You both hir children bée:
Then Reason willes, and Law allowes
 your Mother should haue aide
At both your handes that are hir Sonnes.
 When thus the Iudge had saide,

The

The People laught a good to heare
  this well discussed case
Twixt two deafe men, and thought him fit
  to sit in Iudges place
Upon so blinde a matter that
  was deafe as any rock :
And thus the simple men were shamde,
  the Iustice had a mock.

A promise of olde good will, to an olde
    friend at the beginning of
        New yere.

HE Chuffes for greedie gaine
    and lucers loue expende
  Their New yeares gifts vpon their Lords
    as erie yeare hath ende :
But I in token that
  the yeare his course hath ron,
And proufe that for full Ianus hath
  a nouell yeare begon :
(As Loue and Dutie willes)
  the Herauld of my hart
Here send to you to make a shew
  that Friendship shall not start.
Though yeares doe chaunge by course
  and alter by their kinde :
My olde good will and faith to slip
  I trust you shall not finde.

                L.ij.   Timewes

Timetes will be true,
  his loue shall neuer blin:
But gather strength and grow to more
  than when it did begin.

A Vow to serue faithfully.

IN grœne and growing age, in lustie yœres,
  In latter dayes when siluer bush appœres :
In good and gladsome hap when Fortune serues,
In lowring luck when good auenture swerues
By day when Phœbus shewes his princely pride,
By night when golden Starres in Skies do glide,
In Winter when the groues haue lost their grœne
In Sommer when the longest dayes are sœne,
In happie helth when sicklesse limmes haue lyfe,
In griefull state, amids my dolors ryse,
In pleasant peace when Trumpets are away,
In wreakfull warre when Mars doth beare swáy,
In perillous goulfe amid the sinking sande,
In safer soyle and in the stable lande.
When so you laugh, or else with grimmer grace
You beare your faithfull Friend vnfriendly face,
In good report and time of woorser fame,
I wiil be yours, yea though I lose the game.

Funerall Verse vpon the death of Sir Iohn Horsey Knight.

THat welth assigned is to waste away,
  And stately pompe to banish and decrease.
                             That

That worship weares and worldly wights decay,
And Fortunes gifts though nere so braue do ceals
May well appeere by Horseys hatefull Hierce,
Whose Corse (alas) vntimely Death did pierce.

Who thought thereby as Nature to subdue
By reauing breath and rowne in worldly stage:
So blasted brute to blot, and Fame that flue
Of him that well deserude in all his age
For worship and renowne to haue his share
Among the reast that prayse for Vertur bare.

But seeking waies to wrong this worthy wight,
Shee sowly myst hir purpose in the firie:
For Horsey gaines by deaths outragious spight,
And endlesse fame, whereat his Foes repine:
But eche man else laments and cries alowde
That Horsey was to soone ywrapt in shrowde.

The rich report that ruth in him did raigne,
And pittie lodgde within his louing breast,
The simple say that for no maner gaine
He hath at any time the pore oppreast:
Thus both estates his worthy life commende,
And both lament his ouerhasting ende.

Then ccase (I say) such flushing teares to shed,
Do way thy dole, represse thy ruthfull mone,
For Horsey liues, his soule to Skies is fled,
The onely Corse is closde in Marble stone.
So that thou hast no tause to waile his chaunce,
Whome spitefull death by hatred did auaunce.

L.iij.   The

To his Friend T: hauing bene long studied and
well experienced, and now at length lo-
uing a Gentlewoman that forced
him naught at all.

I Thought good fayth, & durſt haue gagde my hand
For you (Friend T.) ý beautie ſhould now hight
Haue raſde your hart, no: Cupid with his brand
Haue brought thy learned breaſt to ſuch a plight.

I thought Mineruas gift had bœne of powre
By holeſome reade to rote this fanſie out :
But now I ſæ that Venus in an howre
Can bend the beſt, and dawnt the wiſe and ſtoute.

Why ſhouldſt thou ſœke to make ý Tiger tame?
To win a Woulfe ſo cruell by his kinde ?
To ſuffer Æſops Snake thou art to blame
That ſtong the man where he reliefe did finde.

Is naught in hir but Womans name alone,
No Woman ſure ſhe is, but Monſter fell,
That ſcornes hir friend, & makes him die w mone.
Who makes an Idoll of a Diuell of Hell.

Shæ was cut out of ſome Sea beaten rock,
Or taken from the cruell Lyons Tet,
That fœdes hir Friend for friendſhip with a mock
And ſmiles to ſæ him macht in Follies Not.

If thou were wiſe (as thou art full of loue)
Thou wouldſt account hir beautie but a Glaſſe,
And from thy hart ſuch fanſies fond remoue
I loth to ſæ the Lyon wer an Aſſe.

If

If so she were thy faithfull Friend in dæde,
And sought a salue to cure thy cruell sore,
(As now shée séekes to make thy hart to blæde)
God fayth thou couldst account of hir no more.

But wayïng now hir great abuse to thée
A Friend to hir, but to thy selfe a Foe :
Why shouldst thou loue, or so enamoured bée ?
Leaue off be time, let all such dotage goe.

Should I imbrace the man that hates my life ?
Should I account of him that settes me light ?
Should I péeld vp my throate to murthring Knife?
Or séeke for to reclaime a Haggard Kite ?

Hast thou not read how wise Vlysses did
Enstuffe his eares with Ware, and close them vp,
Of Cyrces filthie loue himselfe to rid,
That turnd his Mates to Swine by Witches cup?

And how he did the lyke vpon the Seas
The pleasant noysome Syrens songs tendure,
That otherwise had wrought him great vncase
If once they mought his mates and him allure ?

Put thou the Greekes deuise againe in vre,
Stop vp thine eares this Syren to beguile,
Seale vp those wanton eies of thine, be sure
To lend no eare vnto hir flattring stile.

For all hir talke but to deceit doth tende,
A canckred hart is wrapt in friendly lookes :
Shée all hir wittes to thy decay doth bende,
Thou art the Fish, she beares the byting hookes.

L.iiij.   No

No sauage beast doth force a man a whit
That loues him not: we see the dogged Curre
Fawnes not one him that with ẙ whip doth smite
The Horse hates him ẙ pricks him with the spurre.

And wilt thou loue, or place within thy brest
The cruell Dame that weaues thy web of woe ?
Wilt thou still fawne vpon so false a guest:
In stead of Doue wilt thou retaine a Crowe ?

Beware in time, ere Beautie pierce to farre,
Let fansies go, loue where is loue againe :
For doubtlesse now to much to blame you arre,
To sowe good will and reape but fowle disdaine.

I counsaile thus that may thee best aduise,
For that my selfe did serue a cruell Dame :
The blinde recurde can iudge of bleared eies,
The Triple healde knowes how to heale the lame.

Shake thou betimes the yoke from off thy neck,
For feare the print thereof remaine behind :
A happie man is he that feares no check,
But liues at freedome with contented minde.

¶An Epitaph vpon the death of the worship-
full Maister Richarde Edwardes late Mai-
ster of the Children in the Queenes
Maiesties Chappell.

IF teares could tell my thought,
or plaints could paint my paine,
If dubled sighes could shew my smart,
if wayling were not vaine:

Ii

If gripes that gnawe my brest
　coulde well my griefe expresse,
My teares, my plaints, my sighes, my way
　ling neuer should surcesse.
By meane whereof I might,
　vnto the world disclose
The death of such a man (alas)
　as chaunced vs to lose.
But what auaples to mone?
　If life for life might bee
Restorde againe, I woulde exchaunge
　my lyfe for death with thee.
Or if I might some way,
　to pay thy rawnsome know,
(O Edwards) then beleue me sure
　thou shouldst not lie so low:
That O thou cruell Death,
　so fierce with dint of dart
Due curses on my knees I yeelde
　to thee with all my hart.
For that it list thee trie
　thy foule and cankred spite
On that so rare a péece, on that
　so wise and worthy Wight.
Suffisde thee (since thou must
　be mad) the simple sort
to slea, or on the brutish blood
　of beastes to take thy sport,

　　　　　　　　　　　　　And

And not in furious wise,
   with haste and headlong rage
To kill the flowre of all our Realme
   and Phænix of our age.
The fact doth crie reuenge,
   the Gods repay thine hire,
Deepe darckned Lake of Lymbo lowe,
   and still consuming fire.
His death not I but all
   good gentle harts doe mone :
O London, though thy griefe be great,
   thou dost not mourne alone.
The seate of Muses nine
   where fiftene Welles doe flowe,
Whose sprinckling springs and golden streames
   ere this thou well didst knowe.
Lament to loose this Plant
   for they shall see no more
The braunch that they so long had bred,
   whereby they set such store.
O happie House, O Place
   of Corpus Christi, thou
That plantedst first, and gauest the roote
   to that so braue a bow :
And Christ Church which enioydste
   the fruite more rype at fill,
Plunge vp a thousande sighes, for griefe
   your trickling teares distill.

                              our hast

Whilst Childe and Chappell dure,
  whilst Court a Court shall bée,
(God Edwards) eche estate shall much
  both want and wishe for thée.
Thy tender Tunes and Rimes
  wherein thou woontst to play
Eche princely Dame of Court and Towne
  shall beare in minde alway.
Thy Damon and his Friend,
  Arcyte and Palemon
With moe full fit for Princes eares,
  though thou from earth art gone,
Shall still remaine in fame,
  and lyke so long to bide
As earthly things shall liue, and God
  this mortall Globe shall guide.
For loe, thus Vertue list,
  hir Pupils to aduaunce:
Yet for my part I would that God
  had giuen thée better chaunce.
A longer time on earth,
  thy hastned death before,
But Edwardes now farewell for teares
  will let me write no more.
Well may thy bones be lodgde
  thy fame abroade may flie,
Thy sacred squle possesse a place
  aboue the starrie Skie.
       (ꝙ) Tho. Twine.   **The**

To his Loue that sent him a Ring
wherein was graude,
Let Reason rule.

SHall Reason rule where Reason hath no right?
Nor neuer had? shall Cupid loose his landes?
His claim:his crown:his kingdōe? name of mighte
And yǽld himselfe to be in Reasons bandes?
No,(Friend)thy Ring doth wil me thus in vaine,
Reason and Loue haue euer yet bǽne twaine.

They are by kinde of such contrarie mould
As one mislikes the others lewde deuise,
What Reason willes Cupido neuer would,
Loue neuer yet thought Reason to be wise.
To Cupid I my homage earst haue donne,
Let Reason rule the harts that she hath wonne.

To his Friend Francis Th: leading
his lyfe in the Countrie
at his desire.

MY Francis, whilst you breath your foming steede
Athwart the fields in peace to practise warre,
In Countrie whilst your keneld Hounds doe feede,
Or in the wood for taken pray doe iarre:
whilst you with Haukes the sielie Foule doe slaye,
And take delight a quick retriue to haue,
To see to marke, and hear the Spancls baye
wasting your age in pleasure passing braue:
In Citie I my youthfull yeares doe spende,
At Booke perhaps sometime to weare the day:
where man to man not friend to friend doth lende,
With vs is naught but pitch (my Friend) and pay.

Great

Great store of Corne, but fewe enioy the same,
The owners holde it fast with lymned handes,
we liue by losse, we play and practise game
wee by and sell, the streate is all our landes.
well storde we are of erie needefull thing,
wood, water, Coale, Flesh, Fishe we haue ynow:
(what lack you) wyues and Maides doe daylie sing
The Horne is rife, it sticks on many a brow.
But yet (I say) the Countrie hath no peere,
The Towne is but a toyle, and wearie lyfe:
wo like your Countrie sportes (Friend Francis) heere,
The Citie is a place of bate and strife.
wherefore I thinke thee wise and full of thrift
That fledst the Towne, and hast that blessed gift.

To a Gentlewoman that alwayes willed him to
weare Rosemarie, (a Tree that is alwayes
greene,) for hir sake, and in token
of his good will to hir.

The græne that you did wish mee weare
    aye for your loue,
And on my helme a braunch to beare
    not to remoue:
Was euer you to haue in minde
Whome Cupid hath my Feere assignde.

As I in this haue done your will,
    and minde to doo:
So I request you to fulfill
    my fansie too:
A græne and louing hart to haue,
And this is all that I doe craue.

F 03

For if your flowring hart should chaunge
    his colour grœne,
Or you at length a Ladie straunge
    of mœ be séene:
Then will my braunch against his vse
His colour chaunge for your refuse.

As Winters force can not deface
    this braunch his hue:
So let no chaunge of loue disgrace
    your friendship true:
You were mine owne and so be still,
So shall we liue and loue our fill.

Then may I thinke my selfe to bé
    well recompenst,
For wearing of the Trée that is
    so well defenst
Against all weather that doth fall,
When waywarde Winter spits his gall.

And when wé mœte, to trie me true,
    loke on my Hed,
And I will craue an othe of you
    where Faith be fled:
So shall we both assured bé
Both I of you, and you of mé.

¶An

¶An Epitaph of the Ladie Br.

STaie (gentle Friend) that passest by
and learne this lore of mée,
That mortall things doe liue to die,
and die againe to bée.

For daylie proufe hath daylie taught
and yet doth teache it plaine,
That all our substance comes to naught,
and worldly welth is vaine.

No rawnsome may redéeme thy fleshe
from lothsome lumpes of soyle,
The Wormes will soone thy Beautie freshe
with grœdie gripe dispoyle.

I that was earst of gentle bloud
that neuer sufferd staine,
Haue nothing but a winding shrowds
in stead of all my gaine.

I twise was bound by solemne oth
vnto a louing Make:
Yet twas my luck to burie both,
and eke a thirde to take.

The ioy that fourtie yeares had growne
by those two husbands dayes,
In two yeares space was ouerthrowne
and altred sundrie wayes.

As luck would not allow my choice,
so Death mislikte the same:

                                         Those

Those two agrǽd with common voyce
　my bondage too vnframe.
The Lady (Br) quoth Fortune tho
　hir worship shall not loose:
Then shǽ (quoth Death) shall haue no mo,
　nor other husbande choose.
Thus did they both contend at once
　who mought the friendlist bǽ:
Thus Death and Fortune for the nones
　did make my body frǽ.
¶Pray gentle Friend therefore for me,
　to Mightie Ioue on hie:
For as I am so thou shalt bǽ
　since thou dost liue to die.
Trust neuer Fortunes fickle fate,
　but Vertue still retaine:
Thou mayst in time exchaunge estate,
　yet Vertue will remaine.

　　　Of the time he first began to loue
　　　　and after how he forewent
　　　　　　the same.

Howe may it be that Snow and Ise
　ingender heate?
Or how may Glare and Frost intise
　a feruent sweate?
Or how may Sommer season make
　of heate a colde?

　　　　　　　　　　　　　How

How may the Spring the leaues downe shake
and trées vnfolde ?
Though these two others séeme full rare,
To mée no newes at all they are.

For I my selfe in Winter tide
when colde was rife,
Whote gleames of Cupid did abide
and stormes of strife.
In frostie weather I was warme
and burning whot,
But when the Bées and Birds did swarme,
full colde God wot :
In Winter time began my loue,
Which I in Sommer did remoue.

The assured promise of a
constant Louer.

When Phenix shall haue many Makes,
And Fishes shun the Siluer Lakes .
When Woulfes and Lambes yfeare shall play,
And Phœbus cease to shine by day :
When Grasse on Marble stone shall groe,
And euerie man imbrace his foe :
When Moles shall leaue to dig the grounde,
And Hares accorde with hatefull Hounds :
When Lawrell leaues shall loose their hue,
And men of Crete be counted true :

M. I. When

When Vulcan shall be colde as Ise,
Coræbus eake approued wise :
When Pan shall passe Appollos skill,
And Foles of fansies haue their fill :
When Hawkes shall dread the sielie Fowle,
And men esteeme the nightish Owle :
When Pearle shall be of little price,
And golden Uertue friend to Uice :
When Fortune hath no chaunge in store,
Then will I false and not before.
Till all these Monsters come to passe
I am Timetes as I was.
My Loue as long as lyfe shall last,
Not forcing any Fortunes blast.
No threat, nor thraldome shall preuaile
To cause my fayth onc iote to faile,
But as I was, so wlll I bée,
A Louer and a Friend to thée.

The Pine to the Mariner.

Man of little Wit,
  What meanes this frantick fit,
  To make thy Ship of mée
  That am a slender Trée,
Whome erie blast that blowes
Full lightly ouerthrowes ?
Doth this not moue thy minde
  That rage of roring winde

Do

Did beate my boughes agod
　VVhen earst I grue in VVod?
How can I here auoyde
　The foe that there anoyde?
Thinkst thou now I am made
　A Vessell for thy trade,
I shall be more at ease
　Amid the flasshing Seas?
I seare if Æole frowne,
　Both thou and I shall drowne.

Againe otherwise.

A Vassell to the winde
　when earst I grew in wood,
How shall I fauour finde
　now fléeting in the flod?
For there whilst reaching rotes did holde
　I thought I mought be somewhat bolde.
But now that I am cut
　and framde another way,
And to this practise put
　in daunger crie day.
I seare the sorce of cruell foe,
　my ribbes are thin, my sides be lowe
But if thou venter life,
　then I will hazard lim,
For thée is all my griefe,
　for lightly I shall swim:
　　　　　　　　　　H.s.　　　　　Though

Though top and tackle all be torne,
yet I aloft the surge am borne.

To an olde Gentlewoman, that
painted hir face.

LEaue off good Beroe now
to slicke thy shriuled skin,
For Hecubes face will neuer be,
as Helens hue hath bin.
Let Beautie go with youth,
renownce the glosing Glasse,
Take Booke in hand: that seemely Rose
is woren withred Grasse.
Remooue thy Pecocks plumes
thou cranck and curious Dame;
To other Trulls of tender yeares
resigne the flagge of Fame.

Of one that had a great
Nose.

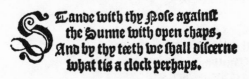

STande with thy Nose against
the Sunne with open chaps,
And by thy teeth we shall discerne
what tis a clock perhaps.

Of

Of one whose Nose was greater
than his hand.

P Proclus, tis in vaine
that thou about doēst ēstande,
Foꝛ well I ēeē thou mindēte to wipe
thy Nares with thy hande.
Truth is that though thou be
fowle fiēted out of frame:
Pet doth this toēsing Nose of thine
in bigneēse paēse the same.
When nœzing thou on Ioue
foꝛ succour ēeēmēte to crie
Thou canēt not heare, thy Nose debarres
the noyēe to Eare to flie.
It beateth back the sounde,
it ētandēs in middle place
Twixt Eare and Mouth, but sure it caētes
a ēhade to all the face.

Of a Nightingale that flue to Colche
to sit abroode.

T Hou ēielie foule what meanes this fooliēh paine,
to flie to Colche tœ hatch thy chickins there:
A Mother thou mayēt hap returne againe,
Medœa will deētroie thy bꝛœde I feare.
                    M. iii.   Foꝛ

For shée that spared not to spoile hir owne,
Wil she stand friend to Fowles ÿ are vnknowne?

Againe of the Nightingale.

What (Philomela) meanes this fond intent
  To hatch thy bróde in fell Medæas lap?
What? doste thou hope hir rigor will relent
  Towarde thy Babes, that gaue hir owne no pap?
But slus them all at once, and at a clap?
  I wote not what thou meanste: vnlesse that shée
Should kill thy Brats, to make the Mother frée.

Of a contrarie mariage.

AN aged Trot and tough
    did marrie with a Lad:
  Againe, a Gallant Girle to
    hir Spouse, a Graybeard had,
A monstrous match (God wote)
    for others she doth wed:
And he bestowes his séede on ground
    that lets it take no hed.
In fayth, a foolish choyce,
    for neither hath his wishe:
For tone doth lack his wife, and to-
    ther fédes on filthie fishe.

Of

Of Dronkenneſſe.

At night when Ale is in,
  like friends we part to bed :
In moroſw graye when Ale is out,
  then hatred is in bed.

Againe of Dronkenneſſe.

When hauing quaſt
  are friendly ouernight :
In dawning dꝛie
  a man tw man a ſpꝛight.

Of the picture of a vaine Rhetorician.

His Ruſe his Table is,
  can nothing be moꝛe true :
If Rufus holde his peace, this péece
  and he are one to bewe.

Of the fond diſcord of the two The- ban brothers, *Octocles* and *Polyniçes.*

In death you part the fire,
  you cut the cruell flame :
If ſo you had deuided Thebes
  you might enſoyde the ſame.

          ℘.iiij.

Of

Of a maruellous deformed man.

TO drawe the minde in Table to the sight
　Is hard : to paint the lims is counted light :
But now in these two are nothing so,
For Nature splayes thy minde to open show.
We sée by proofe of thy vnthriftie déedes,
The couert kinde from whence this filth procéedes.
But who can paint those shapelesse lims of thine,
When eche to vewe thy Carcasse doth repine ?

A Myrrour of the fall of Pride.

SOmetime the Giants did rebell
　　against the mightie Ioue,
　　They thought in Olymp Mount to dwell
　　　and long for that they stroue.
A hundred handes eche Monster had
　by course of cursed kinde :
A stock so stubborne and so mad
　I no where else can finde.
Dame Tellus was their Mother thought
　of pleasant Poets all,
By whome they would haue brought to nought
　the seate Olympicall.
First Briareus began the broyle
　who toke a hill in hand,
And layde it on another soyle
　that thereabout did stand :

Still

Still calling on his monſtrous Mates
  exhorting them the ſame,
And with the reaſt the Gnuffe debates
  how ſtately Gods to tame.
Oſſa was layde on Pyndus back,
  and Pelion on hie :
And thus they thought to bring to ſack
  in time the ſtarrie Skie.
They did enuie the Gods the place
  by nature them aſſignde :
And thought it mæter for a race
  which Tellus bred by kinde.
They would haue had the higheſt throne
  that Ioue had long poſſeſt :
And downe they would the Gods haue throwne
  and Princely powre repreſt.
At length the route began to rore
  in making dreadfull ſound,
The like was neuer heard before
  to Heauen from the ground.
Then Iupiter began to gaze
  and looke about the Skie,
And all the Gods were in a maze
  the Monſters were ſo nie.
They callde a rounſaile then in haſte
  the Gods aſſembled tho :
And common ſentence was at laſt
  that mightie Ioue ſhould throw

                                His

His thunderbolt that Vulcan lame
  prepared for the nonce,
Whereby he might eftsoone make tame
  the haughtie Giants bones.
Then might you see the Mountaines fall
  and hill from hill depart,
And monsters in the valley crawle
  whome Thunder did subuart.
The Mountaines were not raysde so quick
  but downe they fell as fast :
And Giants in a cluster thick
  to Tellus fell at last.
Such plagues had pride in former time,
  the Gods abhorred so
That mortall men should dare to clime
  the Heauens hie to know.
And not alone the heauenly route
  the loftie lookes correct
Of such as prowdly go about
  their Empire to reiect :
But other Gods of meaner state
  (of whome the Poets write)
Such peuish Pecocks pride doe hate
  and seeke reuenge by might.
The grisly God whome flouds obay
  and drenching Seas imbrace,
Who in the waters beares the sway
  where Nereus shewes his face :

                            Whome

Whome forceth he by surge of Seas
  into Charybdis cliues :

Or whome doth Neptune most disease :
  or whome to Scylla driues :

Not him that beares his Sailes alowe,
  nor him that kéepes the Shoare :

Ne yet the Bargeman that doth rowe
  with long and limber Oare.

Not those that haunt the Hauen sure
  and port of perill voide,

They cannot Neptunes wrath procure
  the Chanell that auoide :

But those that voide of carck and care
  and feare of Neptunes yre,

Doe hoise their Sailes and neuer spare
  to further their desyre,

And doe receiue whole Gales of winde
  from mightie Æole sent :

Those, those are they by course of kinde
  that Neptune makes repent.

He spoiles the Sailes, and tackle teares,
  the Mast it goes to wrack :

The Ribbes they rent, the Shipmen feares
  when Gables gin to crack.

Then whereto serues the Pilats pryde
  that hoyst his Sailes so hie :

And where is he that fearde no tide
  nor threatning from the Skie :

                   His

His pride procurde his fearefull fate
　　and fortune that befell
Which Neptune most of all doth hate
　　as Shipmen know right well.
Let Giants fall and Shipmens case
　　a myrrour be therefore
To such as séeke to hie a place,
　　for like shall be their lore.
Narcissus may example bée
　　and myrrour to the prowde,
By whome they may most plainly sée
　　how pride hath béene allowde.
His beautie braue such loftie chéere
　　in him did bréede in time :
That Gods themselues agréeued were
　　with such a haynous crime.
No louing Lasse might him allure,
　　nor Dians Nymphes at all
By ought his friendship might procure :
　　but note ye well his fall.
In Sommer time as Fortune would
　　his Fortune was to bée
In open fielde, where no man could
　　his blazing beautie sée.
At length in raunging to and fro
　　his fortune was to finde
A Fountaine freshe that there did flow
　　as Gods (I think) assignde.

　　　　　　　　　　　　　　　　　　He

He thought forthwith his thirst to quent
  by pleasant trauaile gote,
But there he found or ere he went
  a greater drougth God wote.
In stoping downe to take the taste
  of Christall waters theare,
(Vnhappie Boy) had spide at last
  a little Boy appeare.
Whose beautie braue, and liking looke
  his fansie pleasde so well,
That there himselfe the Boy forsooke
  and to a frensie fell.
He had that he so fondly loude :
  and yet it was not so :
And from himselfe he was remoude
  that thence did neuer go.
He was the Boy that tooke the vewe,
  he was the Boy espide,
And being both he neither knewe,
  such was the ende of pride.
Then gan he shed his teares adowne,
  then gan he make his plaint :
And then at length he fell to grounde
  sore fæbled all with faint.
His spirite that earst so prowde was séene
  conuerted into winde :
But of his Corps a flower gréene
  still there abode behinde.

                        Narcissus

Narciſſus callde (as Poets tell)
   as Narciſſe was before,
In token that to Narciſſe fell
   this moſt vnhappie loze.
I could recite the hiſtozies
   of many other moe,
Whome pieuiſh pzide the miſeries
   of Fortune fozſt to knowe.
But I of purpoſe will let paſſe
   Apollos Baſtard Sonne,
Who Phaeton ycleped was
   when firſt his fame begonne.
I minde not to rehearſe at all
   the charge he tœke in hande,
I wittingly omit his fall
   into Eridan ſande.
But this I ſay aſſuredly
   had it not bœne foz pzide,
The Charret had not gone awzie
   though Phaeton were guide.
But glozie vaine and want of ſkill
   enfozſte his haughtie hart,
Of Phœbe to craue to wozke his will
   in ruling Phœbus Cart.
The like attempt tœke Icarus
   from Creta that did flie
By wings of War with Dedalus,
   when Icar flue to hie.

His Fathers wordes prevailed not
  nor lesson taught before,
Till fained fethers were so whot
  as he could flie no more.
For want of wings then gan he clap
  his breast with open armes
Till downe he fell: such was his hap,
  whose pride procurde his harmes.
When wrastling windes from Æole sent
  besight themselues so long
That East against the West is bent,
  and North puts South to wrong:
Then may you heare the Pine to crack
  that beares his hed so hie,
And loftie lugs go then to wrack
  which seeme to touch the Skie.
When Ioue flings downe his thundring bolts
  our vices to redresse,
They batter downe the highest holts
  and touch not once the lesse.
The Cotte is surer then the Hall
  in proofe we daylie see:
For highest things doe sonest fall
  from their felicitee.
What makes the Phænix flame with fire
  a Birde so rare in sight?
What causeth him not to retire
  from Phæbus burning light?

                      In

In faith if he woulde liue belowe
  as Birds Dame Nature tought,
The Esterlings should neuer knowe
  their Phœnix burnt so oft.
All ye therefore that suretie loue
  and would not haue a fall,
From you the Peacocks pride remoue
  and trust not Fortunes Ball.
Let Phaetons fate be fearde of you
  and Icars lot also :
Remember that the Pine doth rue
  that he so high doth grow.

Of the Clock and the
Cock.

God reason thou allow
  one letter more to mee
Than to the Cock : For Cocks doe sleepe
  when Clocks doe wake for thee.

Of a Tayler.

Though Tayler cut thy garment out of frame,
  And stirie thy stuffe by sowing it amis :
Yet must we say the Tayler makes the same,
To make and marre is one with them ywis.

                                        The

The Louer finding his Loue flitted from
wonted troth leaues to write in
prayſe of hir.

Hough cleane contrarie be my Uerſe
   to thoſe I wꝛote befoꝛe,
Yet let not retchleſſe dꝛome accuſe
   my wandꝛing wits the moꝛe.
As time doth ſhape and ſhew (they ſay)
   ſo ought our ſtile to frame,
In Sommer, Sunne, we næde no fire,
   yet winter aſketh flame :
So I that carſt found cauſe of ſpoꝛt
   and matter to reſoyce,
Of foꝛce by fanſie was pꝛocurde
   to vſe a gladſome voyce.
And now ſince dæpe diſpaire hath dꝛencht
   my hope, I will aſſay
To turne my tune and chaunge my chǽre
   and leaue my wꝋnted lay.
Not farre vnlike the chirping Foule
   in Sommer that doth ſing,
And during Winter hides his head
   till next returne of Spꝛing.
They ſay when altred is the cauſe
   of foꝛce effect doth ſue :
As new repaire of better bloud
   doth cauſe a Hawke to mue.

               N.f.   Though

Though Ætna burne by kindly course
  and belke out fire with fume :
When Sulpher vaine is cleane extinct
  the fire will consume.
Whereby I may conclude aright
  that eche Effect must bée
As is his Càuse : so fruite ensues
  the nature of the Trée.
Then I of force must shape my stile
  as matter is I write :
Unlesse I would be thought to match
  a Fawcon with a Kite.
When winde and waue at Sea doe rore
  that Barck is in distresse,
Then time requires that shipmen should
  their Tackles all addresse.
Then crooked Ancors must be cast
  the shaken Ship to stay
From sincking Sands, and ruthlesse Rocks
  that Shipmen oft affray.
No soner Triton blowes his Trumpe
  and swolen waters quailes,
And Æole makes his windes retire :
  but hoyse they vp the sailes.
Then fléete they forward in the floud,
  then cut they waues in twaine :
Then launch they on (as earst they did)
  with all their might and maine :

So

So I hereafter muſt aſſay
  my wonted tune to chaunge
As time requires, and I in loue
  ſhall finde my Ladie ſtraunge.
If ſhe be one of Creſids crue
  and ſwarue hir former Heſt,
No Lucrece muſt I terme hir then,
  for that were but a ieſt.
Or if ſhe falſe hir fixed fayth,
  Vlyſſes wiues renowne
Unſitting is for hir whoſe loue
  endureth but a ſtowne.
Wherefore, I will as time ſhall ſhape
  and ſhe hir loue prolong,
Applie my Pen, and tell the troth
  as beſt I may in Song.

    He ſorrowes other to haue
      the fruites of his
        ſeruice.

Some men would loke to haue
  a recompence of paine,
And Reaſon wills it ſo to be
  vnleſſe we liſt to faine:
Some would expect for loue
  to haue vnfained hart,
And think it but a fit reward
  for ſuch a god deſart.

              N. H.   But

But I (vnhappie Wight)
   that spend my loue in vaine,
Doe seeke for succour at hir hands
   while other get the gaine.
As thirstie ground doth gape
   to swallow in the shoure :
Euen so fare I poore Harpalus
   whome Cupids paines deuoure.
I holde the Hiue in hande
   and paine my selfe thereby,
While other eate the hidden foods
   that are not halfe so dry.
I plough the soyle with paine
   and cast my soede thereon :
And other come that sheare the sheaues
   and laugh when I am gon.
Mine is the Winters toile,
   and theirs the Sommers gaine :
The Haruest falles out to their share
   that felt no part of paine.
I beare the pinching yoke
   and burden on my back,
And other driue when I must draw,
   and thus I go to wrack.
I fast when other feede,
   I thirst when other drinck :
I mourne when they triumph for ioy,
   they swim when I must sinck.

                       They

They haue the hoped gaine
  whiles J the loſſe indure:
They whole at hart, whilſt J my griefe
  by no meanes can recure,
They ſhrowd themſelues in ſhade,
  J ſit in open Sunne:
They leape as Lambes in luſtie Leaʒe,
  J lie as one bndunne.
They taſte their nightly reſt,
  my troubled head doth wake:
J toſſe and turne from ſide to ſide
  while they their pleaſure take,
J would, but they enioy,
  J craue that is debard,
They haue: what will you moʒe J ſay ꝛ
  their ſeruice is pʒefard.
Thus J pʒocure my woe
  by framing them their ioy:
In ſeeking how to ſalue my ſoʒs
  J bʒœde my chiefe annoy.
So ſhœpe with wooll are clad
  their Maiſters haue the gaine,
So Birds doe builde their Neſts on Bʒakes
  and put themſelues to paine,
But other taſte the fruite
  when ſo their bʒœde is hatcht:
The Neſt remaines, the Birds are gone,
  the Chickens are diſpatcht.

                          N. iij.   Sa

No Bées for Honnie tosse
  in fléeing too and fro,
And sillie wretches take great paines
  for whome they little know.
I think it is procurde
  by griesly Gods aboue
That some should gape, and other gaine
  the fruit of others loue.
But sure if Womans will
  be forger of my wo,
And not the mightie Gods ordaine
  my destinie to be so :
Then must I néedes complaine
  and cursse their cruell kinde,
That in requitall of good will
  doe shew themselues vnkinde.
But whether be the cause,
  hereafter I intende
To fawne on them that force on mée,
  and bowe when other bende.
This one abuse shall make
  me take the better héede
On whome I fire my fansie fast,
  or make a friend in déede.

    The Louer seeing himselfe abusde,
      renounceth Loue.

Though men account it shame
  and folly to repent,

Dr

Or grutcht good will that was bestowde
  when nought saue faith was ment:
Yet can they not denie
  but if the knot be burst,
Then may we shew our selues vnkinde
  that friendly were at furst.
He runnes an endlesse race
  that neuer turnes againe,
And he a fonded Louer is
  that wastes his loue in vaine,
Nought can he iudge of hues,
  that can not see when Guile
In place of friendship cloakes hir selfe
  in forme of forged wile.
And he that plainely sees
  the Trap before his eie
And will not shun from perill, tis
  no matter though he die.
I tell my tale by proufe.
  I speake it not by rot,
To loue a subtile Lasse of late
  was fallen to my lot.
On whome I set such store
  such comfort and delight,
As life it was to see hir face,
  a death to want hir sight.
So I might doe the thing
  that might abridge hir smart,

             N.iiij.   And

And bannish all annoy that grue
  by froward fortunes Art :
What daunger would I dread ?
  or perill seeme to shun ?
None that is here bylow on earth
  or subiect to the Sun.
To shew my selfe a Friend
  to hir, I was my Foe :
She was the onely Idoll whome
  I honorde here belowe.
This is (thought I) the same
  that was Vlysses wife :
Who in the absence of hir Make
  did leade a dolefull life.
Or else tis she at least
  whome Tarquyn did enforce
By beastly rape with piercing sworde
  so to fordoe hir Corse.
But such is hir abuse
  so frowarde eke hir grace,
As loue it may no longer last
  since friendship hides his face.
I did not well aduise
  I built on sincking Sande,
And when I thought she loude me best
  shee bore me but in hande.
Where I had thought a Porte
  and Hauen sure to bée :

There

There founde I hap and dreadfull death,
　　as gazers on may sée.
As Mouse that treades the trap
　　in hope to finde repast,
And bites the bread that bréedes his bane
　　and is intrapped fast :
Like was my dolefull case
　　that fed vpon my wo,
Till now Repentance willes mée all
　　such fansies to forgo.
And (thanked be good hap)
　　now once againe I fléete
And swim aloft, that sanck of late
　　fast hampred by the féete.
Now is my fortune good
　　so Fortune graunt it last:
And I as happie as the best
　　now stormie cloudes are past,
I finde the bottom firme
　　and stable where I passe,
There are no haughtie Rocks at honde
　　ne yet no ground of Glasse.
Good Ancor holde I haue
　　so I may vse it still,
I am no more a bounden Thrall
　　but frée I liue at will.
But that which most torments
　　my minde, and reaues my ioy,

　　　　　　　　　　Is,

Is, for I serude a fickle Wench
that bred mée this annoy,
But Gods forgiue my guilt
and time mispent before
And I will be a sillie Sot
of Cupids crue no more.

Against the Ielous heads that
alwayes haue Louers in
suspect.

When Ielous Iuno saw hir mightie Make
Had Iö turnde into a brutish kinde
More couertly of hir his lust to take:
To work hir will & all his frawd to finde
She craude the Cowe in gift at Ioue his hande,
Who could not well his Sisters sute withstande.

When yélded was hir bone and Hest fulfillde
To Argus charge committed was the Cowe,
For he could wake so well, him Iuno willde
To watch the Beast with neuer sléeping browe :
With hundreth eies that hatefull Hierds hed
Was deckt, som watcht whé som to sléepe were led.

So warded he by day, so wakte by night
And did Dame Iunos will accomplish so,
As neither Ioue might once delude his sight,
Nor Iö part hir pointed pasture fro :
His staring eies on Iö still were bent,
He markt hir march, and sude hir as she went.
                                          Till

Till Ioue at length to ruth and pittie mooue
To sée the spitefull hate that Argus bare
To hir, whome he so feruently had loude
And who for him abode such endlesse care:
His fethred Sonne Cylenus sent from Skies
To reaue the carefull Clowne his watchfull eies.

Who to fulfill his Lorde and Fathers Hest
Tooke charmed Rod in hande and Pipe to playe,
And gyrt him with a sworde as lykte him best
And to the fielde he flue where Argus laye
Disguised like a shepherd in his wæde
That he his purpose might the better spéede.

When eche had other salued in his sort,
To brag vpon his Pipe the Clowne begon,
And sayde, that for that noyse and gallant sport
All other mirthes and maygames he would shon,
His only ioy was on his Pipe to playe:
And then to blow the Rustick did assaye.

In fine when Argus had his cunning showde,
And eche to other chatted had a space
Of this and that as was befalne abrode,
Mercurius tooke his Pipe from out his case
And thereon playde hée so passing well,
As most of Argus eies to slumber fell.

And as they slept with charmed Rod he stroke
The drowsie Wolt to kéepe him in that plight,
And playde so long till time he did prouoke
All Argus eies to byd the beast God night:
                                    Whome

Whome when he sawe in such a slumber led,
He stole the Cowe, and swapt of Argus hed.
   Such was the fine of his dispitous hate,
Such was the bwne and guerdon of his hire,
And all the gwd the carefull Coward gate
For sæking to debarre the Gods desire :
A fit reward for such a gwd desart,
The Cowarde might haue playde a wiser part.
   God sende the lyke and worse to such as vse
(As Argus did) with euer waking eie
The blamelesse sort of Louers to abuse,
That alwayes readie are and prest to prie
The purpose to bewray and couert toyes
Of faithfull friends, and barre their blissefull ioyes.
   I trust there will be found in time of næde
A Mercurie with charmed Twig in hand
And pleasaunt Pipe, their waking eies to fæde
With drowsie dumps, their purpose to withstand :
That iealous heads may learne to be wies
For feare they lose (as Argus did) their eies
   For Cupid takes disdaine and scorne to sæ
His Thralls abusde in such vnsæmely sort,
Who sæke no grædie gaine nor filthie fæ,
But pleasant play, and Venus sugred sport :
A slender hire (God wote) to quite the paine
That Louers bide, or they their loue attaine.

                                    That

That it is hurtfull to con-
ceale secrets from our
Friendes.

A Smart in silence kept
    (as Ouid doth expresse)
Doth moze tozment the payned man
    than him that séekes redzesse.
Foz then it respite takes,
    and leysure to pzocure
Such mischiefe as foz want of helpe
    the longer doth endure.
As if thou set no salue
    whereranckleth swelling soze,
It will in further pzocesse paine,
    and thée tozment the moze.
I sundzie times haue séene
    a wound that earst was small,
In time foz want of Surgions sight
    to greater mischiefe fall :
And eke the balefull blowe
    so grieuous that was thought,
Full quickly curde by Surgions sleight
    if he were quickly sought.
So fareth it by man,
    that kéepes in couert bzeast
The pinching paine that bzéedes within,
    increasing great vnreast :

                                    That

That neuer will disclose
   the secret of his hart,
But rather suffer feruent fits
   and dæper piercing smart.
For why was friendship founde
   and quickly put in vze,
But that th'one of thothers helpe
   should thinke himselfe full sure ?
Why are they like in minde
   and one in erie part ?
Why are they twoo in bodies twaine
   possessing but one hart ?
And why doth one mislike,
   that so offendes his Fære,
But that they two are one in dæde
   it plainely might appære ?
Did Tullie euer dzeade
   his secrets to disclose
To Atticus his louing Friende,
   in whome he did repose
Such credit and such trust
   and in himselfe he might,
To whome full oft with painfull Pen
   this Tullie did indight ?
What euer Theseus thought
   Perythous coulde tell,
With wearie trauell that pursude
   his louing friende to Hell.

                                          vt as

Was Damon daintie founde
  to Pythias at all,
For whome he woulde with Tyran stoute
  as pledge to liue in thrall?
In Pylades was nought
  but that Orestes knewe,
Who priuie was from time to time
  how care or comfort grewe.
Gysippus felt no griefe
  but Titus boade the same:
And where that Titus founde reliefe
  their Gysippe had his game.
When Lælius did laugh
  then Scipio did ioy:
And what Menetus Sonne misliktt
  Achylles did annoy.
Æurialus his thoughts
  and secrets of his hart
To Nysus would declare at large,
  were they of ioy or smart.
All these consoyned were
  in surest league of loue,
Whome neyther Fortune good or bad,
  nor Death might once remoue.
They would not think in minde
  nor practise that at all:
But to that same their trustie Friende
  they would in counsell call.

                                 All

All those therefore that wishe
  their inward paines redresse,
Must to their most assured Friend
  it outwardly expresse.
So may they chaunce to finde
  a salue for secret sore,
Which otherwise in couert kept
  will sone increase to more.

Of the diuers and contrarie
passions and affections
of his Loue.

TO Phisick those that long haue gone
  and spent their time in griefe,
Affirme that Pacients in their paines
  will shun their best reliefe.
They will refuse the Tysants taste
  and wholesome drinkes despise,
Which to recure diseases fell
  Phisitions did deuise:
But when they be debard the same
  which so they shunde before,
They crie and call for Tysants then
  as soueraigne for their sore.
Such is the wayward guise of those
  with pangues that are opprest,
They wish for that they neuer had,
  and shun that they possest.

I

I may to them right well compare
  the Louers diuers thought,
That likes, and then mislikes againe
  that they long earst had sought.
They will not, when they may, enioy
  their hearts desired choise :
They then defie, they then detest
  with lowde and lothsome voice.
They will refuse when time doth serue,
  but when such time is gone,
They sigh and schreach with mournefull erie
  and make a ruthfull mone.
They little think that Time hath wings
  or knoweth how to flie :
They hope to haue it still at hande
  that swiftly passeth bie.
They thinke that Time will tarie them
  and for their fansie stay,
But Time in little time is gone
  it fleeteth fast away.
So standes the sole by fleeting floud
  and looketh for a turne :
But Riuer runnes and still will run
  and neuer shape returne.
What? doe they hope that beauties glasse
  will still continue bright ?
Nay, when the day is gone and past
  by course appeares the night.

           D.s.   F ij

For crooked age his wonted trade
   is for to plough the face
With wrinckled furrowes, that before
   was chiefe of Beauties grace.
Perhaps they thinke that men are mad,
   and once intrapt in loue
Will neuer striue to breake the snare
   nor neuer to remoue.
No Fowler that had wylie Wit
   but will foresee such hap,
That Birds will alway buske and batt
   and scape the Fowlers Trap.
And if their fortune fauor so,
   then who doth mount so hie
As those that guilefull Pitfall tooke
   prepared for to die?
What Fish doth fléete so fast as that
   which lately hangde on hooke?
By happie hap if he escape,
   he will not backwarde looke.
Take time therefore thou foolish Fæme,
   whilst Time doth serue so well:
For Time away as fast doth flée
   as any souud of Bell.
And thou perhaps in after Time
   when Time is past and gone,
Shall lie lamenting losse of Time
   as colde as any stone.

yet

Yet were thou better take thy time
whilſt yet thy Beautie ſerues,
For Beautie as the Flower fades
whome lack of Phœbus ſterues.

Of Dido and the truth of hir death.

Of Dido and the Quæne of Carthage ground,
  Whoſe lims thou ſeeſt ſo liuely ſet to ſight;
Such one I was, but neuer to be found
So farre in loue as Vergill ſeemes to wright,
I liude not ſo in luſt and fowle delight:
  For neither he that wandring Duke of Troie
  Knewe mee, nor yet at Lybie lande ariude;
But to eſcape Iarbos that did note
Mee ſore, of lyfe my Carcaſſe I depriude,
To keepe my Heſt that he would tho haue riude.
  No ſtorme of loue, or dolour made me die,
  I ſlue my ſelfe to ſaue my Sheete of ſhame
Wherein good Sycheus wrapped me perdie:
Then Vergill then the greater be thy blame,
That ſo by loue doſt breede my fowle defame.

Of Venus in Armour.

In complete Pallas ſaw
    the Ladie Venus ſtande :
    Who ſaid, let Paris now be iudge
    encounter we with hande.
                 D.y.   Replide

Replide the Goddesse : what ?
scornste thou in Armour mée,
That naked earst in Ida Mount
so foylde and conquerde thée ?

Of a Hare complaining of the hatred of Dogs.

The scenting Hounds pursude
the hastie Hare of fote :
The siclie Beast to scape the Dogs
did iumpe vpon a rote.
The rotten scrag it burst,
from Cliffe to Seas he fell :
Then cride the Hare : vnhappie mée,
for now perceiue I well
Both lande and Sea pursue
and hate the hurtlesse Hare :
And cake the dogged Skies aloft,
if so the Dog be thare.

To one that painted Eccho.

Thou witles wight, what meanes this mad intēt
To draw my face & forme, vnknowne to thée ?
What meanst thou so for to molesten mée ?
Whome neuer Eic behelde, nor man could sée ?
Daughter to talking tongue, and Ayre am I,
My Mother is nothing when things are waide :
I am a voyce without the bodies aide.
When all the tale is tolde and sentence saide,

Then

Then I recite the latter worde afreshe
In mocking sort and counterfayting wies:
Within your eares my chiefest harbour lies,
There doe I wonne, not seene with mortall eies.
  And more to tell and farther to procæde,
  I Eccho height of men below in grounde:
  If thou wilt draw my Counterfait in dæde,
  Then must thou paint(O Painter) but a sound,

To a cruell Dame for graçe
and pittie.

As I doe lack the skill
    to show my faithfull hart:
  So doe you want good will
    too rue your Louers smart.
The greater is my fire
  the lesser is your heate:
The more that I desire
  the lesse you sæme to sweate.
O quench not so the Coale
  of this my faithfull flame,
With nayes thou frowarde soule,
  let yeas increase the same.
Let vs at length agrée
  whome Cupid made by law
Eche others friend to bée
  in fansies yoke to draw.

O.ij.

A

If I doe playe my part
  at any time amis ,
Then doe bestowe thy hart
  where greater Friendship is.
But if in true good will
  I beare my selfe vpright,
Let mée enioy thée still
  my seruice too requight.
Go thou my fierie Dart
  of scalding whote desire
To pierce hir ysie hart
  and set hir brest on fire.
That I may both prolong
  my painefull pyning dayes,
And eke auendge hir wrong
  that paine for pleasure payes.
I neuer sawe the stone
  but often drops would wast :
Nor Dame but daylie mone
  would make hir yéelde at last.

To a Gentlewoman from whome he tooke a Ring.

What néedes this frowning face ?
  what meanes your looke so coye ?
Is all this for a Ring,
  a trifle and a toye ?

What

What though I reft your Ring?
  I tooke it not to kéepe:
Therefore you néede the lesse
  in such dispite to wéepe.
For Cupid shall be iudge
  and Umpire in this case,
Or who by hap shall next
  approche into this place.
You tooke from mée my hart,
  I caught from you a Ring:
Whose is the greatest losse?
  where ought the griefe to spring?
Kéepe you as well my hart,
  as I will kéepe your Ring,
And you shall iudge at last
  that you haue lost nothing.
For if a Friendly hart
  so stuft with staide loue,
In balue doe not passe
  the Ring you may reprooue
The reauing of the same,
  and I of force must say
That I deserude the blame
  who tooke your Ring away.
But what if you doe wreake
  your malice on my hart?
Then giue mée leaue to thinke
  you guiltie for your part.

                  D.Iij.   **And**

And when so ere I yœlde
  to you your King againe,
Restoze me vp my hart
  that now you put to paine.
Foz so we both be pleasde,
  to say we may be bolde
That neyther to the losse
  of vs hath bought oz solde.

The Louer blames his Tongue that failed to vtter his sute in time of neede.

FOz cause I still pzeserde the truth befoze
  Shamelesse vntruth, and lothsome lœsings loze,
I finde my selfe yll recompenst therefoze
              Off thœ my Tongue.
Foz good desert and guiding thœ aright,
That thou foz aye mightst liue deuoide of spight,
I reaps but shame, and lack my chiefe delight
              Foz silence kept.
When happie hap by hap aduaunst my case,
And bzought mœ to my Ladie face to face,
Where I hir Cozps in safetie might imbzace,
              Thou heldst thy peace.
Thou madst my voyce to cleane amids my thzote,
And sute to cease vnluckylie (God wote)
Thou wouldst not speake, tho ỹ hadst quite fozgote
              My harts behest.

                                    My

My hart by thæ suspected was of guile,
For cause thou ceast to vse a louing stile,
And wordes to forge and frame with finest file
    As Louers wont.
Thou madste my bloud fro paled face to start,
And flie to séeke some succor of the hart,
That wounded was long earst with dreadfull dart
    Off Cupids Bowe.
And thou as colde as any Marble stone
When from my face the chillie bloud was gone,
Couldst not deuise the way to make my mone
    By wordes appære.
And (yæ my teares) that wonted were to flowe
And streame adowne as fast as thawed Snowe,
Were stopt, as then yæ had no powre to showe
    A Louers sute.
My sighes that earst were wont to dim the Skie,
And cause a fume by force of flame to flie,
Were tho as slack, as Welles of wéeping dris
    To showe my Loue.
The hart that late incombred all within
Had fainted quite had not by lokes ybin:
For they declarde the case my hart was in
    By tongues vntroth.

    That all things are as they are vsed.

WAs neuer ought by Natures Art
    Or cunning skill so wisely wrought,
                  But

But Man by practise might conuart
　　To worser vse then Nature thought.
Ne yet was euer thing so ill
　　Or may be of so small a prise,
But man may better it by skill
　　And chaunge his sort by sounde aduise,
So that by proofe it may be séene
　　That all things are as is their vse,
And man may alter Nature cléene,
　　And things corrupt by his abuse.
What better may be founde than flame,
　　To Nature that doth succor pale ?
Yet we doe oft abuse the same
　　In bringing buildings to decaie.
For those that minde to put in bre
　　Their malice, moude to wrath and ire ?
To wreake their mischiefe, will be sure
　　To spill and spoyle thy house with fire.
So Phisick that doth serue for ease
　　And to recure the grieued soule,
The painefull Patient may disease,
　　And make him sick that earst was whole.
The true Man and the Théefe are léeke
　　For sworde doth serue them both at néede,
Sane one by it doth safetie séeke
　　And th'other of the spoile to spéede.
As Law and learning doth redresse
　　That otherwise would go to wrack :

Euen

Euen so doth it oft times oppresse
  And bring the true man to the rack:
Though Poyson paine the drinker sore
  By boyling in his fainting breast,
Yet is it not refusde therefore,
  For cause sometime it brædeth reast:
And mixt with Medicines of prowse
  According to Machaons Arte,
Doth serue right well for our behowse
  And succor sends to dying harte.
Yet these and other things were made
  By Nature for the better vse,
But we of custome take a trade
  By wilfull will them to abuse.
So nothing is by kinde so voide
  Of vice, and with such vertue fraught,
But it by vs may be anoide,
  And brought in trackt of time too naught
Againe there is not that so ill
  Bylowe the Lampe of Phœbus light,
But man may better if he will
  Applie his wit to make it right.

The Louer excuseth himselfe for renowncing
  his Loue and Ladie, imputing the same
  to his fate and constellation.

Though Dydo blamde Æneas truth
  for leauing Carthage shore,

                            others

Where he well entertainde had béene,
   and like a Prince before :
Though Theseus were vnthriftie thought
   and of a cruell race,
That in rewarde of death escapte
   by Aryadnas Lace,
Amid the desart woods so wilde
   his louing Lasse forsooke,
Whome by god hap and luckie lore
   the drowsie Bacchus tooke.
Yet if the Iudges in this case
   their verdit yelde aright,
Nor Theseus nor Æneas fact
   deserue such endlesse spight,
As waywarde Women stirde to wrath
   beare fired fast in minde,
Still séeking wayes to wreake their yre
   vpon Æneas kinde.
For neither lack of liking loue,
   nor hope of greater gaine,
Nor fickle fansies force vs men
   to breake off friendships chaine.
They loth not that they loude before,
   they hate not things possest :
Some other weightie cause they haue
   of chaunge, as may be gest.
And waying with my selfe eche one,
   I can none fitter finde,

                                 Than

Than that to men such blessed hap
  is by the Gods assignde.
The golden Starres that guide their age,
  and Planets will them so:
And Gods (the Rulers of their race)
  procure them to forgo
Their forged faith and plighted truth,
  with promise made so sure,
That is to seeming strong as Steele,
  and likely to endure.
For did not mightie Ioue himselfe
  the swift Cyllenus sende
To will the Troyan Prince in haste
  into Italia bende
And leaue the lyked lande so well,
  and Carthage Queene forsake,
That made him owner of hir hart,
  and all that shee could make :
And such was Theseus lot perdie,
  so hard the Maydens hap,
That shee in desart should be left
  and caught in Bacchus trap.
Should Iason be proclaimde and cride
  a Traitor to the Skies
For that he Medea left at last
  by whome he wan the Flise :
No, such was Oetes Daughters chaunce
  in Cradle hir assignde,

                                 And

And Iasans Birthstarre forst the Gréeke
  to showe himselfe vnkinde :
For if rewardes might binde so fast,
  and knit the knot so sure,
Their faith (no doubt) and lincked loue
  should then of force endure.
For Dido gaue him Carthage Rayes,
  the wealth, and soile withall :
Those other two preserude their liues
  that else had liude in thrall.
Then sithens streaming Starres procure,
  and fatall powers agrée,
And stawled Gods doe condiscend
  that I my friendship floe :
And reaue your Bells and cast you off
  to liue in haggards wies,
That for no priuate stale doe care,
  but loue to range the Skies :
I must not séeme then to rebell
  nor secret Treason forge,
But chaunge my choyce, and leaue my loue
  and fansies fonde disgorge.
I craue of Cupid Lorde of loue
  a pardon for the same,
For that I now reiect his lawes
  and quite renownce his game.

Of Ladie Venus, that hauing loſt hir Sonne
Cupid God of Loue, and deſirous to vn-
derſtand of him againe, declares by
the way the nature of Loue and
affectiohs of the ſame, by
pretie diſcription as
followeth.

What time the Ladie Venus ſought hir little Sonne
That Cupid hight, & found him not, ſhe thus begonne
My friends (quoth ſhe) if any chaunce in open ſtreete
Oz croſſing pathes, & wandzing amozous Elfe to meete,
That Runnagate (I ſay) is mine: who ſo by hap
Shall firſt bzing tidings of the Boy, in Venus lap
Is ſure to ſit, and haue in pzice of taken paine,
A ſugred kiſſe. But he that bzings him home againe,
A buſſe? yea not a buſſe alone doubtleſſe ſhall haue
But like a Friend I will entreate him paſſing bzaue.
I tell you tis a pzoper youth. Marke euery Lim
And member of my ſtraid Sonne that is ſo trim.
Not ſallow white his bodie is, but like to flame,
A fierce and fierie roling eie ſets out the ſame.
A miſchicuous wylie hart in Bzeaſt the Boy doth beare,
But yet his wozdes are Honnie like and ſweete to eare.
His talking tongue and meaning minde aſunder goe,
Smooth filed ſtile foz little coſt he will beſtowe.
But being once inflamde with ire and raging wzath,
A cruell caukred dogged hart the Vzchin hath.
Falſe Foxely ſubtile Boy, and gloſing lying Lad,
He ſports to outward ſight, but inward chafes like mad.
A curled Sconce he hath, with angrie frowning bzowe.
A little hand, yet Dart a cruell ſway can thzowe.
To ſhadie Acheron ſometine he ſlings the ſame,
And deepeſt dainp of hollow Hell thoſe Impes to tame.
Upon his Carkaſſe not a cloth, but naked hee
Of garments goes, his minde is wzapt, and not to ſee.
                                                    Much

Much like a fethred Foule he flies,& wags his wings
Now here now there : ẏ man somtime this Miser wrings
Sometimes againe the Lasse to loue he doth ensorce,
Of neither kind, nor man nor maid,he hath remorce:
A little Bow the Boy doth beare in tender hande,
And in the same an Arrow nockt to string doth stand.
A slender Shaft, yet such a one as farre will flie,
And being shot from Cupids Bow will reach the Skie,
A pretie golden Quiuer hangs there albehinde
Upon his back, wherein who so doth looke, shall finde
A sort of sharpe and lurching shafts, vnhappie Boy
Wherewith his Ladie Mother eke he doth annoy
Sometimes : but most of all the foolish fretting Elfe
In cruell wise doth cruelly torment and vex himselfe.
Doe beate the Boy and spare him not at all,if thou
On him doe chaunce to light : although frõ childish brow
And moysted eies the trickling teares like clouds distill,
Beleeue him not,for chiefly then beguile he will.
Not if he smile vnlose his pyniond armes take heede,
With pleasãt honie words though he thine eares doe feede
And craue a kisse,beware thou kisse him not at all :
For in his lips vile venom lurcks, and bitter Gall.
Or if with friendly face he seeme to yeelde his Bow
And shafts to thee, his proferde gifts (my Friend) forgo
Touch not with tender hand the subtile flattring Dart
Of Loue,for feare the fire thereof doe make thee smart.

Where this that I haue sayde be true,
Yee Louers I appeale to you.
For ye doe knowe Cupidos toyes,
Yee feele his smarts,yee taste his ioyes.
A sickle foolish God to serue,
I tearme him as he doth deserue.

Of the cruell hatred of
Stepmothers.

The Sonne in lawe his Stepdame being dead,
Began hir Hierce with Garlands to comende :
Meane while there fell a stone vpon his head
From out the Tombe that brought the Boy abed,
A pꝛoofe that Stepdames hate hath neuer ende.

Againe.

Glad was ẏ sonne of frowning Beldams death,
To witnesse ioy to deck hir Tomb gan trudge :
A peece of Marbell fell and reft his bꝛeath
As he (good Lad) stode strewing flowꝛes beneath,
A signe ẏ Death dawnts not the mothers grudge.

To *Cupid* for reuenge of his vnkind and cruell
Loue. Declaring his faithfull seruice
and true hart both to the God of
Loue and his Ladie.

If I had bæne in Troyan ground
When Ladie Venus toke hir wound:
If I in Grækish campe had bæne,
Oꝛ clad in armour had bæne sæne:
If Hector had by mæe bæne slaine,
Oꝛ Pꝛince Æneas put to paine :
If I the Machin huge had bꝛought,
By Grecian guile so falsely wꝛought,
Oꝛ raysed it aboue the wall,
Of Troie that pꝛocurde the fall :

                    P.i.   Then

Then could I not thée (Cupid) blame,
If thou didſt put mée to this ſhame.
But I haue alwaies béene as true
To thée and thine in order due,
As euer was there any Wight,
That fayth and truth to Cupid plight.
I neuer yet deſpiſe thy lawe,
But aye of thée did ſtand in awe :
I neuer callde thée Buſſard blinde,
I no ſuch fault in thée did finde,
But thought my time well ſpent to bée
That I imploide in ſeruing thée.
I wiſſe thou wert of force and powre
To conquere Princes in an howre
When thou retaindſt mée as thy man
I thought my ſelfe moſt happie than.
Since this is true that I haue ſalde,
God Cupid let mée haue thy alde,
Helpe mée to wreake my wrath aright
And ſuccor mée to worke my ſpight.
To thée it appertaines of due
Him to aſſiſt that is ſo true :
And thou of reaſon ſhouldſt torment
Such as by wilfull will are bent
To triumph ouer thoſe that ſerue
Thée in the field, and neuer ſwerue,
Go bend thy Bowe with haſtie ſpéede,
And make hir Tigers hart to bléede.

Cauſ

Cause hir that little sets by mæ,
Yet still to stand in awe of thæ.
Let hir perceiue thy feruent fire,
And what thou art in raging ire,
Now showe thy selfe no man to bæ,
Let hir a God both fæle and sæ.
She forceth not my cutting paine,
Hir bowed othes shæ wayes as vaine.
Shæ sits in peace at quiet rest,
And scornes at mæ so dispossest.
Shæ laughes at thæ, and mocks thy might,
Thou art not Cupid in hir sight.
Shæ spites at mæ without cause whie,
Shæ forceth not although I die.
I am hir captiue bounde in Giue
And dare not once for lyfe to striue.
The more to thæ I call and crie,
To rid mæ from this crueltie,
The more shæ sæckes to worke hir ire,
The more shæ burnes with scalding fire.
And all for Cupids sake I bide,
From whose decræs I doe not glide.
Wherefore (I say) go bende thy Bow,
And to hir hart an Arrow throw :
That Dart which breaketh harts of flint
And glues the cruell crasing dint,
Upon hir crabbed breast bestow,
That shæ thy force and powre may know :

That

That shée a Myrrour may be knowne
To such as be thy deadly sone,
So shall they good example take,
How to abuse men for thy sake.
Let hir (good Cupid)vnderstande,
That I am thine both hart and hande,
And to play quittance force a fire,
That shée may frie with whote desire
Of me, whome earst she put to paine,
And this is all that I would gaine.

An Aunswere to his Ladie, that willed him that absence should not breede forgetfulnesse.

Though Noble Surrey sayde
  that absence woonders frame,
  And makes things out of sight forgot,
  and thereof takes his name:
Though some there are that force
  but on their pleasures prest,
Unmindefull of their plighted truth
  and falsely forged hest:
Yet will I not approue
  mée guiltie of this crime,
Ne breake the friendship late begon
  as you shall trie in time.
No distance of the place
  shall reaue thée from my brest;

Not

Not fawning chaunce, nor frowning hap
  shall make mee swarue my Hest.
As soone may Phœbus frame
  his fierie Steades to ronn
Their race from path they wonted were,
  and ende where they begonn:
As soone shall Saturne cease
  his bended browes to show,
And frowning face to friendly Starres
  that in their Circles go:
As soone the Tiger tame
  and Lion shall you finde:
And brutish beastes that sauage were
  shall swarue their bedlam kinde:
As soone the frost shall flame,
  and Ætna cease to burne,
And restlesse Riuers to their springs
  and Fountaines shall returne:
As absence brede debate,
  or want of sight procure
Our faithfull friendships wrrith awrie
  whilst liuely breath indure,
As soone I will committ
  my selfe to Lethes lake
As the (sweete friend) whomme I a Friend
  haue chose for vertues sake.
How may a man forget
  the coale that burnes within:
              P.iij.   Augmen-

Augmenting ſtill his ſecret ſore
  by piercing fell and ſkin:
May Martirs ceaſe to mourne
  or thinke of torments preſt,
Whilſt paine to paine is added aſe
  to further their vnreſt:
May Shipmen in diſtreſſe
  at pleaſure of the winde
Toſt to and fro by ſurge of Seas
  that they in tempeſt finde,
Forget Neptunus rage
  or bluſtring Borias blaſt,
When Cables are in ſunder crackt,
  and tackle rent from Maſt:
Ne may I (Friend) forget
  (vnleſſe I would but faine)
The ſalue that doth recure my ſore
  and heales the ſcarre againe.
I ſend thee by the winde
  ten thouſand ſighes a day,
Which dim the Skies with clowdie ſmoke
  as they doe paſſe away.
Oft gazing on the Sunne
  I count Apollo bleſt,
For that he vewes thee once aday
  in paſſing to the Weſt.
Ob that I had his powre
  and blaſing Lampe of light

                        Then

Then thou my Friend should stand asunde
   to neuer sée the night.
But since it is not so,
   content thy selfe a while :
And with remembrance of thy Friend
   the lothsome time begile.
Till Fortune doe agrée
   that we shall méete againe :
For then shall presence bréede our ioyes
   whome absence put to paine.
And of my olde good will
   (good Friend) thy selfe assure,
Haue no distrust, my loue shall last
   as long as life shall dure.

Of a Thracyan that was drownde by playing on the Ise.

A Thracyan Boy well tipled all the day
Vpon a frozen Spring did sport and play,
The slipper Ise with hiest of bodies sway
   On sodaine brake, & swapt his head away :
It swam aloft, bylowe the Carcas lay.
The Mother came and bore the head away :
When shée did burie it thus gan shée say.
This brought I forth in flame his Hierce to haue,
The rest amids the flood to finde a graue.
       P.iii.   The

The Louer hoping in May to haue had redreſſe
of his woes, and yet fowly miſſing his pur-
poſe, bewailes his cruell hap.

Ou that in May haue bathde in blis
And found a ſalue to eaſe your ſore:
Doe May obſeruaunce, Reaſon is
That May ſhould honord be therfore.
Awake out of your drowſie ſléepe
And leaue your tender Beds of Downe,
Of Cupids Lawes that taken kéepe
With Sommer flowers deck your Crowne.
As ſone as Venus Starre doth ſhowe
That brings the dawning on his back
And chéerefull light begins to growe
By putting of his Foe to wrack:
Repaire to heare the wedded Makes
And late ycoupled in a knote,
The Nightingale that ſits in Brakes
And telles of Tereus truth by note:
The Thruſſell, with the Turtle Doue,
The little Robin eke yſeare
That make rehearſall of their loue,
Make haſte (I ſay) that yée were theare.
Into the fieldes where Dian dwels
With Nimphes enuirond round about,
Haſte yée to daunce about the Wels,
A fit paſtime for ſuch a rout.

Let

Let them doe this that haue receiude
  In May the hire of hoped grace :
But I as one that am bereaude
  Of blissefull state, will hide my face,
And dole my daies with ruthfull voice
As fits a retchlesse Wight to doe :
Since now it lies not in my choise
  To quite mee from this cursed woe.
I harbour in my breast a thought
  Which now is turnde another way,
That pleasaunt May would mee ybrought
  From Scylla to a better bay.
Since all (quoth I) that Nature made,
  And placed here in earth bylowe,
When Spring returnes, of woonted trade
  Doe banish griefe that earst did growe,
And chaungeth eke the churlish chéere
  And frowning face of Tellus hewe,
With vernant flowers that appéere
  To clad the soile with mantell newe :
Since Snakes doe cast their shriueled skinnes,
  And Bucks hang vp their heads on pale,
Since frisking Fishes lose their finnes,
  And glide with new repaired scale :
Then I of force with gréedie eie
  Must hope to finde to ease my smart,
Since eche anoy in Spring doth die,
  And cares to comfort doe conuart.

                             Then

Then I (quoth I) shall reach the port
　And fast mine Ancker on the ground,
Where lyes my pleasure and disport
　Where is my suretie to be found :
There shall my beaten Barke haue rode,
　And I for seruice done be paid,
My sorrowes quite shall be vnlode,
　Euen thus vnto my selfe I said.
But (out alas) it falles not so,
　May is to mée a Month of mone,
In May though others comfort gro,
　My séedes of griefe are surely sowne.
My bitter Teares for water serue
　Wherewith the Garden of my brest
I moist, for feare the séedes should strue,
　And thus I frame mine owne vnrest.
Let others then that féelen ioy
　Extole the merrie Month of May,
And I that tasted haue annoy,
　In praise thereof will nothing say.
But with returne of winters warre
　And blustring force of Borias force againe.
These sower séedes of wo to marre
　By force of winde and wisking raine.
And so perhaps by better fate
　At next returne of Spring, I may
By chaunging of my former state
　Cast off my care, and chaunge my lay.

To

To a fickle and vnconstant
Dame, a friendly
warning.

What may I thinke of you (my Fawlcon free)
That hauing hood, lines, buets, bels of mee,
And wonted earst when I my game did spzing
To flie so well and make such nimble wing,
As might no Fowle foz weightnesse well compare
With thee, thou wert a Bird so passing rare :
What may I deeme of thee (fayze Fawlcon) now,
That neyther to my lure noz traine wilt bow.
But this that when my back is turnde and gon,
Another giues thee rumpes to tyze vpon.
Well wanton well, if you were wise in deede
You would regard the fist whereon you feede.
You would the Hozse deuouring Crow refuse,
And gozge your selfe with flesshe moze fine to chuse.
I wishe thee this foz wonted olde good will
To flie moze high, foz feare the stowping will
Breede him, that now doth keepe thee, out of loue
And thinke his Fawlcon will a Bussard pzoue,
Which if he deeme, oz doe suspect at all,
He will abate thy flesh, and make thee fall,
So that of fozce thou shalt enfozced bee
Too doe by him as nowe thou dost by mee :
That is to leaue the Keeper, and away,
Fawlcon take heede, foz this is true I say.

The

The Louer to his Ladie that gased much
vp to the Skies.

My Girle, thou gazeſt much
vpon the golden Skies :
VVould I were Heauen, I would behold
thee then with all mine eies.

The Penitent Louer vtterly renoun-
cing loue, craues pardon of
forefaſſed follies.

IF ſuch as did amiſſe
and ran their race awrie,
May boldely craue at Iudges hand
ſome mercie ere they die,
And pardon for their gilt
that wilfully tranſgreſt,
And ſawe the bownds before their eies
that vertue had addreſt :
Then I that brake the bancks
which Reaſon had aſſignde
To ſuch as would purſue hir traine,
may ſtande in hope to finde
Some fauour at hir hand :
ſince blinde forecaſt was cauſe,
And not my wilfull will in fault
that I haue ſwerude hir lawes.
Miſguided haue I béene
and trayned all by truſt,

And

And Loue was forger of the fraude,
　and furtherer of my luſt.
Whoſe vele did daze mine eies,
　and darckned ſo my ſight
With errors foggie miſt at firſt,
　that Reaſon gaue no light.
And as thoſe wofull Wightes
　that ſaile on ſwelling Seas,
When windes and wrathfull waues conſpire
　to baniſh all their eaſe,
When heauenly Lamps are hid
　from Shipmens hungrie eies,
And Lodeſtarres are in couert kept
　within the cloudie Skies：
As they without reſpect
　doe follow Fortunes lore,
And run at randome in the flod
　where Æols Impes doe rore,
Till golden creſted Phebe,
　or elſe his Siſters light,
Haue chaſde away thoſe noyſome clouds,
　and put the ſame to flight：
So I (vnhappie man)
　haue followde Loue a ſpace,
And felt the whotteſt of his flame,
　and flaſhing fierie blaſe.
In darkneſſe haue I dwelt,
　and Errours vglie ſhade,

An

Unwitting how to raise a Starre
   from perill to euade.
Few daies came on my head
   wherein was cause of ioy,
But day and night were readie both
   to hasten mine anoy.
Short were my sleepes (God wot)
   most dreadfull were my dreames,
Mine eies (as Conduits of the hart)
   did gush out saltish streames.
Tormented was my Corse,
   my minde was neuer free,
But both repleate with anguish aye
   disseuerde sought to bee.
No place might like mee long,
   no pleasure could endure,
In stead of sport was smart at hande,
   for pastime paine in vre.
A Bondman to my selfe,
   yet free in others sight,
Not able to resist the rage
   of winged Archers might.
Thus haue I spent my time
   in seruage as a Thrall,
Till Reason of hir bountie list
   mee to hir mercie call.
Now haue I made returne,
   and by good hap retirde

From

From Cupids Camp and deepe Dispaire:
   and once againe aspirde
To Ladie Reasons stawle
   where wisedome throned is,
On promise of amends releast
   is all that was amis.
To Plato now I flie,
   and Senecs sound aduise:
A Fatch for Loue, I force not now
   what Chaunce fall on the Dice.

To his Friend that refusde him with-
out cause why but onely
vpon delight of
chaunge.

YOu showe your selfe to bée
   a Woman right by kinde:
   You lyke and then mislyke againe
   where you no cause doe finde.
I can not thinke that loue
   was planted in your brest,
As did your flattring lookes declare,
   and periurde tongue protest.
Thou swarste alone that I
   thy fansie did subdue,
Then why should frensie force thée now
   to show thy selfe vntrue:

Fle

Fie faithlesse woman fie,
   wilt thou condemne the kinde
Bicause of iust report of yll
   and blot of wauering minde?
Too playne it now appeares
   that lust procurde thy loue,
Or else it would not so decay
   and causelesse thus remoue.
I thought that I at first
   a Lucrece had subdude,
But nowe I finde that fansie fonde
   my senses did delude
I déemde that I had got
   a Fawlcon to the fist,
Whome I might quickly haue reclaimde,
   but I my purpose mist.
For (oh) the worser hap
   my Fawlcon is so frée,
As downe shée stoupes to straungers lure
   and forceth least of mée.
God shape was yll bestowde
   vpon so vile a kite,
That Haggard wise doth loue to liue
   and doth in chaunge delight.
Yéeld me thy flanting Hood,
   shake off those Belles of thine,
Such checking Bussards yll deserue
   or Bell or Hood so fine.

                                  With

With Fowles of baſer ſort
　how can you brooke too flie,
That earſt your Nature did to Hawkes
　of ſtately kinde applie?
If want of pray enforſte
　this chaunge thou art too blame;
For I had euer traines in ſtore
　to make my Fawlcon game.
I had a Taſſell eke
　full gentle by his kinde,
Too flie with thee in vſe of wing
　the greater ioy to finde.
No, doubtleſſe wanton luſt
　and fleſhly fowle deſire
Did make thee loath my friendly lure,
　and ſet thy hart on fire
Too trie what mettall was
　in Buſſards to be founde
This, this was it that made thee ſtowpe
　from loftie gate to grounde.
Wherefore if euer luck
　doe let me light on thee,
And Fortune graunt me once againe
　thy keeper for to bee:
Thy diet ſhall be ſuch,
　thy tyring rumpes ſo bare,
As thou ſhalt know thy keeper well,
　and for none other care.

　　　　　　　　D.ſ.　　　　Meanſ

Meanewhile on carren féede,
　thy hungrie gorge to glut:
That all thy lust in daylie chaunge
　and diet new dost put.
Diseases must of force
　such féeding sowle ensue :
No force to me, thou wert my Bird,
　But (Fawlcon) now adue.

To one that vpon surmise of
aduersitie, forewent
hir Friend.

AS too the whyte, and lately lymed house
　The Doues doe flock in hope of better fare,
And leaue their home of Culuers cleane and bare :
As to the Kitchin postes the péeping Mouse
Where Uittailes fine and curious Cates are drest,
And shonns the shop where liuelyhod wareth thin,
Where he before had fillde his emptie skin,
And where he chose him first to be a guest:
As Lyse vnto the lyuing Carcasse cleaue,
But balke the same made readie to the Beare,
So you that earst my Friend to séeming weare,
In happie state : your néedie Friend doe leaue.
Unfriendly are those other, Doue and Mouse
That doe refuse olde harbour for a newe
And make erchaunge for lodge they neuer knewe,
Unfriendly eke the slowe and lumpish Lowse.
　　　　　　　　　　　　　　　　But

But moze vnciuill you that wittie arre
To iudge a Friend, your Friendſhip to fozgo,
Without a cauſe and make exchaunges ſo :
Foz ſciendes are nœded moſt in time of warre.
Put caſe that Chaunce withdzew hir olde gœd will
And frownde on mœ to whome ſhœ was a friend ¢
Is that a reaſon why your loue ſhould end ¢
No, no, you ſhould a ſciend continue ſtill.
Foz true gœd will in miſerie is tride,
Foz then will none but faithfull ſciends abide.

To Maiſter Googes fanſie that begins
Giue Monie mee take friend-
ſhip who ſo liſt.

FRiend *Googe,* giue me ẙ faithfull friend to truſt,
And take the ſickle Coine foz mœ that luſt.
Foz Friends in time of trouble and diſtreſſe
With help and ſound aduiſe will ſone redzeſſe
Eche growing griefe that gripes the penſiue bzeſt,
When Monie lies lóckt vp in couꝛt Cheſt.
Thy Coine will cauſe a thouſand cares to grow,
Which if thou hadſt no Coine ẙ couldſt not know.
Thy Friend no care but comfoꝛt will pzocure,
Of him thou mayſt at nœde thy ſelfe aſſure.
Thy Monie makes the Thœfe in waite to lie,
Whoſe fraude thy Friend ¢ falſehood will deſcrie,
Thou canſt not kœpe vnlockt thy carefull Coine,
But ſome from thœ thy Monie will purloine :

D.ij.   Thy

Thy faithfull Friend will neuer ftart afide,
But take his fhare of all that fhall betide.
When thou art dead thy Monie is bereft
But after life thy truftie Friend is left:
Thy Monie ferues another Maifter than,
Thy fapthfull Friend lincks with none other man.
  So that(Friend *Googe*) I deeme it better I,
  To chofe the Friend and let the Monie lie.

The Louer abufed renown-
ceth Loue.

FO2 to reuoke to penfiue thought
  And troubled head my fo2mer plight,
  How I by earneft fute haue fought
  And griefull paines a louing Wight
Fo2 to accoy, accoy,
  And b2æde my ioy
Without anoy, makes faltifh b2yne
To flufh out of my vapo2d eyne.
¶ To thinke vpon the fund2ie fnares
And p2iuie Panthers that were led
To fo2ge my daylie dolefull cares,
Whereby my hoped pleafures fled,
  Doth plague my hart, my hart,
  With deadly fmart,
Without defart, that haue indurde
Such woes, and am not yet returde,

                ¶ Was

❧Was neuer day came on my bed
Wherein I did not sue for grace,
Was neuer night but I in bed
Vnto my Pillow tolde my case,
    Bayning my brest, my brest,
    For want of rest,
With teares opprest, yet remedie none
Was to be found for all my mone.
❧If she had dained my good will
And recompenst me with hir Loue,
I would haue béene hir Vassell still,
And neuer once my hart remoue:
    I did pretend, pretend,
    To be hir Friend
Vnto the end, but she refusde
My louing hart, and me abusde.
❧I did not force vpon the spite
And venemous stings of hissing Snakes,
I wayed not their words a Mite,
That such a doe at Louers makes:
    I did reioyce, reioyce,
    To haue the voyce
Of such a choyce, and smild to sée
What they reported so of mée.
❧Oh mée most luckie Wight (quoth I)
At whome the people so repine,
I trust the rumor that doth flie
Will force hir to my will incline,
                    M.iij.   A

And like well mée, well mét
   Whome shée doth sée,
Hir loue to bée, vnfainedly,
In whome shée may full well affíe.
¶But now at length I plainely vew
That woman neuer gaue hir brest,
For they by kindly course will rue
On such as séeme to loue rbeth best :
   And will relent, relent
   And be content,
When nought is ment, saue friendly hart
And loue for neuer to depart.
¶Some cruell Tiger lent hir Tet
And fostred hir with sauage Pap,
That can not finde in hart to let
A man to loue hir, since his hap
   Hath so assignde, assignde
   To haue his minde
To loue inclinde, in honest wise
Whome shée should not of right despise.
¶But since I sée hir stonie hart
Cannot be pierst with pitties Launce,
Since nought is gainde but wofull smart,
I doe intende to breake the daunce,
   And quite forgo, forgo
   My pleasaunt Fo,
That paines mée so, and thinkes in fine
To make me like to Circes Swine :

I cleane deſie hir flattering face,
I quite abhorre hir luring lookes :
As long as Ioue ſhall giue meͤ grace
Sheͤ neuer comes within my bookes.
  I doe deteſt, deteſt
  So falſe a Gueſt
That broͤdes vnreſt, where ſhe ſhould plant
Hir loue, if pittie did not want.

Let hir go ſeͤke ſome other Foole,
Let hir inrage ſome other Dolt :
I haue beͤne taught in Platos Schoole
From Cupids Banner to reuolt :
  And to forſake, forſake
  As fearefull Snake,
Such as doe make, a man but ſmart
For bearing them a faithfull hart.

    The forſaken Louer laments that his **La-**
    die is matched with an other.

AS Menelaus did lament
  When Helena to Troie went,
  And to the Teucrian Gueſt applide
  And all hir Countrie Friends deſide :
Euen ſo I feͤle tormenting paine
To lurck in erie little vaine,
And ranſack all my Corſe, to ſeͤ
That ſheͤ hath now forſaken meͤ,
  The faithfull Friend that ſhe conld finde :
  But fickle Dames will to their kinde.
             Q.iiij.   A

A simple chaunge in fayth it was
To leaue the Lyon for the Asse,
Such chopping will but make you bare
And spend your lyfe in carck and care,
You might haue taken better héede
When left the Graine, and chose the wéede:
Your Haruest would the better béene
If you had to your Bargin éene,
   But to recant it is to late,
   Go to, a Gods name to your Mate.
Tis Muck that makes the Pot to play
As men of olde were woont to say,
And women marrie for the gaine
Though oft it fall out to their paine:
And as I gesse thou hast ydoon
When all thy twist is throughly spoon,
It will appéere vnto thy foes,
Thou pluckst a Nettle for a Rose:
   In faith thy Friend would loth to sée
   Thy curssed luck so yll to bée.

Of one that was in reuersion.

ANother hath that I did bie,
   and I enioy that hée imbraste:
   I reape the Graine, and pluck the Peare,
   but he had Peare and Corne at laste.
Which sithens Fortune hath allowde,
   let eyther well contented bée :

I

I hate him not for his delights,
    then let him doe the lyke to mee.
For sowe both be pleasde, I say,
    this bargaine was deuised well:
Let him with present good delight
    as I what time to mee it fell.
If euer he by hap forgo,
    I trust my hope is not in vaine,
I hope the thing I once enioyde
    will to his owner come againe,
Which if be so, then happie I
    that had the first, and haue the laste:
What better fortune may there bee
    than in Reuersion to be plaste.

That all hurts and losses are to be re-
couered and recured saue the
cruell wound of Loue.

The Surgion may deuise
    a Salue for erie sore,
And to recure all inwarde griefes
    Phisitions haue in store
Their Simples to compownde
    and match in mixture so,
As ech disease from sicklie Corse
    they can enforce to go.
The wastfull wrack of welth
    that Merchants doe sustaine,

By

By happie vent of gotten wares
  may be supplide againe.
A Towne by treason lost,
  a Forte by falsehod woon,
By manly fight is got againe
  and helpe of hurtfull Gon.
Thus eche thing hath redresse
  and swéete recure againe :
Saue onely Loue, that farther frets,
  and féedes on inward paine.
No Galen may this griefe
  by Phisicke force expell :
No Reasons rule may ought preuaile
  where lurcking Loue doth dwell.
The Patient hath no powre
  of holesome things to taste :
No Drench, no Drug, nor Sirop swéete
  his hidden harme may waste.
No comfort comes by day,
  no pleasant sléepe by night :
No néedefull nap at Noone may ease
  the Louers painefull plight.
In déepe dispaire he dwels
  till in comes hope of ease,
Which somewhat lessens paines of Loue,
  and calmes the surge of Seas.
His head is fraught with thoughts,
  his hart with throwes repleate :

His

His eies amazde, his quaking hand,
　his stomack lothing meate.
This bale the Louer bides
　and hatefull Hagge of Hell,
And yet himselfe doth déeme that hée
　in Paradyce doth dwell.

Of the choise of his Va-
lentine.

With others I to chose a Valentine
　Addrest my selfe: Ech had his dearest friend
In Scrole ywrit, among the rest was mine.
Sée now the luck by lot that Chaunce doth send
　To Cupids crewe, marke Fortune how it falls,
　And mark how Ven' Imps are Fortús thralls.
The Papers were in couert kept from sight,
In hope I went to note what hap would fall:
I choze, but on my Friend I could not light.
(Such was the Goddesse wil that wildes the Ball)
　But sée god luck, although I mist the same,
　I hapt on one that bare my Ladies name.
Vnegall though their beauties were to loke,
Remembrance yet of hir well feautured face
So often séene, thereby my Sences toke,
Vnhappie though thée were not then in place:
　Long you to learne what name my Ladie hight:
　Account from V. to. A. and spell aright.

　　　　　　　　　　　　　　　　Of

Of an open Foe and a fayned Friend.

Not he so much anoies
  that sayes : I am thy Fo,
As he that beares a hatefull hart,
  and is a Friend to sho.
Of tone we may beware,
  and flie his open hate,
But tother bites before he barck,
  a hard auoyded Mate.

Againe.

If both giue mée the man
  that sayes, I hate in déede:
Than him that hath a Knife to kill,
  yet weares a friendly wéede.

Of a Ritch Miser.

A Misers minde thou hast,
  thou hast a Princes pelfe :
Which makes thée welthy to thine Heire,
  a Beggar to thy selfe.

Of

Of a Painter that painted
Fauour.

Thou (Painter fond) what meanes this mad deuise
Fauour to draw? sith vncouth is the hed
From whence it comes, and first of all was bred:
Some deeme that it of Beautie doth arise,
Dame Fortunes Babie and vndoubted Sonne,
Some other doe surmise this Fauour was:
Againe, some thinke by Chaunce it came to passe,
Another saies of Vertue it begonne.
what Mate is he that daylie is at hand?   Quest
Faire speaking he and glosing Flattrie hight.   Iuns.
what he that slowly comes behind? Iuns. Despight. Quest
what they (I pray) that him inuiron stand?   Quest
wealth, Honor, Pride, and Noble needefull Lawes.   Iuns
And leading Lust that driues to thousand ills.
what meane those wings, & painted quiuering Quills? Quest
Cause vpward aie Dame Fortune Fauour drawes.   Iuns
why blinde is Fauour made? (Iuns.) for cause that he Quest
That is vnthriftie once yplast amownt
From baser step not had in any cownt
Can not discerne his friends, or who they be.
why treades he on the tickle turning wheele?   Quest
He followes Fortunes steps and giddie Gate   Iuns
Unstaied Chaunces aie vnstedfast Mate:
And when that things are swell, can neuer feele.
Then tell me one thing else to pease my minde
My last demaund. what meanes his swelling so?   Quest
How chaunst that Fauour doth so prowdly go?   Iuns
Good haps by course vs Men doe maken blinde.

The Louer whose Lady dwelt fast by a Prison.

One day I hide mee fast vnto the place
where lodgde my Loue, a passing propre dame

For head, hand, leg, lim, wealth, wit, comly grace:
And being there my sute I gan to frame,
The smokie sighes bewrayde my fierie flame.
But cruell shæ, disdainefull, coy and curst,
Forst not my words, but quaild hir Friend at furst.

Whereat I lookte me vp a wofull Wight,
And threw mine eies vp to the painted Skie,
In minde to waile my hap: And saw in sight
Not farre from thence a place where Prisners lie,
For crimes forepast the after paines to trie:
A Laberinth, a lothsome Lodge to dwell,
A Dungeon dæpe, a Dampe as darke as Hell.

Oh happie you (quoth I) that fæle the force
Of girding Gyue, thirst, colde and stonie bed,
Respect of mæ, whose loue hath no remorse:
In death you liue, but I in life am ded,
Your ioy is yet to come, my pleasure fled.
In prison you haue mindes at fræedome aye,
I fræe am thrall, whose loue sækes his decaye.

Unworthy you to liue in such distresse
Whose former faults repentance did bewaile:
More fitter were this Ladie mercilesse
At grate to stand, with whome no teares preuaile:
More worthy she to liue in lothsome Gaile
That murders such as sue to hir for lyfe,
And spoyles hir faithfull Friends wt spiteful knyfe.

Com-

Complaint of the long abſence of his Loue vpon the firſt ac-quaintance.

O Curſed, cruell, canckred Chaunce,
   O Fortune full of ſpight,
Why haſt thou ſo on ſodaine reſt
   from mœ my chiefe delight?
What glorie ſhalt thou gaine perdie
   or purchace by thy rage?
This is no Conqueſt to be callde,
   wherefore thy wrath aſſwage.
To ſœne eclipſed was my ioy,
   my dolors grow to faſt :
For want of hir that is my life,
   my life it can not laſt.
Is this thy fickle kind ſo ſœne
   to hoiſe a man to ioy,
And ere he touch the top of bliſſe
   to brœde him ſuch anoy?
Nowe doe I plaine perceiue and ſœ
   that Poets faine not all,
For churliſh Chaunce is counted blinde
   and full of filthy Gall.
I thought there had bœne no ſuch Dame
   ne Goddeſſe on a whœle:
But now tœ well I know hir kinde,
   tœ ſœne hir force I fœle.

                            And

And that which doth augment my smart
  and maketh more my wo,
Is, for I felt a sodaine ioy
  where now this griefe doth grow.
If thou hadst ment (vnhappie Hap)
  thus to haue nipt my ioy,
Why didst thou show a smyling chéere
  that shouldst haue lookte acoy ?
For griefes doe nothing grudge at all
  but where was blisse before :
None wailes the want of wealth so much
  as he that had the store.
Not he that neuer saw the Sunne
  complaines for lack of light,
But such as saw his golden gleames
  and knew his chéerefull might.
Too late I learne through spitefull chaunce
  that ioy is mixt with wo,
And eche good hap hath hate in horde,
  the course of things is so.
So Poyson lurcks in Suger swéete,
  the Hooke so hides the bayte :
Euen so in gréene and pleasant grasse
  the Serpent lies in wayte.
Vlysses wife I learne at last
  thy sorrow and distresse,
In absence of thy lingring Loue,
  that should thy woes redresse.

                          Great

Great was your griefe (ye Greekish Girlles)
   whilſte ſtately Troie ſtood,
And kept your huſbands from your laps
   in perill of their blood.
All ye therefoze that haue aſſayde
   what tozments lack pzocures
Of that you loue, lament my lack
   which ouerlong endures.
Ye Winds tranſpozt my ſoking ſighes
   to my new choſen Friende,
So may my ſozrow ſwage perhaps
   and dzeerie ſtate haue ende.
Ye Sighes make true repozt of teares,
   that ſo beraine my bzeſt,
As Helens huſbands neuer were
   foz treaſon of his Gueſt.
If thou (my Letter) maiſt attaine
   the place of hir abode,
Doe thou, as Herauld of the hart,
   my ſorrowes quite vnlode.
In thee as in a Myzrour cleere
   oz Chziſtall may ſhe vewe
My pangues, my paynes, my ſighes and teares
   which Tiger's could but rewe.
There ſhall thee ſee my ſecret parts
   encombzed all with mone,
My fainting lims, my vapozd eien
   with hart as colde as ſtone.

        R.ij   I

I know shée can but rue my case
  when thou presents my sute,
Wherefore play thou thy part so well
  that I may reape the frute.
And if (when shée hath read thée through)
  shée place thée in hir lap,
Then chaunge thy chéere thy Maister hath
  his long desired hap.

The ventrous Louer after long absence
    craues his Ladie to meete with
      him in place to enterparle
        of hir auentures.

IF so Leander durst
    from Abydon to Sest
    To swim to Herô whome he chose
    his Friend aboue the rest,
And gage his comely corse
  vnto the sowsing Tyde
To lay his water beaten lims
  fast by hir tender side :
Then I (my Deare) whose gleames
  and ardor doth surpasse
The scorching flame and blasing heate
  that in Leander was,
May well presume to take
  the greatest toyle in hande,

                          To

To reach the place where thou dost lodge
  the chiefe of Venus bande,
For not Leanders loue
  my friendship doth excell,
Nor Hero may compare with hir
  that beares Dame Beauties Bell.
There resteth nought for thee
  but to assigne the place,
The mirrie day, the ioyfull houre
  when I may see thy face :
Appoint the certaine Tide
  and fixed stem of stay,
And thou shalt see thy faithfull Friend
  will quickly come his way
Not dreding any doubt :
  but ventrously will go
Through thick and thin to gaine a glimse
  of thee his sugred fo.
Where when by hap we meete,
  our long endured woes
Shall stint by force of friendly thoughts
  which we shall then discloes.
Then eyther may vnfolde
  the secrets of the hart,
And show how long dislodge hath bred
  our cruell cutting smart.
Then may we freely chat
  of all forepassed ioyes,

          R.H.   And

And put those pensiue pangues to flight
  with new recourse of ioyes.
Then pleasure shall possesse
  the lodge were Dolour lay,
And mirrie blincks put cloudes of care
  and lowring lookes away.
Then kissing may be plide
  and clipping put in vre,
And lingred sores by Cupids salues
  aspire to quick recure.
Oh dræde thou not at all,
  set womans feare a part
And take the courage of a man,
  that hast a manly hart
In hostage ate with thæ
  to vse at thy deuise.
In all affaires and nœdefull houres
  as matter shall arise.
Reuoke to louing minde
  how ventrous Thisbe met
In fearefull night with Pyramus
  where Nynus Tombe was set.
So hazard thou to come
  vnto the pointed place,
To thwart thy Friend, and mœte with him
  that longs to sœ thy face.
Who better will attend
  thy friendly comming there,

                                Than

Than Pyramus of Thysbe did
  his disappointed Fære.
For (oh) their méeting was
  the reauer of their breath,
The crop of endlesse care, and cause
  of either Louers death.
But we so warely will
  our fixed time attende,
As no mishap shall grow thereby.
  And thus I make an ende
With wishing well to thée,
  and hope to méete in place
To enterparle with thée (my Friend)
  and tell my dolefull case.

To Maister Googe his Sonet
out of sight out of
thought.

The lesse I sée, the more my téene,
  The more my téene the greater griefe
  The greater griefe, the lesser séene,
  The lesser séene, the lesse reliefe :
The lesse reliefe the heuier spright,
When P. is farthest out of sight.
  The rarer séene, the rifer sobs,
The rifer sobbes, the sadder hart,
The sadder hart, the greater throbs,
The greater throbs, the worser smart,

K.iij.

The

The wo2ſer ſmart p2oceedes of this
That I my P. ſo often miſſe.
 The nærer too, the mo2e I ſmile,
The mo2e I ſmile, the merier minde:
The mirrie minde doth thought exile,
And thought exilde recourſe I finde
Of heauenly ioyes: all this delight
Haue I when P. is once in ſight.

The Louer whoſe Miſtreſſe feared a Mouſe,
declareth that he would become
a Cat, if he might haue
his deſire.

IF I might alter kinde,
 what thinke you I would bee,
No2 Fiſh, no2 Foule, no2 Fle, no2 Frog,
no2 Squirrell on the Tree.
The Fiſh the hooke, the Foule
 the lymed twig doth catch,
The Fle the Finger, and the Frog
 the Baſſard doth diſpatch.
The Squirrell thincking nought
 that feately cracks the Nut,
The greedie Gaſhauke wanting p2ay
 in d2ead of death doth put.
But ſco2ning all theſe kindes
 I would become a Cat,

Aꝛ

To combat with the créeping Mouse
 and scratch the scréeking Rat.
I would be present aye
 and at my Ladies call,
To gard hir from the fearefull Mouse
 in Parlour and in Hall.
In kitching for his life
 he should not shew his hed,
The Peare in Poke should lie vntoucht
 when shée were gone to bed.
The Mouse should stand in feare,
 so should the squeaking Rat:
All this would I doe if I were
 conuerted to a Cat.

The Louer driuen to absent him
from his Ladie, bawayles
his estate.

When angrie Gréekes w Troians fought
 In minde to sack their welthie Towne,
King Agamemnon néedefull thought
 To beate the neighbour Cities downe,
And by his Princely power to quell
Such as by Priams Realme did dwell.
 Thus forth he trauailde with his traine
Till he vnto Lyrnesus came,
Where cruell fight he did maintaine,
And slue such Wights as were of fame:

K.iiij.   Downe

Downe went the walles and all to wrack
And so was Lyrnes brought to sack.

Two Noble Dames of passing shape
Unto the Prince were brought in fine
That might compare with Paris rape,
Their glimring beauties so did shine:
The Prince chose fairest of the twaine,
And Achyll tother for his paine.

And thus the warlike Chiefetaines liude
Eche with his Ladie in delight:
Till Agamemnon was depriude
Of hir that golden Chryses hight.
For Gods did will as (Poets faine)
That he should yælde hir vp againe.

Which done, he reft Achylles Mate
To serue in Chrysis place at næde,
Not forcing on the fowle debate
That follolwde of that cruell dæde:
For why Achylles grutged sore
To lose the Lasse he wan before.

And what for griefe and great disdaine
The Græke his Helmet hoong aside,
And Sworde that many a Knight had slaine,
And Shield that Troian Darts had tride:
Refusing to approch the place
Where he was woont his foes to chase.

His manly courage was appallde
His valiant hart began to yælde,

His

His brawned armes that earst were gallde
With clattering Armour in the field
Had lost their force, his fist did faint,
His gladsome songs were growne to plaint.

His mouth refusde his wonted foode,
His tongue could feele no taste of meat,
His hanging cheekes declarde his moode,
His feltred beard with haire briset,
Bewraid his sodaine chaunge of cheere
For loosing of his louing Feere.

His eares but sorrowes sounde could heare,
The Trumpets tune was quite forgot,
His eies were fraught with many a teare,
Whome carcking care permitted not
The pleasant slumber to retaine
To quite the sielie Misers paine.

The thousande part of pensiue care
The Noble Greeke endured than
In Bryseis absence, to declare
It farre surmounts the Wit of man:
But sure a Martyr right he liude
Of Bryseis beautie once beriude.

If thus Achylles valiant hart
Were wrapt in web of wailefull wo,
That was inbrde too dint of Dart
His louing Bryseis to forgo,
If thus the sturdie Greeke (I say)
Bewaild the night and wept the day:

Then

Then blame not mée a louing Wight
Whome Nature made to Cupids Bow
To liue in such a piteous plight,
Bewasht with waues of woorser wo,
Than euer was the Grækish Péere
Dispoiled of his Darling déere.

For I of force am faine to flée
The presse, the presence and the place
Of you my Loue a brauer B
Than Bryseis was for sote and face,
For Head, for Hande, for Carkasse éke
Not to be matcht of any Gréeke.

Whose troth you haue full often tride,
Whose hart hath béene vnfolded quight
Whose faith by friendship was descride
Whose ioy consisted in your sight,
Whose paine was pleasure if in place
He might but gaze vpon thy face.

O dolefull Gréeke I would I might
Erchaunge my trouble for thy paine,
For then I hope I should acquite
My griefe with gladsome ioyes againe :
For Bryseis made returne to thée,
Would B. might doe the like to mée.

But to erchaunge my Loue for thine,
Or B. for Bryseis I ne would :
To labour in the Leaden Mine.
And leaue the ground where growes the Golde

I

I minde it not, it follie were
To chose the pare, and leaue the Peare.

That Louers ought rather at first acquain-
tance to shew their meanings by
Pen then by Mouth.

IF all that fæle the fits of loue
And flanckring sparkes of Cupids fire,
By tatling tongues should say to moue
Their Ladies to their fonde desire:
No doubt a number would but gaine
A badge of Follie for their paine.

For Ladyes eyther would suspect
Those sugred wordes so swæte to eare
With secrete poysons baite infect:
Or else would wisely stand in feare,
That all such flame as so did burne
To dustie Cinders soone would turne.

For he that bluntly doth presume
On small acquaintance to display
His hidden fire by casting fume
Of wanton words, doth misse the way
To win the Wight he honours so,
For of a Friend he makes a Fo.

For who is shæ that may endure
The dapper tearmes that Louers vse?
And painted Proems to procure
The Modest Matrons minde to muse?

No,

No, first let writings go to tell
Your Ladies that you loue them well.

And when that time hath triall made
Of perfite loue and faithfull brest,
Then boldly may you further wade
This counsell I account the best:
And this (my Deare) procurde my Quill
To write, and tongue to be so skill.

Which now at first shall flatly showe
(As faithfull Herauld of the hart
The perfite loue to thee I owe
That breedst my ioy, and wilt my smart,
Unlesse at last (*Remembrance*) rue
Upon hir (*Thought*) that will be true.

Wherefore I say, go slender scrole
To hir the sielie Mouse that shonnes,
Salute in friendly sort the soule
Among those pretie beastes that wonnes,
That bit the Pocat forthe Peare,
And bred the soule to such a feare.

¶ An Epitaph of Maister Win
drowned in the
Sea.

Ho so thou art that passest by this place
And runst at random on the slipper way,
Recline thy listning eare to mee a space
Doe stay thy ship & hearken what I saye:

Cast

Cast Ankor here vntill my tale be donne,
So maist thou chaunce the lyke mishaps to shonne.

   Learne this of mée, that men doe liue to die
And Death decayes the worthiest VVightes of all,
No worldly welth or kingdomes can supplie
Or garde their Princes from the fatall fall:
One way to come vnto this lyfe we sée,
But to be rid thereof a thousand bée.

   My gallant youth and frolick yeares behight
Mée longer age, and siluer haires to haue,
I thought my day would neuer come to night,
My prime prouokte me to forget my graue:
I thought by water to haue scapte the death
That now amid the Seas doe lose my breath.

   Now, now the churlish chanell me doth chock
Now surging Seas conspire to bréede my carke
Now fighting flouds enforce me to the rock,
Charybdis VVhelps and Scyllas Dogs doe barke
Now hope of life is past, now, now I sée
That W. can no more a liues man bée.

   Yet I doe well affie for my desart
(VVhen cruell death hath done the worst it may)
Of well renowmed Fame to haue a part
To saue my name from ruine and decay:
And that is all that thou or I may gaine,
And so adue, I thanke thée for thy paine.

                       Againe.

Againe.

O Neptune churlish Chuff, O wayward Wolfe
O God of Seas by name, no God in dæde,
O Tyran, Ruler of the grauell Golfe
Where greater Fish on lesser Spawne doth fæde
Why didst ẙ drench with deadly Mace a Wight
That well deserude to run his course aright ?

O cruell cursed Tide, O weltring Waue
That W. wrought this detestable care,
O wrathfull surge, why wouldst ẙ not vouchsafe
A mid thy rage so good a youth to spare,
And suffer him in luckie Bark to reach
The pleasant port of ease and blissfull beach ?

But what though surging Seas & tossing Tide
Haue done their worst and vttered all their force
In working W. wrack, that so hath tride
The cruelst rage that might befall his Corse :
Yet naythelesse his euer during name
Is fast ingraude within the house of Fame.

Let Fishes fæde vpon his flesh apace,
Let crawling Cungers cræpe about his bones,
Let Wormes awake and W : Carkasse race
For why it was appointed for the nones :
But when they haue done all the spite they can
His good report shall liue in mouth of man.

In stead of stonie Tombe and Marble Graue
In lieu of a lamentable Verse,

Let

Let W. on the fandie Cheafell haue
This dolefull rime in ftead of better Herfe;
Lo, here among the Wormes doth W. woon
That well deferude a farther race to roon.

But fince his fate allotted him to fall
Amid the fowrfing Seas and troublous Tide,
Let not his death his faithfull Friends appall
For he is not the firft that fo hath dide,
Nor fhall be féene the laft: As nie away
To Heauen by waters as by Land they fay.

Praife of his Loue.

APpelles lay the Penfill downe
and fhun thy woonted fkill,
Let brute no more with flattring Trumpe
the Gréekifh cares fulfill:
Clayme not to thée fuch Painters praife
as thou haft done of yore,
Leaft thou in fine be foiled flat
and gained glorie lore.
So féeke not to difgrace the Gréekes
thy louing Natiue land,
But rather from depainting formes
withdraw thy fkilleft hand.
For fo thou ftiffely ftand and vaunt
that thou wilt frame hir like
Whome I extoll aboue the Starres,
thou art a ftately Gréeke,

As

As soone with might thou mayste remoue
  the Rock from whence it growes,
As frame hir featurde forme in whome
  such flouds of graces flowes.
If I might speake vnhurt of hate,
  I would auaunt that kinde
In spite of Rose and Lillie both
  had hir in earth assignde
To dwell among the daintie Dames
  that shée hath placed héere :
Cause, by hir passing feature might
  Dame Natures skill appéere.
Hir Haire surmounts Apollos pride
  in it such beautie raines
Hir glistring eies the Cristall farre
  and finest Saphire staines
A little Mouth with decent Chin,
  a Corall Lip of hue,
With Téeth as white as Whale his bone
  eche one in order due.
A body blamelesse to be found,
  Armes rated to the same:
Such Hands with Azure deckt, as all
  that warre with hir doe shame.
As for the paries in couert kept
  and what is not in sight,
I doe estéeme them by the rest
  not forcing on dispight.

I

If I were foreman of the Queſt
  my verdit to expreſſe,
Forgiue mæ (Phœbus,) of thy place
  ſhæ ſhould thæ diſpoſſeſſe.
P: ſhould be raiſed to the cloudes
  and Phœbus brought alow,
For that there ſhould liue none in earth
  but might hir vertue know.
Thus to conclude and make an ende,
  to vouch I dare bebolde :
As ſoone as Nature hir had made
  all Natures ware was ſolde.

The complaint of a Friend of his ha-
uing loſt his Doue.

What ſhold I ſhed my teares to ſhow mine inward pain
  Since ỹ the Iewell I haue loſt may not be had again.
Yet bootcieſſe though it bee to vtter couert ſmart
It is a meane to cure the griefe, and make a ioyfull hart.
Wherefore I ſay to you that haue enioyde your Loue,
Lament with me in wokull wiſe for looſing of my Doue.
You Turtle Cockes that are your louing Hennes bereft,
And do bewaile your cruell chaunce that you aliue are left:
Come hither, come I ſay, come hie in haſte to mee,
Let eyther make his dolefull plaint amid this drearie tree.
A fitter place than this may no where elſe be found
For friendly Eccho here wil cauſe ech cry to yeeld a ſound.
In youth it was my luck on ſuch a Doue to light,
As by good nature ſwan my loue, ſhe was my whole delite
A freſher fowle than mine for ſhape and beauties hue,
Was neuer any man on earth that had the hap to vewe.
                    S.I.   Dams

Dame Nature hir had framde so perfite in hir kinde
Is not the spiteful man himself one fault in hir could finde.
Hir eie so passing pure, hir beake so braue and fit,
The stature of hir lims so small, hir head so full of wit,
Hir neck of so good spse, hir plume of colour white,
Hir legs & feete so finely made, though seldom sene in sight:
Eche part so fitly pight as none mought chaunge his place,
Nor any Bird could lightly haue so good & braue a grace.
But most of all that I did fansie, was hir voyce,
For swete it was vnto mine eare, & made the hart reioyce.
No sooner could I come in place where she was set,
But vp she rose, and ioyfull would hir Make & louer met.
About my tender neck she would haue clasped tho,
And laid hir beake betwixt my lips, sweete kisses to besto,
And ought besides that mought haue pleasurde me at all,
was neuer man that had a birde so fit to play withall.
when I for ioy did sing, she would haue song with mee,
whē I was wo, my griefe was hirs, she wold not plesāt be
But (oh) amid my ioyes came cruell canckred Death.
And spiting at my pleasures rest my louing bird hir breath
who finding me alack, and absent on a day,
Caught bow in hand, & strak hir down, a bieding as she lay
Since I haue cause to waile the death of such a Doue,
(Good Turtles) help me to lament y lose of my true loue.
The Tree whereon she sat shall be the place where I
will sing my last, & end my life: for (Turtles) I must die.
You know it is our kinde, we can not liue alone,
More pleasant is y death to vs then life when loue is gone
To tell a farther tale my fainting breath denies,
And selfe same death y slue my Doue, begins to close mine
(eies.

That

That Louers ought to shunne no paines
to attaine their Loue.

IF Marchaunts in their warped Keales
commit themselues to Waue,
And dreadfull daunger of the Goulfe
in tempest that doth raue,
To fet from farre and Forraine lands
such ware as is to sell,
And is not in their Natiue soile
where they themselues doe dwell:
If Souldiars serue in perills place
and dread of Cannon shot,
Ech day in daunger of their liues
and Countrie losse God wot,
Whose Musick is the dreadfull Drum
and dolefull Trumpets sounde,
Who haue in stead of better bed
the colde and stonie grounde,
And all tattaine the spoile with spæde
of such as doe withstande,
Which slender is sometime we see
when so it comes to hande:
If they for Lucre light sustains
such perill as ensues,
Then those that serue the Lorde of Loue
no trauaile ought refuse:

                S.y.   But

But lauish of their liuely breath
  all tempeſt to abide,
To maintaine Loue and all his lawes
  what Foꝛtune ſo betide.
And not to ſhꝛink at erie ſhoure
  oꝛ ſtoꝛmie flaw that lights,
Ne yet to yéelde themſelues as thꝛall
  to ſuch as with them fights.
Such are not fit foꝛ Cupids Campe,
  they ought no wages win
Which faint befoꝛe the clang of Trump
  oꝛ Battels bꝛoile begin.
They muſt not make account of hurt,
  foꝛ Cupid hath in ſtoꝛe
Continually within his Campe
  a ſalue foꝛ erie ſoꝛe.
Their Enſigne bearer is ſo ſtoute
  ccleaped Hope by name,
As if they follow his aduiſe
  ech thing ſhall be in frame.
But if foꝛ want of courage ſtoute
  the Banner be bereft,
If Hope by hap be ſtricken downe,
  and no good hope yleft :
Tis time with Trump to blow retreate,
  the Field muſt nædes be woon:
So Cupid once be Captiue tane
  his Souldiars are vndon.

Wherefoꝛe,

Wherefoze, what so they are that Loue
   as waged men doe serue :
Must shun no daunger dzift at all
   ne from no perill swerue,
Kéepe watch and warde the wakefull night
   and neuer yéelde to rest.
Foz feare least thou a waiting nought
   on sodaine be oppzest.
Though hunger gripe thy emptie Maw
   endure it foz a while,
Till time doe serue with good repast
   such famine to beguile.
Be not with chilly colde dismaide,
   let Snow noz Ise pzocure
Thy lustfull lims from painefull plight
   thy Ladie to allure.
That is the spoile that Cupid giues
   that is the onely wight
Where at his Thzalls are woont to roue
   with Arrowes from their sight.
My selfe as one among the moe,
   shall neuer spare to spend
My life, my lims, yea hart and all
   Loues quarrell to defend.
And so in recompence of paines
   and toile of perills past,
He yéelde mée but my Ladies loue :
   I will not be agast,

                           H.iy.   D

Of Fortune, nor hir frowning face,
  I nought shall force hir chæere,
But tend on erie turne on hir
  that is my louing Fæere.

A request of Friendship to *Vulcans* Wyfe made my *Mars.*

Though froward Fortune would ẏ you who are
  So braue a Dame, tó Vulcan shoulden linck :
Yet may you loue the lustie God of warre,
And bleare his eies that no such fraud will thinck.
Tis Cupids charge, and all the Gods agræe,
That you be Fæere to him, and Friend to mæe.

The Louer that had loued *Long* without requitald of good will.

Long did I loue, and likte hir passing well
  Whose beautie bred ẏ thraldom of my thought,
Long did I sue to hir for to expell
The foule disdain ẏ beauties beames had wrought:
Long did I serue, and Long I would haue don,
My minde was bent a thorow race to ron.
  Long when I had loude, sude, and serued so.
As mought haue likte as braue a Dame as shæe,
Hir Friend she forced not but let him go,
Shæe loude at least besides him two or thræe :

                                                Hir

Hir common cheare to erie one that sude,
Bred me to déeme shée did hir Friend delude.
  Great was my griefe at first to be refusde
That Long had lowde with true vnfained hart,
But when I sawe I had béene long abusde
I sorede the lesse from such a Friend to part:
Yet ere I gaue hir vp I gainde a thing
That griefe to hir, and ease to me did bring.

To a Friend that wild him to be-
ware of Enuie.

This sound aduise and counsell sent from you
  With friendly hart ý you (my friend) doe giue,
With willing minde I purpose to ensue,
And to beware of Enuie whilst I liue.
For spitefull it doth nought but malice brue
Aie séeking Loue from faithfull harts to riue,
And plant in place where perfit Friendship grue
A mortall hate, good Nature to depriue:
And those that nip mée by the back behinde,
I trust you shall vntrue reporters finde,

Of Misreporters,

I Hope (mine Owne) this fired Loue of thine
  Is so well staid and rooted déepe in brest
That not, vnlesse thou sée it with thine eine
That I from thée my loue and Friendship wrest,
Thou wilt vntie the knot of thy behest.
                    S.iij.   I

I trust your selfe of Enuie will beware
That wild your friend take héede of Enuies snare.

That no man should write but
such as doe excell.

S Hould no man write (say you,)
but such as doe excell ?
This fonde deuise of yours deserues
a Bable and a Bell.
Then one alone should doe
or verie few in déede :
For that in erie Art there can
but one alone excéede.
Should others ydle bée
and waste their age in vaine,
That mought perhaps in after time
the prick and price attaine :
By practise skill is got
by practise Wit is won.
At games you sée how many doe
to win the wager won,
Yet one among the moe
doth beare away the Bell :
Is that a cause to say the rest
in running did not well ?
If none in Phisick should
but onely Galene deale,

No

No doubt a thousand perishe would
   whome Phisick now doth heale.
Eche one his Talent hath,
   to vse at his deuise :
Which makes that many men as well
   as one are counted wise.
For if that Wit alone
   in one should rest and raine
Then God the skulles of other men
   did make but all in vaine.
Let eche one trie his force,
   and doe the best he can
For therevnto appointed were
   the hand and leg of man.
The Poet Horace speakes
   against thy Reason plaine,
Who sayes tis, somewhat to attempt
   although thou not attaine
The scope in erie thyng :
   to touch the highst degrée
Is passing hard, two doe the best
   sufficing is for thée.

To his Friend, declaring what vertue it is
     to stick to former plighted
       friendship.

The sage and Siluer haired Wights doe thinks
  A vertue rare not to be proude of mind
                When

When Fortune smiles: nor cowardly to shrink
Though chaūged Chaūce do shew hir self vnkind.
But chiefest praise is to imbrace the man
In welth and wo with whome your loue began.

Of two desperate Men.

A Man in déepe dispaire with Hemp in hand
　Went out in haste to ende his wretched daies:
And where he thought the Gallo trée should stand
He found a Pot of Gold: he goes his waies
Therewith eftsoone, and in exchaunge he left
The Rope wherewith he would his breath bereft.

The gréedie Carle came within a space
That owde the good, and saw the Pot behind
Where Ruddocks lay, and in the Ruddocks place
A knottie Cord, but Ruddocks could not find:
He caught the Hemp and hoong himselfe on trée,
For griefe that he is Treasure could not sée.

Of the torments of Hell and the
paines of Loue.

T Hough they that wanted grace
　　and whilome liued héere,
　Sustaine such pangues and paines in Hell
　　as doth by Bookes appéere,
Though restlesse be the rage
　of that infernall route,
That voide of feare and Pitties plaint
　doe fling the fire aboute,

　　　　　　　　　　　　And

And tosse the blasing Brands
   that neuer shall consume,
And breath on sielie Soules that sit
   and suffer furious fume:
Though Tantall, Pelops Sonne,
   abide the Dropsie dry,
And sterue with hunger where he hath
   both Foode and Water by:
Though Tytius doe indure
   his Liuer to be rent
Of Vultures tyring on the same
   vnto his spoile ybent:
And Sysiphe though with paine
   and neuer stinting drift
Doe role the stone from Mountaines top
   and it to Mountaine lift:
Though Belydes doe broile
   and suffer endlesse paine,
In drawing water from the deepe
   that falleth downe againe:
Though Agamemnons Sonne
   such retchlesse rage indure,
By meane of furies that with flame
   his griefull smart procure:
Though Mynos hath assignde
   Prometheus to the tack,
With hand and fote ystretch abrode
   till all his lims doe crack:

                       To

To leade a lothsome life
  and die a liuing death,
Amid his paines to waste his winde
  and yet to want no breath :
Though other stand in Stix
  with Sulpher that doth flame,
And other plunge in Phlegiton
  so gastly for the name :
Though Cerberus, the Kaie
  of Plutos Denne that beares,
With hungrie throte and grædie grips
  the newcome Straunger teares :
Though these condemned Ghostes
  such dreadfull paine indures,
Yet may they not compare at all
  with pangues that Loue procures.
His tiring farre ercædes
  the gnawing of the Gripes,
And with his Whip such lashes giues
  that passe Megeras stripes.
He lets the Liuer lie,
  tormenting aie the Hart :
He strikes and wounds his bounden thrall
  with dubble hedded Dart.
His fire ercædes the flame
  of dæpe Auernus Lakes :
And where he once pretendes a plague
  a spitefull spoile he makes.

His

His foes doe wake by day
  they dread to sleepe the night :
They ban the Sunne, they curse the Moone,
  and all that else giues light.
They passe their lothsome liues
  with not contented minde :
Their dolefull daies drawe slow to date
  as Cupid hath assignde.
To Tantall like, but yet
  their case is worse than his :
They haue that they imbrace, but straight
  are quite bereft of blis.
They waste their winde in sighes
  they bleare their eies with brine :
They breake their bulcks with bowncing griefe,
  their harts with lingring pine.
Though Orpheus were aliue
  with Musick that appeasde
The vglie God of Lymbo Lake,
  and soules so sore diseasde,
By Arte he mought not ease
  the Louers feruent fits,
Ne purchace him his harts desire
  so troubled are his wits.
No place of quiet rest,
  no rowme deuoide of ruth :
No swaging of his endlesse paine
  whose death doth trie his truth.

His

His Chamber serues for nought
  but witnesse of his plaint,
His Bed and Bolster to bewaile
  their Lorde with Loue attaint,
The man for murther caught
  and clodgde with yron colde
To sweare that he more happie is
  than Louers may be bolde.
For he in little space
  his dreadfull day shall sée,
But Cupids thralls in daylie griefes
  tormented daylie bée.
A thousand deaths they bide
  whilst they in life remaine,
And onely plaints and stormie thoughts
  they are the Louers gaine.

¶An Epitaph of the death of Maister
Tufton of Kent.

HEre may wée sée the force of spitefull death
  And what a swaye it beares in worldly things,
It neyther spares the one nor others breath,
  He slayes the Keasers and the crowned Kings.
  Nothing preuailes against his hatefull hande
He beares no suters when they pleade for lyfe,
The richmans purse cānot Deaths powre withstand,
Nor Souldiars sworde compare with fatall knyfe.
                    He

He recketh not of well renowmed fame
He forceth not awhit of golden Fee,
His greatest ioy is to obscure the name
Of such as seeke immortall aie to bee.

For if that wealth, bloud, lynage, or desart
Loue, pittie, zeale, or friendship mought preuaild,
If life well led, if true vnfayned hart
Mought purchase lyfe : then Death had not assaild.

This Tuftons lyfe with curst and cruell blade
Breaking the course of him that ran so right
A race as he no stop at all had made
Had Death not tript this Tufton for despight.

The poore haue lost the ritch haue nothing gaind,
The good haue cause to mourne, the yll to plaine :
For Tufton was to all a Friend vnfaind.
Let Kent cry out that Death hath Tufton slaine,
Yet this there is whereof they may reioyce
That his good lyfe hath won the peoples voyce.

Againe.

Let neuer man presume on worldly wealth,
Let riches neuer breede a loftie minde,
Let no man boast to much of perfite health
Let Natures gifts make no man ouer blinde
For these are all but Bladders full of winde.

Let friendship not enforce a retchlesse thought,
Let no desart or life well led befoze,
Let no renowne or glozie greatly sought

Make

Make man forget his present state the more:
For death is he that kæpes and rids the store.

If eyther health, or gœds had bæne of powre,
If Natures giftes, or friendship and gœd will,
If lyfe forepast, if glories Golden Bowre
Mought haue preuaild, or stopt the dolefull Knill
Of Tufton, then had Tufton liued still.

But now you sæ that Death hath quight vndone
His last of lyfe, and put him to the foile,
Yet liues the bertue that aliue he won,
The times alone are shrowded in the soile:
Thus Death is ende of all this worldlesse toile.

In praise of Ladie P.

PŒmes of Venus stock to bæ
    for beauties comely grace,
  A Grysell for hir grauitie,
    a Helen for hir face:
A second Pallas for hir Wit,
    a Goddesse rare in sight:
A Dian for hir daintinesse,
    shæ is so chaste a Wight.
Doe bew hir Corse with curious eie,
    eche lim from top to tœ,
And you shall say I tell but truth
    that doe extoll hir so.
The Head as chiefe that stands aloft
    and ouer lœketh all,

                        With

With wisedome is so fully fraught
　　as Pallas there did stall.
Two Eares that trust no trifling tales
　　noz credit blazing bzute :
Yet such againe as readie are
　　to heare the humbles sute.
Hir Eies are such as will not gaze
　　on things not wozthy sight,
And where she ought to cast a loke
　　she will not winke in spight.
The golden graines that gredie guestes
　　from fozraine Countries bzing,
Ne shining Phœbus glittring beames
　　that on his Godhead spzing :
No auncient Amber had in pzice
　　of Roman Matrons olde,
May be comparde with splendant haires
　　that passe the Venys Golde.
Hir Nose adozns hir countnance so
　　in middle iustly plaste,
As it at no time will permit
　　hir beautie be defaste.
Hir Mouth so small hir Teeth so white
　　as any Whale his bone,
Hir lips without so liuely red
　　that passe the Cozall stone.
What nœde I to describe hir Chækes :
　　hir Chin : oz else hir Pap :

　　　　　　　　T.j.　　　　　　　　Foz

For they are all as though the Rose
  lodge in the Lillies lap.
What should I stand vpon the rest
  or other parts depaint :
As little Hand with Fingers long,
  my wits are all to faint.
Yet this I say in hir behalfe
  if Helen were hir lœke,
Sir Paris nœde not to disdaine
  hir through the Seas to sœke :
Nor Menelaus was vnwise
  or Troupe of Troians mad,
When he with them, and they with him,
  for hir such combat had.
Leanders labour was not lost
  that swam the surging Seas,
If Hero were of such a hue
  whome so he sought to please.
And if Admetus Darling dœre
  were of so fresh a face,
Though Phœbus kept Admetus flock
  it may not him disgrace.
Nor mightie Mauors wayc the floutes
  and laughing of the rest,
If such a one were shœ with whome
  he lay in Vulcans Nest.
If Bryseis beautie were so braue,
  Achylles nœdes no blame

Who

Who left the Campe and fled the field
    for loosing such a Dame.
If shee in Ida had bene seene
    with Pallas and the rest,
I doubt where Paris would haue chose
    Dame Venus for the best,
Or if Pygmalion had but tane
    a glimse of such a face,
He would not then his Idoll dumbe
    so feruently imbrace.
But what shall neede so many wordes
    in things that are so plaine?
I say but that I doubt where Kinde
    can make the like againe.

The Louer in vtter dispaire of his Ladies
    returne, in eche respect compares
    his estate with *Troylus.*

My case with Troylus may compare,
    For as he felt both sorrow and care:
    Euen so doe I most Miser Wight,
    That am a Troylus outright.
As ere he could atchieue his wish,
He fed of many a dolefull dish,
And day and night vnto the Skies
The sielie Troian kest his eies,
Requesting ruth at Cresids hande
In whome his life and death did stande:

                    T.li.   So

So night and day I spent in wo,
Ere she hir pittie would bestow
To quight me from the painefull plight
That made me be a Martir right.
As when at last he fauour founde,
And was recured of his wounde,
His grutching griefes to comfort grue,
And torments from the Troian flue :
So when my Ladie did remoue
Hir rigour, and began to loue
Hir Uassell in such friendly sort,
As might appære by outward port :
Then who began to ioy but I
That stœde my Mistresse hart so nie ?
Then (as the Troian did) I sœng,
And out my Ladies vertues rœng
So lowde; as all the world could tell
What was the meaning of the Bell.
And as that pleasaunt taste of ioy
That he endured had in Troy,
From swæte to sower did conuart,
When Cresida did thence depart:
So my forepassed pleasures arre
By spitefull Fortune put a farre
By hir departure from this place,
Where I was wont to view hir face.
So Angelike that shone in sight
Surpassing Phœbes golden light.

As

As when that Diomed the Græke
Had giuen the Troian Foe the glæke,
And reft him Cresids comely hue
Which often made his hart to rue,
The wofull Troylus did lament,
And dolefull dayes in mourning spent :
So I bereft my louing Make,
To sighes and sobbings mée betake,
Repining that my fortune is
Of my desired Friend to misse,
And that a guilefull Græke should bée
Estœmde of hir in such degrée.
But though my fortune frame awrie,
And I dispoylde hir companie
Must waste the day and night in wo,
For that the Gods appointed so :
I naythelesse will wish hir well
And better than to Cresid fell.
I pray she may haue better hap
Than beg hir bread with Dish and Clap,
As shée the sielie Miser did
When Troylus by the Spittle rid.
God shield hir from the Lazars lore
And lothsome Leapers stincking sore,
And for the loue I earst hir bare
I wish hir as my selfe to fare :
My selfe that am a Troian true
As shée full well by triall knue.

                              T.ii.   And

And as King Priams woᵣthie Sonne
All other Ladies sœmde to shonne
Foᵣ loue of Cresid: so doe I
All Venus Dearlings quight defie,
In minde to loue them all alœke,
That leaue a Troian foᵣ a Greeke.

The Louer declareth what he would haue
if he might obtaine his wish.

IF Gods would daine to lende
a listning care to mœ
And yœlde me my demaunde at full,
what think you it to bœ?
Not to ercell in scate
oᵣ wield the Regall Mace,
Oᵣ Scepter in such stately soᵣt
as might commende the place.
Foᵣ as their Hawle is hie,
so is their ruine rough,
As those that carst hath felt the fall
declare it well ynough.
Ne would I wish by warre
and bloudie blade in fist,
To goᵣe the grounde with gitlesse bloud
of such as would resist.
Foᵣ Tirants though a while
doe leade their liues in ioy,
Yet Tirants trie in trackt of time
how bloudshed doth annoy.

I

I would none office craue,
   ne Consulship request :
For that such rule is full of rage,
   and fraught with all vnrest.
Ne would I wish for welth
   in great excesse to flow,
Which kéepes the Keyes of discords Denne
   as all the world doth know.
But my desire should farre
   such base requests excell,
That I might hir enioy at will
   whome I doe loue so well,
O mightie God of Gods
   I were assured than
In happie hap him to surpasse
   that were the happiest man.
Then might I march in mirth
   with well contented minde,
And ioy to thinke that I in loue
   such blissefull hap did finde.
What friendly wordes would we
   togither then recite ?
More than my tongue is able tell
   or this poore Pen to write.
Then should my hart reioyce
   and thereby comfort take,
As they haue felt that earst haue had
   the vse of such a Make.

                                        If

If Fortune then would frowne,
  or sought me to disgrace :
The touching of hir cherrie lip
  such sorrowes would displace.
Or if such griefe did growe
  as might procure my smart,
Hir long and limber armes to mée
  might soone reduce my hart.
For as by foming flouds
  the fleating Fishes liues :
To Salamanders as the flame
  their onely comfort giues :
So doth thy beautie (P)
  my sorrowes quite expell :
And makes me fare where I should faint
  vnlesse thou loudste mée well.
And as by Waters want,
  Fish falleth to decay,
And Salamander can not liue
  when flame is tane away :
So absence from hir sight
  whole Seas of sorrowes makes,
Which presence of that Paragon
  by secret vertue slakes.
Would Death would spare to spoyle
  and crooked age to rase
(As they are wont by course of kinde)
  Pees beautie in this case.

                         Yet

Yet though their rigo2 rage,
and pow2e by p2ose be plaine:
If P. should die to mo2row next,
yet P. should liue againe.
Fo2 Phænix by his kinde
to Phænix will returne,
When he by fo2ce of Phæbus flame
in scalding Skies doe burne.
Then P. must nædes reuiue
that is a Phænix plaine:
And P. by lack of liuely b2eath
shall be a P. againe.

O f a Gentlewoman that wilde hir Louer to
weare greene Bayes in token of hir
stedfast loue towards him.

B: Tolde me that the Bay would aye be græne,
And neuer chaunge his hue fo2 winters th2et:
Wherefo2e (quoth shæ) that plainely may be sæne
What loue thy Ladie beares, the Law2ell get.

A b2aunch aloft vpon the Helmet weare,
P2esuming that vntill the Law2ell die
And lo2e his natiue colour, I will beare
A faithfull hart, and neuer swerue aw2se.

I (siely soule) did smile with ioyfull b2ow
Hoping that Daphnis would retainde hir hue
And not haue chaungde: & lykewise that the vow
My Ladie made would make my Ladie true.

D

O Gods, beholde the chaunce, I wore the Trée,
And honord it as stay of stedfast Loue :
But sodainely the Lawrell might I sée
To looke as browne as doth the brownest Doue.

I marueld much at this vnwonted sight ;
Within a day or two came newes to mée
That shée had chaungde, & swarude hir friendship
Wherefore affie in neither trull nor trée. (quight
For I perceiue that colours lightly chaunge,
And Ladies loue on sodaine waxeth straunge.

¶An Epitaph of Maister Edwards some-
time Maister of the Children of
the Chappell, and Gen-
tleman of Lyncolns
Inne of Court.

YE Learned Muses nine
and sacred Sisters all,
Now lap you chéerefull Cithrons downe
and to lamenting fall.
Rent off those Garlands gréene,
doe Lawrell Leaues away,
Remoue the Myrtell from your browes
and stint on strings to play.
For he that led the daunce
the chiefest of your traine,
(I meane the man that Edwards height)
by cruell death is slaine.

Yée

Yée Courtyers chaunge your chéere,
    lament in wailefull wise
For now your Orpheus hath resignde
    in clay his Carcas lyes.
O ruth, he is bereft
    that whilst he liued héere
For Poets Pen and passing Wit
    could haue no English Péere.
His vaine in Uerse was such,
    so stately eke his stile
His feate in forging sugred Songs
    with cleane and curious file,
As all the learned Greekes
    and Romaines would repine
If they did liue againe, to vewe
    his Uerse with scornefull eine.
From Plautus he the Palme
    and learned Terence wan,
His writings well declarde the Wit
    that lurcked in the man.
O Death thou wodste in dread
    that Edwards by his Art
And Wisedome would haue scapte thy shaft
    and fled thy furious Dart.
This feare enforste thy fist
    thy cursed Bow to bende,
And let the fatall Arrow flie
    that Edwards life did ende.

                                    But

But spite of all thy spite
  when all thy hate is tride,
(Thou cursed Death) his earned praise
  in Mouth of Man shall bide.
Wherefore (O Fame) I say
  to trumpe thy lips applie,
And blow a blast that Edwards brute
  may pierce the golden Skie.
For here bylow in earth
  his name is so well knowne:
As eche that knew his life, laments
  that hée so soone is gone.

¶An Epitaph on the death of Maister
  Arthur Brooke drownde in paf-
    sing to New Hauen.

AT point to ende and finishe this my Booke,
  Came good report to mée, and wild me write
A dolefull Verse, in praise of Authur Brooke
That age to come lament his fortune might.

  Agréede (quoth I) for sure his Vertues were
As many as his yeares in number few:
The Muses him in learned laps did beare,
And Pallas Dug this daintie Bab did chew.

  Apollo lent him Lute for solace sake
To sound his Verse by touch of stately string,
And of the neuer fading Baye did make
A Lawrell Crowne, about his browes to cling,

In

In prouse that he for Myter did excell
As may be iudge by Iulyet and hir Mate:
For there he shewde his cunning passing well
When he the Tale to English did translate.

But what?as he to forraine Realme was bownd
With others moe his soueraigne Quæne to serue,
Amid the Seas vnluckie youth was drownd,
More spædie death than such one did deserue.

Aye mæ, that time(thou crooked Delphin)where
Wast thou, Aryons help and onely stay,
That safely him from Sea to shore didst beare?
When Brooke was drownd why wast ŷ thē away?

If sound of Harp thine eare delighted so
And causer was that he bestrid thy back,
Then doubtlesse ŷ moughtst wel on Brooke bestow
As good a turne to saue him from the wrack.

For sure his hande Aryons Harp exceld,
His pleasant Pen did passe the others skill,
Who so his Booke with iudging eie beheld
Gaue thanks to him, and praisde his learned quill.

Thou cruel Goulf what meanst thou to deuoure
With supping Seas a Iewell of such fame?
Why didst thou so with water marre the Flowre
That Pallas thought so curiously to frame?

Unhappie was the Hauen which he sought,
Cruell the Seas whereon his Ship did glide,
The winds to rough that Brooke to ruin brought,
Unskilfull he that vndertooke to glide.

But

But sithens teares can not reuoke the ded,
Nor cries recall a drowned man to lande:
Let this suffice textall the life he led
And print his prayse in house of Fame to stande
That they that after vs shall bée and liue
Deserued praisse to Arthur Brooke may giue.
(φ) G. T.

Of the renowmed Lady, Lady Anne Coun-
tesse Warwick.

AN Earle was your Sire a worthie Wight,
A Cowntesse gaue you Tet, a Noble Dame,
An Earle is your Fére, a Mars outright,
A Cowntesse eke your selfe of bruted fame:
A Brother Lorde, your Father Earles Sonne,
Thus doth your line in Lordes and Earles ronne.

You were well knowne of Russels race a childe,
Of Bedfords blod that now doth liue an Earle,
Now Warwicks wife, a warlick man in fielde,
A Venus Pére, a ritch and Orient Pearle,
Wherefore to you that Sister, Childe, and Wife
To Lorde and Earles are, I wish long life.

You Alpha were when I this Boke begonne
And formost, as became your state, did stande,
To be Omega now you will not shonne,
(O Noble Dame) I trust: but take with hande
This ragged rime, and with a courteous loke
And Cowntesse eie peruse this trysling Boke.

The

The Authours Epilog₍
to his Booke

The countnance of this Noble Cowntesse marck
When she thy Verse with eie that Saphire like
Doth shine suruayes, let be thy onely carck
To note hir Lookes: and if she ought mislike
Say that thou shouldst haue hid it from hir sight,
Thy Authour made the best for hir delight,

  The worst he willde in couert scrole to lurke
Untill the Beare were ouerlickt afresh,
For why in deepe this hastie hatched wurke
Resembleth much the shapelesse lumpe of flesh
That Beares bring forth: So when I lick thee ouer
Thou shalt (I trust) thy perfite shape recouer.

FINIS.

Imprinted at London
by Henry Denham,
dwelling in Pater-
noſter Rovve, at
the ſigne of the
Starre.

Anno Domini
1 5 6 7.

Cum Priuilegio.

322

E. Malone.

TRAGICAL

Tales, tranſlated by
TVRBERVILE.
In time of his troubles, out of
ſundric Italians, with
the Argument and
Lenuoye to
eche Tale.

Nocet empta ... lere volup...

Imprinted at Lon-
don by Abell Ieffs, dwelling
in the Foreſtreete without
Crepelgate at the
ſigne of the Bel.
Anno Dom. **1 5 8 7.**

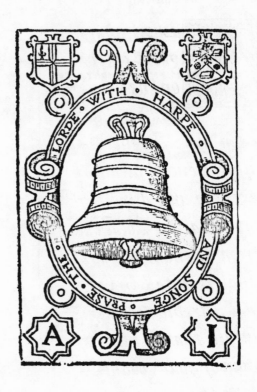

TO THE WORSHIP
full his louing brother, Nicho-
las Turberuile, Esquire.

Lbeit your many and great curtesies bestowed on me, deserue sundry and no slender thankes from me : Neuerthelesse, mine insufficiencie pleading for mine excuse, and disabilitie dealing in my behalfe, doe hope to receiue from you no lesse good liking for a small requitall, than he that yeelds you a treble recompence. Let it suffise that I liue no vnmindfull man of your goodnesse, nor will be found vngratefull for your gentle-

A.ij.   *nesse*

nesse, if euer fortune fouour my de-
sires, or alow me mean to make le-
uell with your good desarts. Till
when I present you this little boke,
as well the vndoubted badge of my
good remēbrāce, as the gretest part
of my slender substance. Following
herein seabeaten soldiers, and mi-
serable mariners, who in auncient
age, after their happy ariuals, ac-
customed to hang vp in the temple
before their sacred Goddes, their
brokē oares, & ragged sayles, with
such like reliks, the assured monu-
ments of their lamētable fortunes
and perfit pledges of late escaped
dangers. VVhich cōmendable cu-
storae

ſtome of thoſe thankfull Etbnicks
I both alow for good, and follow at
this inſtant, as fully apperteyning
to my prcſent ſtate, in dedicating
to you theſe few Poeticall parers,
and penſiue Pamphlets, the ruſul
records of my former trauel, in the
ſorowful ſea of my late miſaduen-
tures: which hauing the more ſpe-
dily by your carefull and brotherly
endeuour, ouerpaſſed & eſcaped,
could not but offer you this treatiſe
in lieu of a more large liberalitie,
& in ſteed of a greater gift, preſu-
ming of good acceptance at your
hãdes, who haue alwayes been my
moſt aſſured ſhielde, and ſtrongeſt.

A. iii   n.

stay in all my life. Wherefore take
these (I pray you) in no worse part
than I meane them, and at lea-
sure for your pleasure peruse them,
excusing my lacke of learning, and
brooking my want of cunning, both
which defaults and imperfections,
might haue bene sufficient to haue
staied my hastie hande: but that I
euer chose rather to be reputed of
straungers vnskilfull, than to be
condemned of my best friendes for
vngratefull: for the one proceedes
for lacke of industrie, but that o-
ther growes for want of humani-
tie. I leaue to trouble you further,
recommending you to the Tragi-
call

call tales, where if aught delight
you, I pray you peruſe it, if aught
offend you, eftſoone refuſe it : if a-
ny hiſtory deſerue reading, of cur-
teſie reſpeƈt it :if any ſeeme vnwor-
thy, doe boldly reieƈt it. If fauour
not the beſt ſo well, as I will wiſhe
your trouble in ſurneying the euill,
whoſe indeuour was onely to this
ende, to doe you pleaſure and ſer-
uice, for your auncient goodneſſe
towardes me, that am your boun-
den brother, and wholy to reaſt
yours during life.

George Turberuile.

To his verie friend

Ro.Baynes.

MY worde, thy wish, my det, and thy desire,
 I meane my booke (my Baynes) lo here I send
To thee at last, as friendship doth require,
Though reason willes it rather left vnpend,
For that the same the Authour should not shendt
But blush who lust, so thou do like the worke,
I am content it shall no longer lurke.

Peruse ech page as leysure giues thee leaue,
Reade ore each verse thus ragged as they lie,
Let nothing slip whereby I may receiue
The hatefull checke of curious readers eie:
For well I know how haut thy muse doth flie:
Wherefore I yeeld this foule mishapen Beare,
Vnto thy choise, to tender or to teare.

Wherein if ought vnworth the presse thou finde,
Vnsauorie or, that seemes vnto thy taste,
Impute it to the troubles of my minde,
VVhose late mishap made this be hatcht in haste,
By clowdes of care best beauties be defaste :
Likewise be wittes and freshest heads to seeke,
VVhich way to write, when fortune list to stroke.

VVho knew my cares, who wist my wailefull woe,
(As thou my friend art priuie to the same)

                                                    Or

Or vnderstoode how griefe did ouergrow
The pleasaunt plot which I for myrth did frame,
VVould beare with this, and quite me clean of blame
For in my life I neuer felt such sittes,
As whilst I wrote this worke did daunt my wittes.

For as the Pilot in the wrathfull waue,
Beset with stormes, still beaten too and fro
VVith boysteous bellowes, knowes not howe to saue
His sielie barke, but lets the rudder goe,
And yeeldes himselfe whither tempest list to blowe,
So I amidde my cares had slender skill,
To write in verse, but bowde to fortunes will.

The more thy paine, thy trouble and thy toile,
That must amend amisse eache faulte of mine,
Yet grudge not (Baynes) with share to turne the soile,
In sorte as though the same were wholie thine,
The charge whereof, loe here I do resine
For want of health, my friend at large to thee,
Since that my limmes with greef surcharged be.

Apollos lore I quite haue layde aside,
And am enforst his Phisicke to peruse,
I hate the Harpe, wherein was all my pride,
I hunte for hearbes, I lothe Mineruas muse,
My want of health, makes me my bookes refuse:

                   The

The bloming rage that erst inspirde my braine,
Saturnus chilling humour doth restraine.

Wherefore sith I confesse my want of skill,
And am to seeke to better this my booke,
See (Baines) thou runne vnto Parnassus hill,
To Helicon, or else that learned brooke,
Which Pegase made, when he the soile fosooke :
For well thou knowst, where Clio and the rest,
Do tune their Lutes, and pipe with pleasant brest.

I can no more, but for thy mickle paine,
Yeeld thousand thankes vpon my naked knee,
And if thou neede the like supply againe,
Assure thy selfe then I will pleasure thee :
So friends vnto each other bounden be,
(Wy Baynes) Adew, this little booke of mine,
When thou hast done, may best be termed thine.

       Thy friend, George Turberuile.

Ro. Baynes to the Reader,
in the due commendation
of the Author.

WHat waight of graue aduice, what reſon left vnſaught,
What more, of Pallas braine hath taſt, than Poets pens
haue taught.
Whoſe powdred ſaues are mixt, with pleaſure, and delight :
Aduiſing this, forewarning that, directing ſtill the right.
Which vaine though Grecians firſt, & Romaines after found :
Yet now the ſame in Engliſh phraſe, doth gorgeouſly abound.
A vertue lately wonne, to this our natiue ſoile :
By ſuch as ſeeke, their countrey praiſe, though to their grea-
ter toile.
Among the reſt, who hath, employed therein more paine ?
Or who than Turberuill hath found, in verſe a ſweeter vaine?
Whoſe quill, though yet it tread, the path of greene delight :
The ſame who vewes, ſhall find his lines, with learned reaſon
dight.
And as to elder age, his ſtayed braine ſhall grow :
So falling from, his riper penne, more graue conceits may flow.
The while, let ech man reape, the pleaſure that he lends.
The coſt is free, his charge but ſmall, an others wealth that
ſpends.
The ſubiect here, is ſuch, as differs farre from pelſe :
I deeme thee wiſe, thy iudgement good, the thing will praiſe
it ſelf.

Qui nihil ſperat nihil diſperat.

¶The Authour here declareth
the cause why hee wrote these Hi-
stories, and forewent the tanslation of the
learned Poet *Lucan.*

I Undertooke Dan Lucans verse,
 and raught hys horne in hand,
To sound out Cæsars blooddy broiles
 and Pompeis puisant bande:
I meant to paint the haughtie hate
 of those two marshall men,

And had in purpose ciuill swords
 of rusull Rome to pen:
Of rusull Rome to penne the plagues
 when Cæsar sought to raigne,
And Pompey pitying Countries spoyle,
 would doe him downe againe.
I had begonne that hard attempt,
 to turne that fertile soyle.
My bullocks were alreadie yokte,
 and flatly fell to toyle.
He thought they laboured meetlie well,
 Tyll on a certaine night:
I gazde so long vpon my booke
 in bed by candle light.
Till heauy sleep full silie came
 and muffled so mine eye,

       That

That I was forſt with quill in hand
   in ſlumber downe to lie.
To whom within a while appeard
   Melpomene, the Muſe,
That to intreat of warlike wights,
   and dreadfull armes doth vſe.
Who me beheld with graue regard,
   and countnance fraught with feare:
And thus the gaſtly Goddeſſe ſpake,
   her wordes in minde I beare.
And art thou woxe ſo wilfull, as
   thou ſeemeſt to outward eye?
Darſte thou preſume with pimped quilles
   ſo prowde a pitch to flie?
Remember how ſonde Phæton farde,
   that vndertooke to guide:
Apollos charge, by meane of which
   that wilfull wanton dide.
Eare thou doe wade ſo farre, reuoke
   to minde to bedlam boy,
That in his forged wings of waxe
   repoſed too great a ioy :
And ſoard ſo neare the ſcorching blaze
   of burning Phœbus brande,
As feathers failde, and he fell ſhort
   of what he tooke in hand.
In this thy hauty heart thou ſhewſt,
   too playne thy pryde appeares,

                         How

How durſt thou deale in field affaires;
   leaue off, vnyoke thy Stœres.

Let loftie Lucans verſe alone,
   a deed of deepe deuiſe:

A ſtately ſtile, a peereleſſe pen,
   a worke of weightie pryce.

More meete for noble Buckhurſt braine;
   where Pallas built her bowre,

Of purpoſe there to lodge her ſelfe,
   and ſhew her princely powre.

His ſwelling vaine would better blaſe,
   thoſe Royall Romane peeres:

Than any one in Brutus land,
   that liude theſe many peeres.

And yet within that little Iſle
   of golden wittes is ſtore,

Great change and choiſe of learned ymps
   as euer was of yore.

I none diſlike, I fancie ſome,
   but yet of all the reſt.

Sance enuie, let my verdite paſſe,
   Lord Buckurſt is the beſt.

Wee all that Ladie Muſes are,
   Who be in nuber nine:

With one accord did bleſſe this babe,
   each ſaid, This ympe is mine.

Each one of vs, at time of birth,
   with Iuno were in place:

                        And

And each vpon this tender childe,
    bestowd her gift of grace.
My selfe among the moe alowde
    him Poets praised skil,
And to commend his gallant verse,
    I gaue him wordes at will.
Minerua luld him on her lappe,
    and let him many a kisse:
As who would say, when all is done,
    they all shall yeeld to this.
This matter were more meet for him,
    and farre vnfit for thæ:
My sister Clio, with thy kinde,
    doth best of all agree.
Shee deales in case of liking loue,
    her lute is set but lowe:
And thou wert woute in such deuise,
    thine humour to bestow.
1 As when thou toldest the Shepheards tale,
    that Mantuan carst had pend:
2 And turndst those letters into verse,
    that louing Dames did send
Vnto their lingring mates, that faught
    at sacke and siege of Troy:
3 And as thou didst in writing of
    thy Songs of sugred ioy.
4 Mancynus vertues fitter are,
    for thee to take in hande,

                  Tha:

Than glitering gleaues, and wreakfull warres,
   that all on slaughter stand.
The Giants proud, aspiring pompe
   when they so fondly stroue,
And hopde with helpe of heaped hilles
   to conquere mightie Ioue,
Is not for euery wit to wield,
   the weight too heauy weare,
For euery Poet that hath wrote
   in auncient age to beare.
Unlesse that Lucan, Virgill, or
   the great renowmed Greeke,
Could vndertake those boysteous broiles,
   the rest are all to seeke.
Each slender ship that beares a saile,
   and flittes in quiet flood:
Is not to brooke the byllow, when
   the roaryng Seas be wood.
Alcydes slippers are too wide
   for euery wretch to weare:
Not euery childe can Atlas charge,
   Upon his shoulders beare.
Not euery Dick that dares to drawe
   a sword, is Hectors peere,
Not euery woodman that doth shoote,
   hath skill to chose his Deere.
No beast can match the Lions might,
   his force is ouer fell:

               Though

Though euery little starre doe shine,
　yet doth the Sunne excell.
Not euery bryer, or tender twigge,
　is equall to the Pyne,
Nor euery Prelate that can preache,
　is thought a deepe deuine.
Not euery fish that flittes amyd
　the floud with feeble finne,
Is fellowe to the Delphine swifte,
　when he doth once beginne.
The peeuishe puttocke may not preace
　in place where Eagles are:
For why their kingly might exceedes,
　their puissance passeth farre.
All which I speake to let thee wyte,
　that though thou haue some skill,
Yet hast thou not sufficient stuffe
　this Authors loome to fill.
Too slender is thy feeble twiste,
　thy webbe is all too weake:
Before thy worke be halfe dispatchte,
　no doubte thy warpe will breake.
Wherefore renounce thy rash deuice,
　thy yeelding force I knowe:
And none so well as I can iudge,
　the bente of *Lucans* bowe.
Thinke of the toade in *Æsops* tale,
　that sought to matche the Bull,

T　　　　　　　　　　　For

For highnesse,and did burst at length,
  his bowels were so full,
So thou,vnlesse thou take good heede,
  translating *Lucans* warre.
Shalt spoyle thy Lute, & stroy thy strings,
  in straining them too farrs.
I heare aduise,and eke commaunde
  that thou no farther goe:
Laye dawne thy Lute,obey my will,
  for sure it shall be so.
With that my drousie slumber fledde,
  my senses came againe:
And I that earst was drownde in dreames,
  behelde the *Goddes* playne,
Whose frouning phrase & spitefull speach
  had daunted so my witte,
As for my life I wist not howe,
  to shape an aunswere fitter.
Each worde(me thought)did wound me so,
  eache looke did lurche my harte:
Eache sentence bredde my sorrowes such,
  eache lyne was like a darte.
But yet at laste with manly minde,
  and mouth vnfraught of feare,
Vnto this loftie learned *Muse*,
  these wordes I vttred there:
O noble Impe,and daughter deare
  to mightie Ioue his graces

Z

It much relieues my weakened wittes
    to sée thy heauenly face.
For which ten thousand thanks I yelde
    thée heere with bended knée:
And counte my selfe the blessedst man
    aliue, thine eyes to sée.
Thy presence makes me to presume,
    thou holdst me verie deare:
But (out alas) thy wordes were such
    as I was lothe to heare.
Controlements came frō haughtie breast,
    for that I vndertooke
With English quill to turne the verse
    of learned *Lucans* booke.
And shall I (Lady) be mislykte
    to take in hande a déd,
By which vnto my natiue soyle
    aduantage may succéde:
By which the ciuill swordes of *Rome*
    and mischiefes done thereby,
May be a mirrour vnto vs,
    the like mishappes to flie:
I yéelde my brayne too barraine farre,
    my verses all too vyle,
My pen too playne, with metre méete
    to furnish *Lucans* style:
Whose déepe deuise, whose filed phrase,
    and Poets péerelesse pen,

       B ii.   **Would**

Would clope the cunningst head in court,
   and tyre the lustiest men.
But yet sith none of greater skill,
   and ryper witte would write
Of *Cæsar* and *Pompeius* warres,
   a woorke of rare delight:
I thought it good as well to passe
   the idle time away,
As to the worlde to set to vewe
   howe discorde breedes decay:
To turne this princely Poets verse,
   that simple men might see
Of Ciuill broyles and breach at home,
   how great the mischeiues bee.
But sith it standes not with your wills
   who lady Muses are,
That one so dull as I, should deale
   in case concerning warre:
I am content to plie vnto
   your pleasures out of hande,
It bootes me not against the will
   of heauenly states to stande.
Yet being that my present plight
   is stufte with all anoye,
And late mishaps haue me berefte
   my rimes of roisting ioye:
Syth churlish fortune clouded hath
   my glee, with mantell blacke,

                         Of

Of foule mischaunce, wher by my barke
  was like to bide the wꝛacke:
(Good ladie)giue me leaue to wꝛite
  some heauy sounding verse,
That by the vewe thercof,my harmes
  the readers heart may perse.
With that the Goddesse gaue a becke,
  and yælded my request,
And vanisht streight without offence,
  and licensc me to reste.
Then I to reading *Boccas* fell,
  and sundꝛie other moe
Italian Authours,where I found
  great stoare of states in woe,
And sundꝛie soꝛtes of wꝛetched wights,
  some slayne by cruell foes,
And other some that thꝛough desire
  and Loue their lyues did lose:
Some Tyꝛant thirsting after bloud,
  themselues were fowly slayne:
And some did sterue in endlesse woes,
  and pynde with bitter payne.
Which gaue me matter sitte to wꝛite:
  and herevpon it grewe
That I this Tragicall deuise,
  haue sette to open viewe.
Accept my paynes, allow me thankes,
  if I deserue the same,
      B iii.   It

If not, yet lette not meaning well
    be payde with checke and blame.
For I am he that buylde the bowre,
    I hewe the hardened stone,
And thou art owner of the house,
    the paine is mine alone.
I burne the bee, I holde the hyue,
    the Sommer toyle is myne:
And all bicause when winter commes,
    the honie may be thine.
I frame the foyle, I graue the golde,
    I fashion vp the ring,
And thou the iewell shalt enioye,
    which I to shape doe bring.
Adieu (good Reader) gaze thy fill,
    if aught thine eyes delight:
For thee I tooke the worke in hande,
    this booke is thine of right.

ᛞEP*ƒT ᴀT H Ɛ S*
and Sonnettes
annexed to the Tragical hi-
ſtories, By the
ᴧuthor.

VVith ſome other broken pam
phlettes and Epiſtles , ſent to certaine
his frends in England, at his
being in Moſcouia.
Anno 1 5 6 9.

Omnia probate.
Quod bonum eſt tenete.

A farevvell to a mother Cofin,
at his going tovvardes
Mofcouia.

GOe poſt you penſiue lynes,
  and papers full of woe,
Make haſte vnto my mothers handes,
  hir ſonnes farewell to ſhowe.
Doe marke her lookes at firſt,
  ere you your meſſage tell,
For feare your ſodayne newes, hir minde
  doe fancie nothing well.
But ſithen nædes you muſt
  my trauailes trouth vnfolde,
To offer vp her ſonnes farewell,
  and laſt adewe, be bolde.
I know ſhe will accept
  your comming in good parte,
Till time ſhe vnderſtand by you
  that I muſt nædes departe.
But when you make reporte
  that I am ſhipte from ſhore,
In minde to cut the foming Seaſ,
  where winter wyndes do roe rore?
Then woe be vnto you,
  that mournefull meſſage beare,
For doubtleſſe ſhe with trembling handes
  will you in ſunder teare:

                T   But

But(mother)let your sonne
   perswade you in this case,
For no man sure is borne to leade
   his life in one selfe place.
I must no longer stay
   aduantage is but vile
The cruel lady fortune on
   your sonne will neuer smile.
My countrey coast where I
   my Nurses milke did sucke,
Would neuer yet in all my life
   allowe me one good lucke.
With cost encrease my cares,
   expences nip me nære,
Loue waxeth cold,no frendship doth
   in natures brest appære.
Where slender is the gaine
   and charges grow too hie
Where liuing lackes and money melts
   that should the want supply:
From thence tis time to trudge
   and hire the hackney post
To shift to ship,to leaue the land
   and sæke a better coast.
Sith I haue all my yeres
   in studies fond applide
And euery way that might procure
   a better chaunce haue tride.

                Yet

Yet better not my state
   but like a sotted dolt
Consume my time that goes about,
   to mend a broken bolt.
Sith I haue liude so long
   and neuer am the nære
To bid my natiue soile farewel,
   I purpose for a yære.
And more perhaps if nède
   and present cause require:
They say the countrey is too colde
   the whotter is the fire.
Moscouia is the place,
   where all good furres be sold
Then pray thée (mother) tel me how,
   thy sonne shall dye with colde.
Put case the snow be thicke,
   and winter frostes be great:
I doe not doubt but I shal finde,
   a stoue to make me sweat.
If I with credite goe,
   and may returne with gaine
I hope I shalbe able wel
   to bide this trauayles paine.
The slouthfull Groome that sits,
   at home and tels the clocke:
And feares the floud because therein
   lies hidden many a rocke.
       T.ii.   As

As hee abydes no woe,
   no welth he doth deserue,
Let him that will not cut the loafe
   for lacke and famine serue.
The Catte deserues no fish
   that feares her foote to weate,
Tis time for me in profite now
   mine idle braynes to beate.
I trust I shall returne
   farre better than I goe,
Increase of credite will procure
   my simple wealth to growe:
Meane while I wishe thee well
   (good mother mine)to fare,
And better than my selfe,who yet
   was neuer voyde of care.
Sith neede obeyes no lawe,
   and needes I must to barcke,
Farewell,and thinke vpon thy sonne,
   but haue of him no carcke.
The Gods I hope will heare
   the sute that you shall make,
And I amid the Sea shall fare
   the better for your sake.
If euer fortune serue,
   and bring me safe to lande,
The harde mishappes of trauayle you
   by me shall vnderstand.

                 And

And whatsoeuer straunge
　　oz monstrous sight I see.
Assure thy selfe at my returne
　　I will declare it thee.
Thus euery thing hath ende,
　　and so my letters shall,
Euen from the bottom of my bzest,
　　I doe salute you all.
What so becomes of me
　　the mightie Gods I craue,
That you my frendes, a blessed life
　　and happie deathes may haue.

That nothing can cause him to forget
　　his frend, vvherein is toucht the
　　　　hardnes of his tra-
　　　　　　uayle.

IF boystrous blaste of fierce and froward wynde,
　If weltring waues, and frothie foming Seas,
　If shining Sunne by night against his kinde,
　If lacke of lust to meate, and want of ease,
　If feare of wzacke, and force of rouing foe,
　If raged Rockes that in the riuers lie:
　If frozen floodes where sliding Sledds doe goe,
　If cruell colde vpon the mountaines hye,
　If seldome sleapes, if sundzie soztes of care,
　If bare skin beddes, oz else a bozded bench,
　　　　　T iii.　　　　　　　If

If lacke of kindly cates and courtly fare,
If want of holsom drinck the thirst to quench,
If stinking Stoues, if Cunas and bitter bragge,
If sauage men, if women foule to sight,
If riding poast vpon a trotting Nagge,
If homely yammes, in stead of Innes at night:
If these (I say) might make a man forget
So true a frend, then thou art out of minde.
But in good fayth, my fancie firme was set,
No Russie mought the true loue knot vnbinde.
Venus be iudge, and Cupid in this case,
Who did pursue me aye from place to place.

He declares that albeit he were imprisoned in
Russia, yet his minde was at libertie, & did
daily repaire to his frend.

Now finde I true that hath bene often told,
    (*No man may reaue the freedome of the mind,*)
Though kepers charge in chaines the captiue hold,
Yet can he not the Soule in bondage binde:
That this is true, I finde the proofe in me,
Who Captiue am, and yet at libertie.

    Though at my heele a cruell clogge they tye,
And ranging out by rigor be restraynde,
Yet maugre might, my minde doth frœly flye
Home to my frend, it will not be enchainde:
No Churles checke, no Tyrants threat can stay
A Louers heart, that longs to be away.

                                    I do

The Planets are the pride of heauen,
  and chæfest lampes of light:
Yet other starres doe yelde a shew
  and helpe to clære the night.
Likewise though diuers write in verse
  and doe exceeding wel:
The remnant must not be refusde,
  because they doe excell.
Ill may we misse the slender shrubs
  for all the princely Pine:
No more we scorne the baser drinkes
  though most we way the wine.
Which makes me hope that though
  my Muse doth yelde but slender sound:
And though my Culter scarcely cuts,
  or breakes the marble ground.
Yet sithens that I meant with verse,
  to sæde the Readers eyes:
And to that purpose bent my braines
  these fancies to deuise.
I trust he takes it wel in worth
  and beares with what he findes.
And thereunto the Reader aye
  the writers trauaile bindes.
Which if he doe I haue my hire,
  who happy then but I?
That wrote this worke for grateful men,
  to vewe with thankfull eye.

And

Her hearc is golden wyer, her shineng eyes
Two Dyamondes that glister passing bright,
Amids her lylye chœkes, the Rubie lyes,
Her tœth of pearle, lippes louely red and white,
All other limmes doe aunswere well the same,
Now iudge of both which is the brauer dame,

La mia donna
bella è buona.

To his frend promising that though
her beautie fade, yet his
loue shall last.

IWotte full well that bewtie cannot laste,
  No rose that springs, but lightly doth decay,
And feature like a lillie leafe doth waste,
Or as the Cowslip in the midst of May:
I know that tract of time doth conquer all,
And beuties buddes like fading floures do fall.

That famous Dame fayre Helen, lost her hewe
Whê withred age tô wrinckles chaungd her chêks,
Her louely lookes did loathsomnesse ensewe,
That was the A per se of all the Grêkes:
And sundrie moe that were as fayre as shee
Yet Helen was as freshe as fresh might bê.

              No

No force for that, I price your beautie light,
If so I finde you stedfast in good will:
Though fewe there are that doe in age delight,
I was your friend, and so doe purpose still,
No change of lookes shall bréede my change of loue
Nor beauties want, my first goodwill remoue.

    Per gentilezza,
       Tanto.
    Non per bellezza.

From the citie of Mosqua, to his friend in England.

GO burning sighes, and pierce the frozen skie,
 Slack you ý snow with flames of fancies fire
Twixt *Brutus* land, and *Mosqua* that doe lie:
Goe sighes I say, and to the *Phenix* flie,
Whome I imbrace, and chieflie doe desire,
Report of me that I doe loue her best,
None other Saint doth harbour in my brest.

Tell her that though the colde is wont by kinde
To quench the cole, and flames do yéeld to frost,
Yet may no winters force in *Russia* binde
My heart so heard, or alter so my minde,
But that I still imbrace her beautie most:
I went her friend, and so cotinue still,
Frost cannot freat the ground of my good will.

    Ardo e ghiaccio.

      T. v.   To

To his miſtres, declaring his life only to depend of her lookes.

The Salamander cannot liue
 without the help of flaming fire:
To bath his limmes in burning coales,
 it is his glee and chiefe defire.
The litle fiſh doth loue the lake,
 dame nature hath aſſigned him:
To liue no longer then he doth
 amid the ſiluer channel ſwimme.
Chameleon feedes but on the ayre,
 the lacke whereof is his decay:
Theſe three doe periſh out of hand,
 take fire, floods, and ayre away.
Iudge you (my deere) the danger then
 of very force that muſt enſue:
Vnto this careful heart of mine,
 that cannot liue withouten you.
I am the fiſh, you are the flood,
 my heart it is that hangs on hooke:
I cannot liue if you doe ſtoppe,
 the floudhatch of your frendly brooke.
I ſilly Salamander die,
 if you maintaine not frendſhips fire:
Quenche you the coale and you ſhal ſee
 me pine for lack of my deſire.
You are the pleaſant breathing ayre,

       and

and J your poore Chameleon,
Barre me your breath and out of hand
    my life and sweete delight is gone.
Which sith tis so(good mistresse) then
    doe saue my life to serue your turne
Let me haue ayre and water stil
    let me your Salamander burne.
My death wil doe you litle good,
    my life perhaps may pleasure you:
Rewe on my case and pitie him,
    that sweares himself your seruant true,
J beare the badge within my brest,
    wherin are blazde your colours braue:
Loue is the only liuery,that
    J at your curteous hand doe craue.
J doe desire no greedy gaine,
    J couet not the massye golde:
Embrace your seruant(mistres)then,
    his wages wil be quickly toide.
As you are faire so let me finde
    your bountie equall to your face:
J cannot thinke that kinde so nere,
    to beauties bower would rigor place,
Your comely hewe behight me hope,
    your louely lookes allow mee life.
Your graue regard doth make me vaine,
    you fellow to Vlisses wife,
Which if be true then happy J,
                            that

that so in loue my fancie set,
In you doth rest my life, my death,
　by slaying me no gaine you get.
The noble minded Lion kils
　no yeelding beast by crueltie,
And worthie dames delight to saue
　their seruants liues by curtesie.

Virtuti comes inuidia.

My Spencer, spite is vertues deadly foe,
　The best are euer sure to beare the blame,
And enuie next to vertue still doth goe,
But vertue shines, when enuie shrinkes for shame.

　In common weales what beares a greater sway
Than hidden hate that hoordes in haughtie brest?
In princes courtes it beares the bell away,
With all estates this enuie is a guest.

　Be wise, thy wit will purchase priuie hate,
Be rich, with rents flocke in a thousand foes
Be stout, thy courage will procure debate,
Be faire, thy beautie not vnhated goes.

　Beare office thou, and with thy golden mace,
Commes enuie in, and treades vpon thy traine,
Yea, be a Prince, and hate will be in place,

　　　To

To bid him stand aloofe it is in vaine.

So that I see, that Boccas wordes be true:
for ech estate is pestred with his foe,
Saue miserie, whom hate doth not ensue,
The begger only doth vnspited goe:

Yet beggers base estate is not the best,
Though enuie let the begger lie at rest.

*Sola miseria e senza
inuidia,   Boccacie.*

*That though he may not possible come
or send, yet he liues mindfull of his
mistresse in Moscouia.*

WHo so hath read *Leanders* loue,
which he to Ladie *Hero* bore,
And how he swamme through *Aelles* flood,
twixt *Abydon* and *Sestus* shore.
To gaine his game, to liue at lust,
to lap him in the Ladies lap,
Will rue his paines, and scarce exchange
his case to haue *Leanders* hap,
But happy I account his case,
for hauing past those narrow Seas,

Yet

He was assured to lodge alofe,
 with Hero in the towre of ease.
He neuer went but did enioy,
 his mistres whom he did desire.
He seldome swamme the foming floud,
 but was assured to quench his fire.
The torch it hung vpon the towre,
 the lampe gaue light to shew the way:
He could not misse the darkesome night
 it shone as cleere as sunny day,
Thus happy was Leanders lot,
 but most vnhahpy mine estate:
For swimming wil not serue my turne
 to bring me to my louing mate.
The flouds are frozen round about,
 the snow is thick on euery side:
The raging Ocean runnes betwixt
 my frend and me with cruel tide.
The hilles be ouerwhelmde with hoare
 the countrey clad with mantels white
Each tree attirde with flakes of yce,
 is nothing els saue snow in sight.
The mighty Volgas stately streame
 in winter slipper as the glasse:
Abides no boate, how should I then
 deuise a meane a way to passe?
And Suchan that in summer time,
 was easie to be ouergone:

       wich

With Boreas blast is bound as harde,
  as any flint oʒ marble stone,
Frō passage Dwina doth deny,
  whose streame is stopt and choakt with snow.
There is no way foʒ any barge,
  much lesse foʒ any man to goe:
I cannot foʒ my life repaire,
  to thē to ease my pʒesent paine:
There is no passage to be had,
  til summer slake the snow againe.
Meane while yet maist thou make accōpt,
  that I doe stil remember thē.
In Rusia where I leade my life,
  and long againe at home to be.
No foʒce shall cause me to foʒget
  oʒ lay the care of loue aside:
Time is the touchstone of good will,
  wherby my meaning shalbe tride.
If I might haue conueid my lines,
  vnto thy hands, it would haue easde;
My heauy heart of diuers doubts,
  my message might my minde appeasde:
But (friend) indure this long delay
  my selfe wil come when time shal serue
To tell thē newes and how I fare:
  meane while stand fast & do not swerue
Pʒesume that as I was thine owne,
  euenso I doe continue still.

                 I

I know hir not whose beautie shall remoue
 or change my first good will.
Thy face hath pierst my brest so farre,
 thy graces else so many bee,
As if I would, I cannot choose
 but loue, and make account of thee.

To a faire gentlevvoman, false to hir friend.

VVIthin the garden plot of thy faire face,
 Doth grow a grasse of diuers qualities:
A matter rare within so little space,
A man to find such sundry properties:
For commonly the roote in euery trée,
Barcke, body, boughes, bud, leafe, and fruit agré.

First for the roote is rigor in the brest,
Treason the trée, that springeth of the same,
Beautie the barcke that ouerspreds the rest,
The boughes are braue, and climing vp to fame,
Braules be the buds that hang on euery bowe,
A blossom fit for such rootes to allowe.

Loue is the leafe that little time endures,
Flattrie the fruit which treasons tree doth beare,
Though beauties barste at first the eie allure,
Yet at the last ill will the worme, doth weare
Away the leafe, the blossoms, boughes, and all,
And rigors roote, makes beauties buds to fall.
  Par essere ingrata, *Non sarai amata.*

           A

A farewell to a craftie deceitfull
Dame.

AS he that lothes the powders smel,
   must neuer pease where Gunners bée:
So he that hates a double dame,
   must neuer haue to do with thée.
For craft I sée, is all thy rate,
   thy smoothest lookes betoken guiles:
In womans wombe thou féedst a foxe,
   that bites thy friend on whom he smiles.
Had Nature wist thy déep deceits
   before thy birth, I thinke that kind,
To saue thy name, and ease thy friends,
   had seald thine eies, and kept thée blind.
For what is she that beares a face
   of greater trust, and more good will:
Yet who is she that hath a heart
   more prone to pay the good with ille
Thy beautie led me on to loue,
   thy lookes allured my looking eyes
Thy doublenesse now bréeds despaire,
   thy craft doth cause my wofull cries.
I could requite dissembling loue,
   and gloze perhaps as well as you:
But that I take but small delight
   to change mine ancient friends for new.
Yet will I not be sotten so,

        U   as

as stil to let my loue to losse,
I better know what mettall is,
    than to exchange the gold for drosse.
Good will is euer woorth good will,
    if both the ballance egall bee :
But sure too massie is my loue,
    to make exchange of loues with thee.
Wherfore I say, vnknit the knot
    wherwith thy loue was falsly tide,
Thou lackst a graine to make vp weight,
    men say, (good measure neuer lide.)
Go seeke some other to deceiue,
    too wel I know thy craftie call :
My mouth is very well in taste,
    to iudge the hony from the gall.
That you are gall, I may auow,
    for hony hath no bitter tast :
The wine of your good will is spent,
    you keep the dregs for me at last.
Wherfore I do renounce the caske,
    I leaue the lees for other men :
My hap was ill, my choice was worse,
    I yeeld you vp to choose agen.

        Spare to speake, Spare to speede.

MY Spencer spare to speake,
    and euer spare to speed,
                        Vnlesse

Unlesse thou shew thy hurt, how shall
　the Surgeon know thy nœde?
Why hath a man a tongue,
　and boldnesse in his brest,
But to bewray his minde by mouth,
　to set his hart at rest?
The fisherman that feares
　his corke and coard to cast,
Or spred his net to take the fish,
　wel worthy is to fast.
The forrestman that dreads
　to rouse the lodged Bucke,
Bicause of bramble brakes, deserues
　to haue no hunters lucke.
Where words may win good wil,
　and boldnesse beare no blame,
Why should there want a face of brasse
　to bourd the brauest dame?
Unlesse thou cast thy lure,
　or throw hir out a traine:
Thou seldome shalt a Falcon, or
　a Tassell gentle gaine.
Though lookes betoken loue,
　and makes a shew of lust,
Yet speech is it that knits the knot
　whereto a man may trust.
Assure thy selfe, as he
　that feares caliuer shot,

　　　　　U. 2.　　　　Can

Can neuer come to scale a fort,
   or skirmish woorth a grote:
So he that spares to speake,
   when time and place are fit,
Is sure to misse the marke, which else
   he were in hope to hit.
Giue him an iuie leafe
   in stead of pipe to play,
That dreads to bourd a gallant dame
   for feare she say him nay.
Where venture is but small,
   and bootie very great,
A coward knight will hazard there
   in hope to worke his feat.
Wherfore when time shall serue
   (my *Spencer*) spare to blush,
Fall to thy purpose like a man,
   and boldly beat the bush.
Who so accounts of losse,
   doth seldom gaine the game:
And blushing chookes be often hard,
   for feare of after shame.
No doubt, a Lady doth
   imbrace him more, that dares
To tell his tale, than such a one
   that of his language spares,
Deceit is dreaded more,
   and craft doth rifer raigne,

In

In one that like an image sits,
  than him that speaketh plaine.
Yea, though thy mistresse make,
  as though she loued no wine,
Remember *Aesops* Foxe, that was
  too lowe to reach the vine.
Take this for certaine troth,
  the best and brauest bowe,
Will stoupe, if so the cause be good,
  thou knowest my meaning now.
Experience hath no pære,
  it passeth learning farre:
I speake it not without my booke,
  but like a man of warre.
Wherfore be bold to board
  the fairest first of all,
Aye Venus aides the forward man,
  and Cupid helps his thrall.

  Wearie of long silence, he breakes
    his mind to his mistresse.

NOt much vnlike the horse
    that fœles himself opprest
With weightie burthen on his backe,
  doth long to be at rest:
So I, whose boiling brest,
  with fansies floud did flow,
          U.3.   Had

Had great desire my great good will
   with painting pen to show,
To ease my wofull hart
   of long endured paine,
And purchace quiet to my mind,
   whom loue welnie hath slaine.
Beléeue my words (deare dame)
   dissembling is a sinne,
Not mine, but thine these many days
   my captiue hart hath bin.
But shame, and coward feare,
   the louers mortall foes,
Would neuer condescend that I
   my meaning should disclose.
Till now at length desire
   my wonted ease to gaine:
Did bid me sue for grace, and said
   I should not sue in vaine.
For as thy beautie is
   farre brauer than the rest,
So bountie must of force abound
   within thy noble brest.
Oh, séeke not thou to shed
   or sucke of yéelding blood:
Alas, I thinke to murther me
   would do thée little good.
Whom if you séeme to rue,
   as I do hope you will,

          In

In prayse of your good nature then
  my hand shall shew his skill.
Lo here in pawne of loue,
  I vowe my selfe to thee :
A slaue, a seruant, and a friend
  till dying day to bee.

He vvisheth his dreames ei-
ther longer or truer.

Short is the day wherein :
  I doe not thinke of thee :
And in the night amid my sleepe,
  thy face(deare dame)I see.
The dreame delights me much,
  it cuts my care away;
Me thinkes I kisse and clip thee oft,
  the rest I blush to say.
Who happy then but I,
  whilest sleepe and slumber last
But who(alas)so much a wretch,
  as I when sleepe is past.
For with the sliding sleepe
  away slips my delight:
Departing dreames doe driue away
  thy countnance out of sight.
And then in place of glee,
  in glydes a crew of care:

My panting hart laments, that I
  do féele my bed so bare.
For thou that wert the cause
  of comfort, art not there :
And I poore silly wofull man,
  in sobs the night do weare.
Then curse I cankred chance,
  that made me dreame of thée,
And fansie fond, that sed it selfe
  with dreames that fained bée.
Thus weares away the night
  consumde in carefull paine :
Those restlesse banners beating still,
  vpon my busie braine.
Then drawes the dawning on,
  I leaue my couch, and rise,
In hope to find some pleasant toy,
  that may content mine eyes.
But out alas, I can
  not sée so faire a sight,
That can my heauie hart relleue,
  and daintie eies delight.
Each beautie that doth blaze,
  each visage that I sée :
Augments my care, in causing me
  to long and looke for thée.
Thus waste I all the night
  in dreames without desire :

Thus

Thus driue I on my dayes in loue,
　that scalds like scorching fire.
yet well content therewith,
　so that, at my returne
Thou pitie me, who for thy sake
　with Cupids coles do burne.
I am the Turtle true,
　that sits vpon the tree:
And waile my woe without a make,
　and onely wish for thee.

　　Vnable by long and hard trauell to banish
　　　　loue, returnes his friend.

WOunded with loue, and piercing deep desire
　Of your faire face, I left my natiue land,
With *Russia* snow to slacke mine English fire,
But well I see, no cold can quench the brand
That Cupides coles enkindle in the brest,
frost hath no force where friendship is possest.
　The Ocean sea for all his fearefull floud,
The perils great of passage not preuaile,
To banish loue the riuers do no good,
The mountains hie cause Cupid not to quaile,
Wight are his wings, and faster flies as fast,
As any ship for all his sailes and mast.
　The riuer *Dwina* cannot wash away
With all his waues the loue I beare to thee,

　　　　　　　　　　Nor

Nor Suchan swift loues raging heate delay,
Good will was graft vpon so sure a trée.
Sith trauaile then, nor frost can coole this fire:
From Mosqua I thy frend wil home retire.

That he findeth others as faire, but not
so faithfull as his frend.

I Sundry sée for beuties glosse
　　that with my mistresse may compare:
But few I finde for true good wil
　　that to their frends so frendly are,
Looke what she saies I may assure
　　my selfe thereof, she wil not faine:
What others speake is hard to trust
　　they measure all their words by gaine.
Her lookes declare her louing minde,
　　her countnance and her heart agrée:
When others laugh they looke as smooth,
　　but loue not halfe so wel as shé:
The gréefe is hers when I am grypde,
　　my fingers ache is her disease:
With me though others mourne to sight,
　　yet are their hearts at quiet ease.
So that I marke in Cupids court,
　　are many faire and fresh to sée:
Each where is sowen dame beuties séde
　　but faire and faithfull few there bée.

　　　　　　　　　　Tra-

Trauailing the desert of Russia, he complay-
neth to Eccho, vvith request that she
comfort his afflicted state.

YOu hollow hilles and vallies wide,
 that wonted are to yelde agayne:
The latter cause of louers cries
 resound and help me to complaine.
Repeate my piteous pensiue plaints,
 recite my tale when I haue done:
howle out ye hilles and let me heare
 my voice among your rockes to run.
It wil delight my dazed spirites,
 when I report my mistresse name:
Amid my plaint to heare the hilles,
 at euery call to call the same.
Good Eccho shew me thy good will,
 is no man here but thou and I:
Take vp my tale as I lament,
 and say (Alas) as I doe crie.
Was neuer man that did enioy,
 a better dame then I haue done:
But now (Alas) she is alacke,
 helpe Eccho, helpe, I am vndone
Besides mine absence from her sight,
 another doth possesse my place.
And of my haruest sheares the sheaues,
 helpe Eccho, helpe, lament my case.

 I

I know not when I ſhal returne,
   oꝛ when to ſee that ſwæte againe:
Foꝛ(out alas)ſhe is away
   good eccho helpe to eaſe my pains.
But nought I ſæ it doth auaile,
   thy talke encreaſeth but my woe:
It irkes me to recite her name,
   and miſſe the ſaint I honoꝛ ſo.
Wherefoꝛe ſith bœtleſſe be complaints,
   and clepings cannot right my caſe:
I bid thæ(Eccho)here adew
   I will goe ſæke to ſæ her face.
The face that Paris would haue choſe,
   if he had ſæne her in the mount:
God faith the lady Venus had
   bæn had as then in ſmall account.
And as foꝛ Pallas and the third,
   I meane the mighty Junos grace:
I know right wel they would haue hid
   themſelues,and neuer pꝛeſt in place.
Foꝛ nature made hir not to match,
   but to excæde and paſſe the reſt:
Thꝛice happy he that can attaine
   her loue,and to be liked beſt.

He craues his miſtreſſe to accept his wryting be-
   ing otherwiſe inſufficient to vvinne
      good liking from her.

As

As many are the meanes,
    to fall in fancies frame:
So diuers be the driftes of men,
    for to atchieue the same.
For some to winne their loues,
    and purchase priuy grace:
With curious tonges like carpet knightes
    doe pleade a fained case.
And all to please the eares,
    and mate their mistresse minde:
Of this and chat they tell their tales,
    as they fit leasure finde.
Some other wanting chatte,
    not hauing words at wil:
With nimble ioynts, and fingering fine,
    on Lutes doe shew their skil.
By sugred sound to winne,
    their ladies to their loue:
With earnest care those wanton wightes,
    Apollos practise proue.
And such as skilfull are,
    in daunsing doe desire
To practise that whereby to set,
    their fronions harts on fire.
Whose breast is sweete to eare,
    bestraines his voice to sing:
Thereby vnto his greedy lust
    his mistresse minde to bring.

                        The

The martial man at armes,
   to muster doth delight:
And loues to shew his helmed head,
   before his Ladies sight.
In hope to purchase praise,
   and after praise some grace:
For vvomen loue a valiant man
   that dares defend their case.
Thus each one doth attempt,
   and puts the thing in vre
That fittest is to gaine good will,
   so Faulkners vse the lure.
But I vnhappy wight,
   that can doe nought of these:
How might I doe, or what deuise
   my mistresse minde to please.
Where neither tongue can talke
   nor finger frame with Lute:
Nor footing serue to daunce: alas,
   how should I moue my sute?
Not pleasant is my voice
   vnable to delight:
I can doe nought vnlesse it be
   with pen to shew my plight.
I only can in verse,
   set out a dame to show:
And on a wel deseruing frend,
   a frendly praise bestow.

                        Thus

Thus must I hunt for loue
 wherefoe (good Lady) then
In lieu of other finer skilles,
 accept my ragged pen.
Let me by writing win,
 what others doe by arte:
And during life you shal assure,
 you of a louing hart.
No vertue shalbe lodgde
 within your curteous brest:
But I wil blaze the same abroad,
 as brauely as the best.
And as for beuties praise,
 I wil procure that fame
Shal sound it out so loud, that all
 the world shal read thy name.
So as by louing me,
 you shal haue loue againe:
And eke the harts of thousands mo
 for you good wil attaine.
I neuer was mine owne
 sith first I sawe your face:
Nor neuer wil, but euer yours,
 if you wil rue my case.

The meane is best.

The fire doeth frye, the frost doeth freese
 the colde breedes care, the heate doeth harme,
                                        The

The middle point twixt both is best,
  nor ouer-cold, nor ouer-warme.
I dreame it not the happy life
  the needie beggers bag to beare:
Ne yet the blessed state of all
  a mightie Kaisars crowne to weare.
That one is closed with sundry cares,
  and dies ten thousand times a day:
That other still in danger goes,
  for euery traitors hand to slay.
The highest hill is not the place
  whereon to build the stately bower:
The deepest vale it is as ill,
  for lightly there doth rest the shower.
The sailing ship that keepes the shore,
  vpon the rocke is oft enrent:
And he that ventures out too farre,
  and tries the stream with waues is hent.
For there the wind doth worke his will,
  there Neptunes churlish imps do raignt
The middle way is safe to saile,
  I mean the mean betwixt the twain.
So that the meane is best to choose,
  not ouer hie, nor ouer lowe:
Wherfore, if you your safetie loue,
  imbrace the meane, let mounting goe.

To

To his friend Edward Dancie
of Deceit.

Dancie, deceit is rifer now a day,
Then honest dealing, vertue is but vile,
I sée dissembling beares the bell away:
Craft hath a cloke to couer all his guile,
And vnderneath the same a knife doth lurke,
When time shall serue a shamefull spoile to worke.

Each man almost hath change of fates now,
To shift at pleasure, when it may auaile:
A man must giue no credit to the brow,
The smoothest smiling friend will soonest faile,
No trust without a triall many yéeres,
All is not gold that glistringly appéeres.

Who so shall make his choice vpon a man
To loue, and like, must warily looke about,
A faithfull friend is like a coleblacke Swan.
We may not trust the painted sheath without,
Vnlesse good lucke continue at a stay,
Farewell thy friends, like foules they flie away.

Of the right noble L. VVilliam, Earle
of Pembroke his death.

Though betters pen the praise
of him that earned fame,

X   Yet

Yet pardon men of meaner skill
   if they attempt the same.
Good will may be as great
   in simple wits to write,
In commendation of the good,
   as heads of deeper sight.
Wherfore among the rest
   that rue this Earles want,
My selfe will set my Muse abroach,
   although my vaine be scant.
This Realme hath lost a lampe,
   that gaue a gallant show :
No stranger halfe so strange to vs
   but did this Noble know.
His vertues spred so farre,
   his worthy works so wide,
That forrain princes held him deere,
   where so he was imploid.
Whose wit such credite won
   in countrey seruice still,
That Enuie could not giue the checke,
   nor rancor reaue good will.
He euer kept the roume
   that prince and fortune gaue :
As curteous in the countrey, as
   in court a Courtier braue.
To low and meanest men
   a lowly mind he bore,

                        No

No hawtie hart to stoute estates,
  vnlesse the cause were more.
But than a Lions hart
  this dreadfull Dragon had:
In field among his foes, as fierce,
  as in the Senate sad.
Had *Pallas* at his birth
  for *Pembroke* done hir best,
As nature did: then *Pembroke* had
  surmounted all the rest.
For though that learning lackt
  to paint the matter out:
What case of weight so weightie was,
  but *Pembroke* brought about ꝫ
By wit great wealth he wonne,
  by fortune fauour came:
With fauor friends, and with the friends,
  assurance of the same.
A Princes euer praisd
  aduaunst and staid in state:
From first to last commended much,
  in honors stoole he sate.
Beloued of *Henry* well,
  of *Edward* held as dere:
I doubt whether sonne or father loued
  him best, as might appere.
Queene *Mary* felt a want,
  if *Pembroke* were away:

        X.2.   So

So greatly she affied him,
    whilest she did beare the sway.
And of our pæerelesse Quæne,
    that all the rest doth passe,
I nœd not write, she shewd hir loue
    whose Steward Pembroke was.
Sith such a noble then
    by death our daily foe,
Is reft this realme, why do we not
    by teares our sorowes show?
Why leaue we to lament?
    why kæpe we in our cries?
Why do we not powre out our plaints
    by condites of the eies?
Our noble prince, our pæres,
    both pœre and rich may rue,
And each one sorow Pembroke dead,
    that earst him liuing knew.
Yt ioy in one respect,
    that he who liued so hie,
In honors seat his honor saued,
    and fortunde so to die.
Which stocke of noble state
    sith cruell death hath reft,
I wish the branches long to bud,
    that of the rœte are left.
And prosper so aliue as did this noble trœ,
    and after many happy dayes,

                    to

to die as well as hée.

Finding his Mistresse vntrue, he exclaimeth thereat.

SUnne, cease to shine by day,
 restraine thy golden beames :
Let starres refuse to lend their light,
 let fish renounce the streames.
Sea, passe thy kindly bounds,
 set ebbe and flood aside :
Brasse leaue to grow, yet gallant plants,
 depart with all your pride.
Send Tyber backe againe,
 and to thy spring returne :
Let firie coles begin to fréeze,
 let ise and water burne.
Wolues leaue to slay the Lambs,
 hounds hunt the Hare no more :
Befriend to foules, ye hungry haukes
 whom ye pursude before.
For kind hath altred course,
 the law that nature set,
Is broken quite, hir orders skornd,
 and bands in sunder fret.
Loue is accounted light,
 and friendship forced nought :
My selfe may well proclaime the same,
 that loue hath dearly bought.

      K.7.   I

I fortund once to like
    and fansie such a dame :
As sundry serud, but none atchieud
    hir feature was hir fame.

Long sute and great desart,
    with triall of my trust:
Did make hir fansie me againe,
    she found me perfit iust.

But ere I felt the blisse,
    that louers do attaine :
I bode a thousand cruell fits,
    ten thousand kinds of paine.

Till ruth by reason grew
    and rigor layd apart :
On me she did bestow hir loue,
    that best deserued hir hart.

Then mirth gan counterpoise
    the griefs I felt before :
And if I had endured smart
    I ioyed than the more.

She past me many vowes,
    and sundry sorts of hest :
And swore I was the onely wight
    whom she did fansie best.

Then happy who but I,
    that did beleeue the same :
As who is he that would refuse
    to credite such a dame?

D

O friend when J (quoth she)
　　shall alter my good will,
And leaue to loue thee passing well,
　　thy fansie to fulfill:
When J for gallant gifts,
　　for mucke or glittring gold:
for comely limmes of courtly knights,
　　delightfull to behold:
for Kaisars kingly crowne
　　thy friendship do desie:
O Gods (quoth she) renounce me then,
　　and let me monster die.
These words and sacred vowes
　　might quicklie credit gaine:
for who in such a case would glose
　　or go about to faine?
Yet now for all hir spéech
　　and glauering talke she vsed,
She is reuolted, and hir friend
　　too fowlie hath abusd:
Though not against hir kind,
　　(for Ladies are but light,)
And soone remooue but cleane against
　　their othes and promise quite.
But what should we expect
　　from thornes, no Rose perdie:
The figtrée yéelds a fig, on vines
　　the grapes in clusters bée.
　　　　X.4.　　　　　Which

Which sith I find at last
   though greatly to my paine:
Loe here I do defie the face
   in whom such craft doth raigne.
Farewell thou shamelesse shrew,
   faire Cresides heire thou art:
And I sir Troylus earst haue bæn,
   as prowcth by my smart.
Henceforth beguile the Grækes,
   no Troyans will thæ trust:
I yælo thæ vp to Diomed,
   to glut his filthie lust.
And do repute my selfe
   herein a blessed man,
Who, finding such deceit in thæ,
   refuse thy friendship can.
For sundry times we sæ,
   the sots that serue in loue,
Can neuer purchase frædom, nor
   their frantike rage remoue.
But who so hath the grace
   to banish fond desire,
I count him blest of mightie Ioue,
   for few or none retire.
So swæte is sinfull lust,
   the venome is so vile:
As Circes cup no sooner might
   the bowsing Græks beguile.

                       Now

Now hang abroade thy hookes.
  bestowe thy baytes elsewhere,
Thy pleasant call shall haue no power
  to lure my cunning eare.
Itride thy twigges too much,
  my feathers felt thy lime:
To giue thee vp, and shunne thy shiftes,
  I coumpt it more than time.

A warning that she be not
vncourteous.

I Chuse you not to change,
  I entred band to bide:
But plighted promise crackt by you
  I count my selfe vntide.
No hest is to be held,
  no vow of balew, when
You dames the coller slip:
  by craft to compasse men.
Presume not of good wil,
  because I swore you loue:
For faithful frends vpon abuse,
  their fancy may remoue.
Which lincke of loue vndone
  repentance comes too late:
The fort is wonne when trueth is slaine
  and treason keepes the gate.
                L.v.   Ne

No teares can purchase truce,
  no wæping winnes good wil:
Trewe loue once lost by due desart,
  is not renewde by skil.
Good meaning may not serue,
  to fæde your frends withall:
As wit in words,so trueth in dædes,
  appæres,and euer shal.
Who so doth runne a race,
  shall surely sweate amaine
And who so loues,shal hardly gloze
  or secret hidden paine.
Way wel my loue at first
  recall to retchlesse thought,
The fiery fittes,the pensiue panges,
  which I ful dærely bought.
Before I tooke the tast,
  of what I lykte so well:
And then consider careles,how
  to Iunos yoke you fel.
Forget not how for gaine
  and mucke your match was made:
When I the while(poore man)was forst
  a wæry life to trade,
The Lions loue refusde
  the noblest beast of all:
Unto a sotte you yokt your selfe,
  and wore a willing thrall.

                          Then

Then who wionld foꝛce but I,
   oꝛ hold the iewel dære.
That on anothers finger sits
   and hath done many a paꝛe.
And long is like to doe,
   the hoꝛge that gapes foꝛ hawes,
That hang so fast, may groynd his tuskes
   and die with emptie iawes.
I speake it not of spight,
   but sure you ill deserue:
A man that meanes so wel as I,
   sith you doe dayly swerue.
A foole by foule abuse,
   shall haue you moꝛe at becke:
Then he that euer loued you well
   and neuer gaue you checke.
Which shewes that either wit,
   oꝛ faithful loue you lacke:
Beware in time, misliking growen,
   may not be bended backe.
When Cresid clapt the dish,
   and Laʒerlike did goe:
She rewde no doubt that earst she did,
   the Troyan handle so.
And might she then retirde,
   to beuties auncient towꝛe:
She would haue stucke to Priams sonne,
   of faithful loue the floure.

                            But

But fond,too late she found
    that she had bæn too light:
And ouerlate bewaild that she
    forwent the worthy knight.
Impzint it in your brest,
    and thinke that Ladies lot
May light on you,with whom your frend
    is causlesse thus forgot.
I would be loth to loue,
    and leaue with losse againe:
I smarted once,and you(none els)
    the ground of all my paine.
Time tries the trusty minde,
    which time doth councell me
To deale my loue by equall wright
    least I deceiued be.
Where counsel nor aduice,
    can take no better holde:
The losse is light:for colour I
    imbzace not glowing golde.
No moze I way a frend,
    foz feature of her face:
Her dealing wel must binde good will,
    vpzightly iudge my case.
I wholly was your owne,
    and lesse you loue alœke:
The match betwixt vs two is marde,
    and I your frend to sæke.

                                        If

If any els deſerue
  a ſhare oʒ better part:
Let me but know pour mind, and then
  adue with all my hart.
J ſound the trumpet now,
  that warning geues to pou:
To leaue to loue beſides my ſelfe,
  to whom the whole is due.
J tell pou this betimes,
  as one that would be loath
By pour deſert to chooſe againe,
  and bʒeake mine auncient oth.
Which if by foʒtune fall,
  allowe pour ſelfe the thankes:
Whoſe parts vnkind may foʒce a man
  to play vnfriendly pʒankes.

To one whom he had long loued, and at laſt was
    refuſed vvithout cauſe, and one imbra-
      ced that leaſt deſerued it.

     Che prende diletto di far fʁode
     Non ſi delamentar, ſi altri le inhaana.

If lyking beſt with fancy firmely ſet,
If louing moſt, with retchleſſe care of ſtate,
  If true good will, whom time could neuer fret,
If pardoning faultes, which now J rewe too late,

                    If

If good ſtil done, and euer meant to you:
Are not of force to make your frendſhips true.

If foule abuſe and tearmes of loathſome ſound,
If miſchiefe meant, and ſeldome good beſtowed,
If black defame and credit brought to ground
If baſe reportz ſo raſhly ſpread abroad,
Can winne good wil, and binde a ſuret band:
Then he that loues and beares you not in hand.

Then happy he that workes your déepe decay,
And ſlaunder ſéekes to both your open ſhames,
For he doth laugh and beare the bel away,
Unlucky I with whom ſo il it frames,
As now at laſt in guerdon of my toyle:
I reape refuſe and bide this ſecond foile.

Wel may he laugh that is my deadly foe,
And I lament impatient of my paine,
Il may ſhe fare whoſe craft hath cauſde my woe,
And fickle faith deceiued me thus againe.
But I too blame as many foulers bée:
Who had the bird in hand and let her flée.

More wiſe then you the babe that féeling flame
And once indangerd of the burning blaze,
Doth ſtraight refuſe the touching of the ſame,
But you much like the gnat doe loue to gaze,

                                                    And

And flée so long about the candle light:
Is both wil seare your wings and carcasse quight.

The slaue that serues his prentiship in paine
Not halfe so much a wretch as wretched I,
for he doth end his yéeres with certaine gaine,
Where I haue leaue the hardest hap to trie,
And hopelesse quite of what by due was mine
To grone in gréefe, and with my paines to pine.

Wel, wel, content, sith chaunce and you agrée
Itake my hap though cleane against my wil
Enforst by you my faith and frend I flée,
You must by kinde remaine a woman stil,
Who lookes to haue the crowe to change his blacke
Before it chaunce perchance his eyes may lacke.

Sith you can rule (as by report you may,)
(And that to rule is it you women craue)
Begin your raigne, God graunt he doe obey
That long in yoke hath kept you like a slaue,
I feare, I wish, I hope the time wil bée:
When Louedaies made for lucre wil not grée.

Sticke fast to him who bolsters your estate,
forgiue the faults that haue bén done amisse,
forget reports, cling closely to your mate,
But thinke on him sometime that wrote you this,

If

If euer chaunce doe make your bondage frée
God send your second choyce like this to bée.

And as foz him whose helping hand hath done,
The best it might to wozke my cruel wóe,
I trust in time when all the thzéde is sponne,
Shall déepely rewe that he abusde me so.
That womans spite all other spites excéedes:
It doth appære by both your cursed dédes.

If my desert to him had bén so ill,
Then could I not on him haue laid the blame,
If mine abuse to you had crackt good will,
Yours were the pzaise and mine the open shame,
I loued you both, and yet doe reape at last.
But hate from both, foz all my frendship past.

1. *Due volte me hai ingannato.*

2. *Supplicio al mondo non e dato,*
   Maggior, quanto pate vn che inamorato.

3. *Qual lieni foglie, le dome sono, e crude piu che tasso*
   Piu che Tigre inclementi, & disdegnose,
   Piu che orse, & piu che luge empie e rabbiose.
   Hanno piu inganni, che non hanno capelli in cape.

4. *O quante, arte & inganni ha il sesso feminino.*
   O quanti lacci? O quanti nedi, e groppi?
   Per far huomini venir deboli e zorpi.

   A lio ingrata, troppo amata.

An Epitaph vpon the death of Henry
Sydhnam, and Giles Bampfield
Gentlemen.

As rise as to my thought repaires
    that dzearie doleful day,
And most vnluckie houre (alas)
    that hent my friends away:
So oft my bzest is like to bnrst,
    and ribs to rend in twaine:
My liuer and my lungs giue vp,
    my hart doth melt amaine.
And to decipher inward griefs
    that crush my carcasse so:
The sluces of mine eyes do slip,
    and let their humoz go.
Out flies the floud of bzackish teares,
    whole seas of sozow swell:
In such abundance from my bzaine,
    as wo it is to tell.
Why do I then conceale their names?
    what means my sluggish pen,
To hide the haps and lucklesse loe
    of these two manly men.
Sith silence bzæds a smothering smart,
    where sundzy times we sæ:
That by disclosing of our mindes
    great cares digested bæ.
Wherfore my mournfull Muse begin, &c.

              Y   So

So Fortune would, the cankred Kernes,
   who seldom ciuil are,
Detesting golden peace, tooke armes,
   and fell to frantike war.

Up rose the rude and retchlesse rogues
   with dreadfull darts in hand:
And sought to noy the noble state
   of this our happy land.

Whose bedlam rage to ouerrule,
   and fury to confound:
The L. of Essex chosen was,
   a noble much renownd.

Away he went awaited on
   of many a courtly knight:
Whose swelling harts had fully vowed
   to daunt their foes in fight.

Among the rest (I rue to tell)
   my *Sydnh.am* tooke the seas:
Gyles Bampsfield eke abord he leapt,
   his princes wil to please.

Whose martial minds and burning brests
   were bent to beare the broile:
Of bloodie wars, and die the death,
   or giue the foe the foyle.

And treble blessed had they béen,
   if fortune so had willed:
That they with hawtie sword in hand
   had died in open field.

For

For fame with garland of renowne
   vndoubted decks his hed :
That in defence of Prince and Realme,
   his life and blond doth shed.
But out (alas) these gallant imps
   before they came to land :
To shew their force and forward harts,
   by dint of deadly hand.
Before they fought amid the field,
   or lookt the fee in face :
With sodain storme in Irish streame
   were drownd, a wofull case.
Up rose with rage a tempest huge,
   that troubled so the surge,
As shipmen shrunke, and Pylot knew
   not how to scape the scourge.
And yet no dread of doubtfull death,
   no force of fretting fome :
Nor wrath of weltring waues could stay,
   those martiall mates at home.
Not angry *Aeols* churlish chaffe,
   that scoules amid the skies :
Nor sullen Neptunes surging suds
   mought daunt their manly eyes.
Unworthy they (O gods) to feed
   the hungry fish in flood :
Or die so base a death as that,
   if you had thought it good.

           P.2.   But

But what you will, of force befals,
   your heauenly power is such,
That where and how, and whom you list,
   your godheds daily tuch.
And reason good, that sithence all
   by you was wrought and done:
No earthly wight should haue the wit
   your wreakefull scourge to shonne.
Well, *Sydhnam,* *Bampfield,* and the rest,
   sith wailing doth no good:
Nor that my teares can pay the price
   or ransome of your blood.
Sith no deuise of man can make
   that you should liue againe :
Let these my plaints in verse suffise
   your soules, accept my paine.
If ought my writing be of power
   to make your vertues known:
According to your due deserts
   which you in life haue shown.
Assure your selues, my mournfull Muse
   shall do the best it can:
To cause your names and noble minds,
   to liue in mouth of man.
And so adue, my faithfull friends,
   lamenting lets my quill :
I loued you liuing, and in death,
   for euer so I will.

                    Ac:

Accept my writing in good worth,
   no fitter means I find
To do you good, now being dead,
   nor ease my mourning mind.
No better life than you haue led
   vnto my selfe I wish:
But happier death, if I might chuse,
   than so to feed the fish.
The gods allow my lims a tombe
   and graue wherein to lye :
That men may say, thrise happy he,
   that happened so to die.
For kindly death is counted good,
   and blessed they be thought :
That of their friends vnto the pit,
   vpon the beere are brought.
But for my selfe, I reckon those
   more blest a thousand fold,
That in the quarel of their prince,
   their liues and blood haue sold.
As you mine ancient mates did meane,
   for which the mightie Ioue:
In heauen shal place your souls, although
   your bones on rocks do roue.

A letter begun to a Gentlewoman of some
account, which was left of by means
of the aduise of a friend of his,
who said she was foresped.

YOur beautie (madame) made
   mine eye to like your face:
And now my hart did cause my hand,
   to sue to you for grace.
The ground of my good wil,
   by feature first was cast,
Which your good noble nature hath
   for euer sealed fast.
When plants be surely pight,
   than lightly will they proue,
No tree can take so déep a roote
   as grifts of faithfull loue.
If I had feared disdaine,
   or thought that hawtie pride
Had harbourd in that brest of yours,
   which is the pecocks guide.
Then should I not haue durst
   these verses to indite,
But waying well your curteous kind,
   I tooke the hart to write.
In hope that Venus gifts
   are matcht with Pallas goods,
And that true frendship floures wil spring
   of blasing beauties buds.

                        For

For seldom shal you find
  a dame of your degræ:
And of such featnres, but hir lookes
  and maners do agræ:
Which if in proofe I find,
  as I presume I shall,
Then happy others, but I compt
  my fortune best of all.
And to expresse my ioy,
  my hands I mean to clap:
As who would say, loe I am he
  that haue this blessed hap.
Let not my hopes be vaine,
  in your hand lies my life:
And if you list to cut my throte,
  you haue the fatall knife.
For wholy on your lookes
  and mercy stayes the thræd
That holds my lims togither now,
  the gods haue so decræd.
I am your bounden thrall,
  and euer mean to be:
I will not change my choice, &c.

       N.4.   *To*

*To his friend not to change, though iea-
lousie debarre him hir company.*

CHange not thy choyce (my dǽre,)
　　stand stable in good will,
Let ancient faithful loue appǽre
　　betwixt vs louers still.
A wisdom friends to win,
　　as great a wit againe :
A gotten friend, that faithfull is,
　　in friendship to retaine.
Thou sǽst how hatred hewes
　　the chips of our mischance :
And iealousie doth what it may,
　　the Viper to aduance.
Whose prying eyes are prest
　　to hinder our intent,
But malice oft doth misse his marke,
　　where two good wils be bent.
So carefull *Argus* kept
　　the faire well featured cowe :
Whose watchful eies ful seldome slept,
　　according to his vowe.
And yet at length he lost
　　his head, and eke his hire :
For Mercury his cunning crost,
　　to further Ioues desire.

　　　　　　　　　　So

So curſt Acriſius cloſde
 the mayden in the mewe
Where he aſſuredly ſuppoſed
 to kéepe the virgin true.
Yet Danae did conceaue
 within the ſecret towre:
And did in lap receiue the god,
 that fel in golden ſhowre.
Way what good wil he beares,
 that liues in ſuch diſtruſt:
he fares as doth the wretch that feares
 his golde, and lets it ruſt.
Whoſe hungry heaping minde
 for all his looking on:
Is ſt abuſde, and made as blinde
 as any marble ſtone.
I craue but your conſent,
 when time and place agrée:
And that you wil be wel content
 to yelde your ſelfe to me.
Who euer wil regard,
 the honor of your name:
And looke what pleaſure may be ſparde,
 wil only craue the ſame.
No checke ſhall taint your chéeke,
 by proofe of open acte:
I neuer wil vnwiſely ſéeke,
 to haue your credit crackte.

    P.b.   My

My loue excels his lust.
  my fancy his good wil:
My trueth doth farre surmount his trust
  my good deserts his il.
Wherfore (my deare) consent
  vnto my iust request:
For I long sith haue loued you wel,
  and euer meant you best.
So shal you haue my heart,
  stil redy at your call:
You cannot play a wiser part
  then cherish such a thrall.

To his frend not to forget him.

Where liking growes of lust,
  it cannot long endure:
But where we finde it graft on loue,
  there frendships force is sure.
Where wealth procures good wil,
  when substance slides away
There fancy alters all by fittes,
  and true loue doth decay.
Where beutie bindes the band,
  and feature forceth loue.
With crooked age or changed face,
  there frendship doth remoue.

No

No one of these (my deare)
  that fickle thus dee fade:
Did bend my brest, oz fozst thy frend
  to follow Cupids trade,
But meere good wil in dæde
  not graft on hope of gaine:
I loue without regard of lust
  as pzoofe hath taught you plaine.
I way no wauering wealth
  I fozce not of thy face:
No graunt of pleasure przickes me on
  thy person to embzace.
No hope of after hap,
  ingenders my good wil:
I loue thæ when I saw thæ first,
  and so I loue thæ stil
Wherfoze requite with care
  the man that meanes you so:
It lies in you to yeld him easte,
  oz plague his hart with woe.
You were not bzed of rockes,
  no marble was your meate:
I trust I shal so good a dame,
  to loue me best intreate.
You know I beare the blame,
  your selfe are nothing strætt
He loues me not foz louing you,
  noz you foz louing me.

                    Con-

Consider of the case
    and like where you are lodde:
It is against your kinde to please
    where you are so reproude.
His frendship is in doubt,
    you stand assured of me:
He hates vs both, I cannot loue,
    the man that hateth thee.
His frantike words of late,
    bewraide his folly plaine:
Assure your selfe he loues you not,
    his glosing is for gaine.
Which purpose being brought,
    to his desired passe:
The sotte wil shew himselfe a beast,
    and proue a wayward Asse.
By reason rule his rage,
    by wisdome master wil:
Embrace your frend in spite of him,
    that meanes you no good wil.
A time in time may come,
    if gods wil haue it so:
When we each other shal inioy,
    to quite each others woe.
Which time if time agree,
    to pleasure vs withall:
Our honie wil the sweeter seeme
    that we haue tasted gall.

                          Till

Till when vse womans wit
   therein you know my minde:
I neuer was, nor neuer wil
   be found your frend vnkinde.

A vowe of Constancie.

First shal the raging flouds
   against their course runne:
By day the moone shal lend her light,
   by night the golden sunne.
First fickle fortune shall
   stand at a stedy stay:
And in the sea the shining starres
   shal moue and keepe their way.
First Fish amid the ayre,
   shal wander to and fro:
The cloudes be cleere, in beuty eke
   the cole exceede the snowe.
First kinde shal alter all
   and change her wonted state:
The blind stal see, the deafe shal heare,
   the dumbe shal freely prate.
Before that any chaunce,
   or let that may arise
Shalbe of force to wrest my loue
   or quench in any wise.
The flame of my good will,
   my faithful fancies fire:

                         Saue

Saue cruel death shal nothing daunt,
   oz coole my hote desire,
Desire that guides my life
   and yeldes my hart his foode:
Wherfoze to be in pzesence stil,
   with thee, would doe me good
Which pzesence I pzesume
   thou neuer wilt deny:
But as occasion serues,
   so thou to frendship wilt apply.
Til when I giue thee vp,
   to good and happy chaunce:
In hope that time to our delights,
   wil seeke vs to aduance.
Adue (deere frend) to thee,
   that art my only ioy:
Moze faire to me then Helen was
   to Priams sonne of Troy.
And constant moze in loue,
   then was Vlisses make
Of whose assured life and zeale,
   so much the Poets spake.
Lesse light then Lucrece eke
   whom Tarquins lust defilde:
As curteous as the Carthage Queene,
   that fowly was beguilde.
To quite all which good parts,
   this vow I make to thee:

I

I will be thine as long as I
  haue power mine owne to be.

Another Epitaph vpon the death of Henry Sydhnam, and Gyles Bampfield gent.

If teares might ought auaylc to ftynt my woe
If fobbyng fighes breathd out from penfiue breft
Could eafe the gryping greefes that payn me fo
Or pleafure them for whom I am diftreft
Neyther vvould I fpeke vvyth teares to fret my face:
Nor fpare to lpend redoubled fighes apace.

2 But fith neyther dreary drops nor fighes haue power
To doe me good, or ftand my frends in fteede
Why fhould I feeke vvyth forovves to deuoure
Thofe humors that my fayntyng lymmes fhould feede.
Bootelefle it vvere therefore I vvyl aſſay
To fhevv my felfe a frend fome other vvay.

3 Some other vvay, as by my mournyng pen,
To doe the vvorld to vvit vvhat vvyghts they vvere
Whose deaths I vvayle, vvhat frendly forvvard men
And to thys land they both dyd beare
Alas, I rue to name them in my verfe:
Whofe only thought my trembling hart doth pearfe.
                                          But

4 But yet I must of force their names vnfolde,
(For things concealde are seldome when bewaild,
Tone Sydnham was, a manly wight and bolde,
In whom neither courage haute, nor feature faylde,
Faythful to frends vndaunted to his foes
A lambe in loue, where he to fancy chose.

5 The second neere vnto my selfe allyde,
Gyles Bamsield hight. (I weepe to wryte his name,)
A gallant ympe, amyd his youthfull pryde:
Whose seemely shape commended natures frame,
Deckte of the gods in cradle where he lay:
With louely lymmes, and parts of purest clay.

6 Themselues might boast them bryths for gentle bloud
The houses are of countenaine Whence they came
And vaunt I dare their vertues rare as good,
As was their race and fitted to the same.
There wanted nought to make them perfect blest:
Saue happy deathes which clouded all the rest.

7 When rascall Irysh hapned to rebel,
(who seld we see doe long continue true)
Vnto the Lord of Esser lotte it fell,
To haue the lotte those outlawes to subdue.
Who went away to please the Prynce and state:
Attended on of many a doughty mate.

8 Whose names although my dreary quil conceale,
Yet they (I trust) wil take it wel in worth
For noble mindes employd to common weale,
Shall finde a stemme to blaze their prowes foorth.
My dolefull muse but this alone entends:
To wryte and wayle my frends vnhappy endes.
　　　　　　　　　　　　　　　　　9 Thei

9 Away they would,and gaue their laſt adew,
with burning hearts to ſlay the ſauage foe,
Beſtride their ſteads,and to the ſea they flew,
where weather roſe,and water raged ſo,
As they (alas) who meant their countrey good,
were forſt to loſe their liues in Iriſh flood.

10 Thoſe eyes ſhould haue lookt the foe in face,
were then conſtraind to winke at euery waue,
Thoſe valiant armes the bilowes did imbrace,
That vowd with ſword this realms renowne to ſaue:
Thoſe manly minds that dreaded no miſhap,
Were ſouſt in ſeas,and caught in ſuddaine trap.

11 Proud Eole Prince,controller of the winds,
With churliſh Neptune,ſoueraigne of the ſeas
Did play their parts,and ſhewd their ſtubburn kinds,
whom no requeſt nor prayer might appeaſe,
The Troyan Duke bid not ſo great a brunt,
when he of yore ſor Lauine land did hunt.

12 And yet theſe wights committed none offence,
To Iuno,as ſir Paris did of yore,
Their only trauell was for our defence,
Which makes me waile their ſodain deaths the more,
But what the Gods do purpoſe to be done,
By proofe we ſee,mans wiſdom cannot ſhun.

13 Ye water Nimphes,and you that Ladies be,
Of more remorſe,and of a milder mood:
Than Neptune or king Eole,if you ſee
Their balefull bodies driuing on the floud,
Take vp their lims,allowing them a graue,
who well deſerued a richer hearſe to haue.

14 Whereon do stampe this small deuice in stone,
That passers by, may read with dewed eyes,
When they by chance shall chance to light thereon.

{ Loe Sydhnam here, and Bampfields body lies :
{ Whose willing harts to serue their prince and realme,
{ shortned their liues amid this wrathfull streame.

Ante obitum, supremáque funera fœlix.

Deo iubente, fato cedunt mortalia.

A louer decciued, exclaimes against
the deceiuer and hir
kind.

HOw much a wretch is he
that doth affie so well
In womans words, and in hir hart
doth lodge his loue to dwell :
Beléeues hir outward glée,
and tickle termes to trust,
And doth without regard of time,
apply to womans lust:
Sith that hir wandring will,
and most vnstable mind:
Doth daily tosse and turne about,
as leaues amid the wind.
Who lothes hir most, she loues,
and him that sues for grace,

She

She sharply shuns, and proudly scornes,
  and ebbes and flowes apace.
(O gods what haue I done:
  alas, at length I spie:
My former follies, and discerne
  how much I marcht awry.
To plant assured trust,
  in tickle womans brest:
That Tygerlike sance mercy liues,
  and euer shuns the best.
And yet she knowes I loue,
  and how I waste away:
And that my hart may haue no rest,
  nor quiet night or day.
Which sith to hir is knowen,
  and how I hold hir chiefe:
Why cruell and vnkind, doth she
  not pitie of my griefe?
(Who is so perfect wise,
  that may such malice brooke,
Of womans prcud disdaine,
  or beare their braules with quiet looke?
Without an open shew
  of lothsome lurking smart:
That racks the ribs, that beates the brest,
  and plagues the pensiue hart.,
O me vnhappy wight,
  most wofull wretch of all,

      Z.2.   How

How do I lose my libertie,
  and yœld my selfe a thrall.
In seruing hir,that cleane
  against all law and right :
Consumes my life,destroyes my days,
  and robs my reason quite.
O loue,cut off hir course,
  and bridle such a dame:
As skornes thy skill,and leaues thy laws,
  and makes my griefe hir game.
If (as I dœme) thou be,
  the soueraigne of the skies:
Of Elements and Nature eke,
  that all in order ties.
Wreake both thy wrong sustaind,
  and eke thy damage done
To me,on hir,whom flatly thou,
  perceiuest vs both to shun.
Conuert hir frosen hart,
  to coles of scalding fire
Where rigor raigns,and enuie dwels,
  with poisoned wrathfull ire.
¶ She,cruell,knowes my loue,
  and how as Saint,I shrine
Hir beautie in my brest,
  and how with pearcing pains I pine :
And how a thousand times,
  each day I die,she knowes,

                              Yet

yet mercilesse, no mercy she,
   nor signe of sorow showes.
She bound me to the stake,
   to broile amid the brands:
At point to die a Martyrs death,
   all which she vnderstands.
Yea, though she know it well,
   yet she conceiues a ioy:
At all my bitter grief, and glads
   hir selfe with mine annoy.
O most disloyall dame,
   O bloudy brested wight:
O thou, that hast consumd by care,
   my hart and courage quite.
O thou for treason that
   Iugurtha, and the Iew
Doest far excell, and from thy friend,
   withholdst thy fauour dew.
O traiterous of thy troth,
   of all good nature bare:
Loe here of my poore wounded hart,
   the gash cut in by care.
I see thou seest my sore,
   and yet thou wilt be blind:
Thou stopst thine eares, and wilt not hear
   the griefs that I do find.
¶ Where is become thy loue,
   and ancient great good will:

That

That earst was borne: wheres that desire
　　that forst thée to fulfill
Thy pleasures past with me
　　in cabbin where we lay?
What is become of those delights?
　　where is that sugred play?
Wheres all that valiance now,
　　and profers proudly made?
Wheres those imbrasings friendly,
　　where is that blessed trade
And signs of persit loue,
　　which then thou putst in vre?
And which for any gift of mine,
　　mought yet right well endure.
❡ Full shadowlike they thift,
　　and can no longer bide:
Like dust before the wind they flie,
　　your other mate doth guide.
And strikes so great a stroke,
　　he wrests your wits as round
As flittering leaues, that from the Asshe
　　or pine are shaken downe.
Full lightly womans loue,
　　is altred euermore:
It may not last, there is exchange
　　continually in store.
And reason: *For by kind*
　　a woman is but light,

　　　　　　　　　　　　Which

Which makes that fansie from hir brest,
   is apt to take hir flight.
℃ I had good hope at first,
   when hap did me allure,
To like of thæ, that this thy loue,
   was planted to endure.
I neuer feard a fall,
   on ground that lay so gréne:
Where path was plaine for me to passe,
   and bottom to be séene.
I doubted no decay,
   nor feard no after smart:
Thy beautie did me not despaire,
   thy lookes assured thy hart.
But who beléues the lookes
   of any of your race,
May soone deceiue himselfe,
   There lies no credite in the face.
Well, sith thy froward mind,
   doth like to heare my mone:
And mine vnhappy planet giues
   consent, that I alone,
Without thy loue shall liue,
   and lacke the lampe of light:
To cleare mine eies, that far excels
   all other stars in sight.
Unto the hawtie skies,
   and people here below:

I

I will my griping griefs expresse,
    and surge of sorowes show.
In hope that direfull death,
    with dreadfull dart of force:
Will couch my carcase in the graue,
    and there conuey my corse.

Yet ere I die, receiue this Swan-
            like song,
    To ease my hart, and shew thine
            open wrong.

O Wauering womans will,
    that bends so soone about:
Why doest thou so reuolt in hast,
    and shutst thy friend without.
Against the law of loue,
    O thrise vnhappy hee:
That doth beleue thy beauties be ames,
    and lokes of gallant glee.
For neither thraldom long,
    that I poore wight aboue:
Nor great good will by sundry signs,
    and outward gesture shewed.
Had force to hold thy hart,
    and keep thee at a stay:

                                        No

No good deſart of mine might ſtop
  that would of foꝛce away.
Yet of this cruel lotte,
  and fel miſchance, I finde
Noꝛ know no cauſe, but that thou art
  ſpꝛong out of womans kind.
I iudge that Nature, and
  the Gods that gouerne all
Deuiſde this wicked ſhameles ſe.te
  to plague the earth withall.
A miſchiefe foꝛ vs men,
  a burden bad to beare:
Without whoſe match too happy we,
  and too too bleſſed were.
Euen as the Beares are bꝛead,
  the Serpent and the Snake.
The barking Wolfe, the filthy flie
  that noyſome fleſh doth make.
The ſtinking wæde to ſmell
  that growes among the graine:
Euen ſo I thinke the Gods haue made
  your race vs men to paine.
Why did not kinde foꝛeſæ
  and nature ſo deuiſe
That man of man without the help,
  of woman mought ariſe?
As by the art of hande
  of apples apples ſpꝛing:
              J.b.   Ant

And as the pearetrǽ graft by kind
    another peare doeth bring.
But if you marke it wel,
    the caufe is quickly ſcene:
It is foʒ that thou Nature art
    a woman though a Quéne.
O dames I would not wiſh
    you peacocklike to looke
Oʒ puft with pʒide to vaunt that man
    of you his being tooke.
Foʒ on the bʒyar oft
    a gallant Roſe doth grow
And of a ſtincking wǽde an herbe
    oʒ floure freſh to ſhew.
Ye are exceſſiue pʒoude,
    ſtuſt vp with ſtately ſpite:
Uoyd of good loue, of loyall trueth
    and all good counſel quite.
Raſh, cruel cauſleſſe, curſt,
    vnkinde without deſert
Boʒne onely foʒ the ſcourge of him
    that beares a faithful hart.
I rather wiſh to die,
    then liue a vaſſaile ſtil
Oʒ thʒall my ſelfe vnto a dame
    that yeldes me no good wil.
The woʒmes ſhal ſooner féde
    vpon my happy hart:

                                    Within

Within my graue, then I for loue
  of you wil ſuffer ſmart.
Loue deere dames,
  the gaſtly ghoſtes of hel
Shal plague your bones
  that gloze and loue not wel.

To his cruel miſtreſſe.

GEue looſers leaue to ſpeake,
  let him that feeles the ſmart
Without controlment tel his tale,
  to eaſe his heauy hart.
To thee (proude dame) I poynt,
  who like the beaſt of Nile:
By teares procureſt thy frend to loue
  and ſlaieſt him all the while.
By weeping firſt to winne
  and after conqueſt made
To ſpoyle with ſpite thoſe yelding impes
  that follow Cupids trade.
Condemnes thy cancred kinde,
  more glory were for thee
To ranſacke none but rebel harts
  and let the reſt goe free.
Kinde wiſt not what ſhe wrought
  when ſhe ſuch beuty lent
Unto thoſe gallant limmes of thine
  to monſtrous miſchiefe bent.

For

For either fowler face
    she would haue yelded thée:
Oz better moode and milder minde
    to make remoze of me.
Thou bearest two burning brands,
    below those browes of thine:
And I the brimstone in my brest,
    which makes my hart to pine.
Eche lowzing looke of yours,
    frets farther in my hart:
And nips me néerer then
    the force of any other dart.
And to increase my care,
    thou makest thy beutie moze:
An oyle(God wotte)vnto my fire,
    no salue to ease my soze.
If thou a woman were,
    of ruth and due remozse:
Thou wouldst allow me loue,
    and not so proudly plague my corse.
I sue for mercy now,
    with hands lift vp on hie
Which if I misse I am assurde,
    within fewe dayes to die.
And if I may not haue
    the thing I would enioy:
I pray the Gods to plague thée
    as they did the dame of Troy.

I

I meane that Creside coy
   that linkt her with a Greeke:
And left the lusty Tropan Duke,
   of all his loue to seeke.
And so they wil I trust
   a mirror make of thee:
That beuties darlings may beware
   when they thy scourge shal see.
I neuer meant thee wel,
   in all my life before:
But now to plague thy foule abuse,
   I hate thee ten times more.
for reason willes me so,
   my frends to loue and serue
And cruel Ladies like thy selfe,
   to wish as they deserue.
henceforth if any limme,
   of mine perhap rebel:
And thee whom I of right should loth
   doe loue or fancie wel.
I quite renounce the same
   he shall no more be mine
to vse or stand in stead, then I
   doe purpose to be thine.
And thus I make an end
   of loue, and lines at once
The frounce consume the flesh of her,
   that feedes vpon my bones.

         The

The Author being in Mosco-
uia, wrytes to certaine his frendes in Englande
of the state of the place, not exactly, but at all
aduentures, and minding to haue descry-
bed all the Moscouites maners, brake
off his purpose vpon some
occasion.

The three Epistles followe.

To his especiall frende, master Edwarde
Dancie.

My Dancie dære, when I
recount within my brest:
My London frends and wonted mates
and thœ aboue the rest.
I fœle a thousand fittes
of dæpe and deadly woe:
To thinke that I from sea to land,
from blisse to bale did goe.
I left my natiue soyle,
ful like a retchlesse man
And vnacquainted of the coast,
among the Russies ranne.
A people passing rude,
to bices vile enclinde:
Folke fitte to be of Bacchus traine,
so quaffing is their kinde.　　　Drinke

Drinke is their whole desire,
 the pot is all their pryde:
The sobzest head doeth once a day,
 stand nœdeful of a guyde.
If he to banquet bid his frends,
 he wil not shrinke
On them at dinner to bestow
 a dosen kindes of drinke.
Such licour as they haue
 and as the countrey giues:
But chæfly two, one called Kuas,
 whereby the Musick liues.
Small ware and waterlike
 but somewhat tart in taste:
The rest is Meade, of hony made
 wherewith their lips they baste.
And if he goe vnto
 his neighbour as a guest:
He cares for litle meate, if so
 his drinke be of the best.
Perhaps the Mousick hath
 a gay and gallant wife:
To serue his beastly lust ye: he
 will leade a bowgards life.
The monster moze desires
 a boy within his bed
Then any wench, such filthy sinne
 ensues a drunken head.

                          The

The woman to repay,
    her drousie husbands dettes:
From stinking stoue vnto her mate
    to baudy banquet gets.
No wonder though they vse
    such vile and beastly trade:
Sith with the hatchet and the hand,
    their chiefest Gods be made.
Their Idolles haue their hearts
    on God they neuer call:
Vnlesse it be (Nichola Bough)
    that hangs against the wall.
The house that hath no God,
    or painted saint within:
Is not to be resorted to,
    that roofe is full of sinne.
Besides their priuate Gods,
    in open places stand
Their crosses, vnto which they crouch,
    and blesse themselues with hand.
Deuoutly downe they ducke,
    with forhead to the ground:
Was neuer more deceit in ragges,
    and greasie garments found.
Almost the meanest man
    in all the countrey rides:
The woman eke against our vse,
    her trotting horse bestrides.

                                    In

In sundzy colozs they
   both men and women go :
In buskins all, that money haue
   on buskins to bestow.
Eche woman hanging hath
   a ring within hir eare :
Which all of ancient vse, and some
   of very pzide do weare.
Their gate is very graue,
   their countenance wise and sad :
And yet they follow fleshly lusts,
   their trade of liuing bad.
It is no shame at all,
   accounted to defile
Anothers bed, they make no care
   their follies to concile.
Is not the meanest man
   in all the land, but he
To buy hir painted colours doth
   allow his wife a fee.
Wherewith she decks hir selfe,
   and dies hir tawnie skin :
She pzancks and paints hir smokie face,
   both bzowe, lip, cheeke and chin.
Yea those that honest are
   (if any such there bee)
Within the land, do vse the like,
   a man may plainly see.

            A a   Vpon

Upon some womens chéekes
   the paint ing how it lies :
In plaster sort, for that too thicke
   hir face the harlot dies.
But such as skilfull are,
   and cunning dames in déd:
By daily practise do it well,
   yea sure they do excéd.
They lay their colours so,
   as he that is full wise :
May easily be deceiued therein,
   if he do trust his eies.
I not a little muse
   what madnesse makes them paint
Their faces, waying how they kéepe
   the stoue by méere constraint.
For seldom when, vnlesse
   on church or mariage day .
A man shall sée the dames abzode
   that are of best aray.
The Russie means to reape
   the profit of hir pzide :
And so he mewes hir, to be sure
   she lie by no mans side.
Thus much (friend *Dancie*)
   I did meane to wzite to thée :
To let thée wite, in Russia land,
   what men and women bée.

                        Here

Hereafter I perhaps
  of other things will write:
To thee and other of my friends,
  which I shall see with sight.
And other stuffe besides,
  which true report shall tell:
Meane while I end my louing lines,
  and bid thee now farewell.

     To Spencer.

IF I should now forget
  or not remember thee:
Thou (*Spencer*) mightst a foule rebuke
  and shame impute to me.
For I to open shew
  did loue thee passing well:
And thou were he, at parture whom
  I loathd to bid farewell.
And as I went thy friend,
  so I continue still:
No better proofe thou canst desire
  than this, of true good will.
I do remember well
  when needs I should away:
And that the poast would licence vs,
  no longer time to stay.
Thou wroongst me by the fist,
  and holding fast my hand:

     Aa. 2.   **Didst**

Didst craue of me to send thee newes,
 and how I likte the land.
It is a sandie soyle,
 no very fruitfull vaine:
More wast and wooddie grounds there are
 than closes fit for graine.
Yet graine there growing is,
 which they vntimely take:
And cut or ere the corne be ripe,
 they mowe it on a stake.
And laying sheafe by sheafe,
 their haruest so they drie:
They make the greater hast,
 for feare the frost the corne destrie.
For in the winter time,
 so glarie is the ground:
As neither grasse nor other graine
 in pastures may be found.
In comes the cattell then,
 the sheepe, the colt, the cowe:
Fast by his bed the Mowsicke
 then a lodging doth alowe.
Whom he with fodder feeds,
 and holds as deare as life:
And thus they weare the Winter with
 the Mowsicke and his wife.
Eight monthes the Winter dures,
 the glare it is so great:

        As

As it is May before he turne
  his ground to sowe his wheate.
The bodies eke that die,
  vnburied lie till then:
Laid vp in coffins made of firre,
  as well the poorest men.
As those of greater state,
  the cause is lightly found:
For that in winter time
  they cannot come to breake the ground.
And wood so plenteous is
  quite throughout all the land:
As rich and poore at time of death,
  assured of coffins stand.
Perhaps thou musest much,
  how this may stand with reason:
That bodies dead, can vncorrupt,
  abide so long a season.
Take this for certaine troth,
  as soone as heate is gone :
The force of cold the body bindes
  as hard as any stone.
Without offence at all,
  to any liuing thing:
And so they lie in perfit state,
  till next returne of spring.
Their beasts be like to ours,
  as far as I can see :

Aa. 3.   For

For shape and show, but somwhat lesse
   of bulke and bone they bee.
Of wattrish taste the flesh not firme,
   like English biefe:
And yet it serues them very well,
   and is a good reliefe.
Their sheep are very small,
   sharpe singled, handfull long:
Great store of fowle on sea and land,
   the moorish reeds among.
The greatnes of the store
   doth make the prices lesse :
Besides, in all the land they know
   not how good meat to dresse.
They vse neither broach nor spit,
   but when the stone they heat,
They put their vitails in a pan,
   and so they bake their meat.
No pewter to be had,
   no dishes but of wood:
No vse of trenchers, cups
   cut out of birch are very good.
They vse but wooden spoones,
   which hanging in a case:
Each Mowsike at his girdle ties,
   and thinks it no disgrace.
With whittles two or three,
   the better man the mo .

                      The

The chiefest Ruſtics in the land,
   with ſpone and kniues do go.
Their houſes are not huge
   of building, but they ſay
They plant them in the loftieſt ground
   to ſhift the ſnow away.
Which in the Winter time
   eche where full thicke doth lie:
Which makes them haue the moꝛe deſire
   to ſet their houſes hie.
No ſtone woꝛke is in vſe,
   their rooſes of rafters beé:
One linked in another faſt,
   their wals are all of treé.
Of maſtes both long and large,
   with moſſe put in betweéne,
To keép the foꝛce of weather out,
   I neuer carſt haue ſeéne.
A groſſe deuiſe ſo good,
   and on the rooſe they lay:
The burthen barke, to rid the raine
   and ſudden ſhowꝛes away.
In euery roome a (ſtoue)
   to ſerue the winter turne:
Of wood they haue ſuffiſing ſtoꝛe,
   as much as they can burne.
They haue no Engliſh glaſſe,
   of ſlices of a rocke

Hight

Hight Sluda, they their windowes make,
    that English glasse doth mocke.
They cut it very thin,
    and sowe it with a thread,
In pretie order like to panes,
    to serue their present need.
No other glasse good faith
    doth giue a better light:
And sure the rocke is nothing rich,
    the cost is very slight.
The chiefest place is that
    where hangs the God vp it:
The owner of the house himselfe,
    doth neuer vse to sit.
Unlesse his better come,
    to whom he yelds the seat:
The stranger bending to the god,
    the ground with browe must beat.
And in that very place,
    which they most sacred deeme:
The stranger layes a token that
    his guest he doth esteeme.
Where he is woont to haue
    a Beares skin for his bed:
And must in stead of pillow
    clap his saddle to his hed.
In Russia other shift
    there is not to be had:

for

for where the bedding is not good,
   the bolsters are but bad.
I mused very much
   what made them so to lie
Sith in their countrey downe is rife,
   and feathers out of cry.
Unlesse it be because
   the countrey is so hard:
They feare by niceues of a bed,
   their bodies would be marde.
I wisht thee oft with vs,
   saue that I stoode in feare
Thou wouldst haue loathed to haue layd,
   thy limmes vpon a beare
As I and Stafford did,
   that was my make in bed:
And yet we thanke the God of heauen,
   we both right wel haue sped.
Loe thus I make an end,
   none other newes to thee:
But that the countrey is too colde
   the people beastly be.
I write not all I know,
   I touch but here and there
for if I should, my pen would pinch,
   and eke offend I feare.
Who so shal reade this verse,
   contecture of the rest:

                        And

And thinke by reason of our trade
   that I doe thinke the best.
But if no traffick were,
   then could I boldly pen
The hardnes of the soyle,
   and eke the manners of the men.
They say the Lyons pawe
   geues iudgement of the beast:
And so may you deeme of the great
   by reading of the least.

To Parker.

My Parker, paper, pen
   and inke were made to write,
And idle heads that litle doe,
   haue leysure to endite
Wherfore respecting these,
   and thine assured loue,
If I would write no newes to thee
   thou mightst my pen reprooue.
And sithens fortune thus,
   hath shoued my ship from shore:
And made me seeke another Realme
   vnseene of me before.
The manners of the men,
   I purpose to declare
And other priuate points beside,
   which strange and geason are.

                  The

The Ruſſie men are round
  of bodies, fully faſt
The greateſt part with bellies big,
  that ouerhang the waſt,
flat headed foz the moſt,
  with faces nothing faire.
But bzowne by reaſon of the ſtoue,
  and cloſenes of the apze.
It is their common vſe,
  to ſhaue oz els to ſheare,
Their heads: foz none in all the land,
  long lolling lockes doe we are.
Vnles perhaps he haue
  his ſoueraigne Pzince diſpleaſde
foz then he neuer cuts his heare,
  vntil he be appeaſde.
A certaine ſigne to know
  who in diſpleaſure be:
foz euery man that vewes his head
  wil ſay, loe this is he.
And during all the time,
  he lets his locks to grow:
Dares no man foz his life,
  to him a face of frendſhip ſhow.
Their garments be not gay,
  noz handſome to the eye:
A cap aloſt their heads they haue
  that ſtandeth very hie.

                         Which

Which(Colpack)they doe tearme
　　they weare no ruffes at al
The best haue collars set with pearle
　　Rubasca they doe call.
Their shirts in Russie long
　　they worke them downe before
And on the sleeues with coloured silkes,
　　two ynches good or more.
Aloft their shirts they weare
　　a garment iacket wise
Hight Onoriadka, and about
　　his bourly wast he ties
His Portkies, which in stead,
　　of better breeches be.
Of linnen cloth that garment is
　　no coopeece is to see
A paire of yornen stockes
　　to keepe the cold away:
Within his bootes the Russie weares,
　　the heeles they vnderlap.
With clouting clamps of steele,
　　sharpe pointed at the toes:
And ouer all a Suba furde,
　　and thus the Russie goes.
Wel butned is the Sube
　　accoding to his state
Some silke, of siluer other some
　　but those of poorest rate

　　　　　　　　Doe

Doe weare no Subes at all
  but grosser gownes to sight:
That reacheth downe beneath the calfe,
  and that Armacha hight.
These are the Russies robes,
  the richest vse to ride
from place to place, his seruant runnes
  and followes vp his side.
The Cassocke beares his scalt,
  to force away the raine:
Their bridles are not very braue,
  their saddles are but plaine.
No bittes, but snaffels all,
  of byrche their saddles be:
Such fashioned like the Scottish seates,
  broad flats to kæpe the knæ.
From sweating of the horse,
  the paunels larger farre
And broader be than ours
  they vse short stirrops for the warre,
For when the Russie is
  pursude by cruel foe
he rides away, and sodenly,
  betakes him to his bowe.
And bendes me but about
  in saddle as he sits
And therewithall amid his race,
  his following foe he hittes.

                              Their

Their bowes are very short,
　　like Turky bowes outright:
Of sinewes made with byrchen barke,
　　in cunning maner dight.
Small arrowes, cruel heads,
　　that fel and forked be:
Which being shot from out those bowes
　　a cruel wayes wil flee.
They seldome shooe their horse,
　　vnlesse they vse to ride
In poast vpon the frozen floods,
　　then cause they shal not slide
He sets a slender talke,
　　and so he rides his way:
The horses of the countrey goe,
　　good fourescore beasts a day
And all without the spurre
　　once prick them and they skip,
But goe not forward on their way,
　　the Russie hath his whip
To rap him on the ribs
　　for though all booted be
Yet shal you not a paire of spurs
　　in all the countrey see,
The common game is chesse
　　almost the simplest wil
Eoth geue a checke and eke a mate,
　　by practise comes their skil.

　　　　　　　　　　　　　　Againe

Againe the dice as fast,
   the poorest roges of all
Wil sit them downe in open field
   and there to gaming fall.
Their dice are very small,
   in fashion like to those
Which we doe vse, he takes them vp,
   and ouer thumbe he throwes,
Not shaking them a whit,
   they cast suspiciously:
And yet I deeme them voyd of arte,
   that dicing most apply.
At playe when siluer lackes,
   goes saddle, horse and all:
And each thing els worth siluer walkes,
   although the price be small.
Because thou louest to play,
   frend Parker, otherwhile
I wish thee there, the weary day,
   with dicing to beguile.
But thou were better farre
   at home, I wist it wel
And wouldst been loath among such loutes
   so long a time to dwel.
Then iudge of vs thy frends,
   what kind of life we had.
That neere the frozen pole to wast
   our weary dayes were glad.

                        In

In such a sauage soyle,
   where lawes doe beare no sway
But all is at the king his wil,
   to saue or els to slay.
And that saunce cause God wot,
   if so his minde be such
But what meane I with kings to deale
   we ought no Saints to touch.
Conceaue the rest your selfe,
   and deeme what liues they leade:
Where lust is law, and subiectes liue
   continually in dread.
And where the best estates,
   haue none assurance good
Of lands, of liues, nor nothing falles
   vnto the next of bloud.
But all of custome doeth
   vnto the Prince redowne:
And all the whole reuenue comes
   vnto the king his crowne.
Good faith I see thee muse,
   at what I tel thee now
But true it is, no choyce
   but all at Princes pleasure bowe.
So Tarquine ruled Rome,
   as thou remembrest well:
And what his fortune was at last,
   I know thy selfe canst tell.

                    Where

Where will in common weale,
 doth beare the onely sway :
And lust is law, the prince and realme
 must needs in time decay.
The strangenesse of the place is such
 for sundry things I see :
As if I would, I cannot write
 each priuate point to thee.
The cold is rare, the people rude,
 the prince so full of pride :
The realm so stord with monks & nunnes,
 and priests on euery side.
The mauers are so Turkylike,
 the men so full of guile :
The women wanton, temples stuft
 with idols that defile.
The seats that sacred ought to be,
 the customs are so quaint :
As if I would describe the whole,
 I feare my pen would faint.
In summe I say, I neuer saw
 a prince that so did raigne :
Nor people so beset with Saincts,
 yet all but vile and vaine.
Wild Irish are as ciuil as
 the Rusties in their kind :
Hard choice which is the best of both,
 each bloodie rude, and blind.

    L t.   If

If thou be wise, as wise thou art,
  and wilt be rulde by mee :
Liue still at home, and couet not,
  those barbarous coasts to see.
No good befals a man that seekes,
  and finds no better place :
No ciuil customs to be learnd,
  where God bestowes no grace.
And truly ill they do deserue,
  to be beloued of God:
That neither loue, nor stand in awe
  of his assured rod.
Which (thogh be long) yet plagues at last
  the vile and beastly sort
Of sinfull wights, that all in vice
  do place their chiefest sport.
Adieu friend *Parker*, if thou list,
  to know the Russies well:
To *Sigismundus* booke repaire,
  who all the truth can tell.
For he long earst in message went,
  vnto that sauage king:
Sent by the *Pole*, and true report
  in each respect did bring.
To him I recommend my selfe,
  to ease my pen of paine :
And now at last do wish thee well,
  and bid farewell againe.

                           To

To his friend Nicholas Roscarock to induce him to take a wife.

Roscarocke, sith my raging prime is past,
And riper age with reasons learned lore,
Well staied hath my wits that went so fast,
And cold the heat that hent my brest of yore:
I cannot choose but write some solemne stuffe,
for thee to read, when thou art in thy ruffe.

I see thee muse what should the matter be,
Whereof I meane to treate, thou bitest thy lip,
And benost thy browe as though I were not he
That had a tricke my Cornish friend to trip:
Well, to be short, it toucheth mariage vow,
An order which my selfe haue entred now.

A sacred yoke, a state of mickle praise,
A blessed band, belikt of God and man,
And such a life, as if in former dayes
I had but knowen, as now commend I can,
God faith I would not wasted so my prime,
In wanton wise, and spent an idle time.

An idle time, as sundry gallants vse,
I meane my London mates, that tread the streete,
And golden wits with fond conceits abuse,
And base deuises farre for such vnmeet.
                    Eb.2.   Leauing

Leauing the law, and casting bookes aside,
Wherby in time you mought your countries guide.

Your daily practise is to beat the bush,
Where beauties birds do lodge themselues to lie:
You shoote at shapes and faces deare a rush,
And bend your bowes, your feeble strengths to trie.
Of closure you somtimes do common make,
And where you list, abroad your pleasures take.

You count it but a game to graffe the horne
That inward growes, and seldom shewes without:
The silly man you skoffe and laugh to skorne,
And for his pacience deeme him but a lout.
By day you gaze vpon your Ladies lookes,
By night you gad to hang your baited hookes.

Thus do you lauish frolike youth away,
With idle words not woorth a parched pease,
And like to wanton colts that run astray,
You leape the pale, and into euery lease.
Where fitter far it were to marry wiues,
And well disposd to lead more sober liues.

Reuolt in tyme, least time repentance bring,
Let each enioy his lawfull wedded mate,
Or else be sure, your selues in time shall sing
The selfesame note, and rue your harmes too late.

F oz

For commonly the wrong that we entend,
Lights on our heads and shoulders in the end.

Perhaps thou wouldst as willing wedded be,
As I my selfe and many other moe:
But that thou canst no perfit beautie sée,
For which thou wilt thy single life forgoe.
Both yong & faire, with wealth & goods thou séekst,
Such one she is, whom thou *Roscarocke* léekst.

Be rulde by me, let giddy fansie go,
Imbrace a wife, with wealth and coyne enough:
Force not the face, regard not feature so,
An aged grandame that maintains the plough.
And brings thée bags, is worth a thousand peates,
That pranck their pates & liue by Spanish meates.

That one contents hir self with now and than,
Right glad if she might sit at Venus messe
Once in the moneth, the youthfull Damsell can
Not so be pleasd, hir rage must haue redresse,
As oft as pleasure pricks hir lims to lust,
Els all the matter lies amid the dust.

Wherfore I iudge the best and wisest way
Were wise to wed, and leaue to range at will,
In maried life there is assured stay,
Where otherwise to follow euery Gill,
　　　　Bb. 3.　　　　Frœds

Bredes wracke of wealth, of credit, ease, and blisse,
And makes men run their races quite amisse.

Experto credere tutum est.

A gentlewomans excuse for executing vn-
lawfull partes of loue.

Erst *Sylla* tooke no shame, for *Minos* sake
Hir father *Nysus* purple pate to sheare,
Medea for the loue of *Iason* brake
The bands of kind, and slew hir brother deare,
Forwent hir worthy Sire, and kingly crowne,
And followed him the rouer vp and downe.

For *Theseus* when in Labirinth he lay
In dread of death, the monster was so nie,
Faire *Ariadna* did deuise a way
To saue his life, vnlesse that *Ouid* lie,
And yet the beast, hir brother was in deed,
(Whom *Theseus* slue) and sprang of *Minos* seed.

At siege of *Troy* whilest *Agamemnon* fought,
Aegistheus wan Quéene *Clitemnestras* hart,
So as when he returnd and little thought
Of death, this dame began to play hir part,
She slew the prince to folow former lust,
And thought the fact to be excéeding iust.

                                      Faire

Faire *Phyllis* flew hir felfe, vnhappy dame
Through loue: and did not *Dydo* do the like
For Prince *Aeneas* who to *Carthage* came,
When he was forft, by fhowres the fhore to feeke:
What more vnkindly parts can man deuife,
Than Quæns for loue their honors to defpife?

Now iudge my cafe, my fault vprightly fcan,
Dæme my defart, by this it may be geft,
I am by nature made to loue a man,
As *Sylla*, *Phyllis*, *Dido*, and the reft,
If they and I haue done amiffe for loue,
Let kind be blamd, that thereunto did mœue.
 The wifeft men as farre as I can fee,
 Haue been enthrald through loue as well as we.
 Amor vince ogni cofa.

Of his Conftancie.

WE way not waxe, for all his gallant hew,
 Bicaufe it vades and melts againft the fire,
We more regard a rocke of marble blew,
For that no force doth caufe it to retire,
The builder makes his full account, that it
Will firmly ftand at a ftay, and neuer flit.

So may you (fwæte) be fure, that my good will
Is no good will of waxe, to wafte away,
 When

When fond desire of fansie hath his fill,
My loue is like the marble for his stay,
Build thereupon, and you shall surely find,
No blast of chance to change my stedfast mind.

Blacke shall you sée the snow on mountains hie,
The fish shall féed vpon the barren sand,
The sea shal shrinke, and leaue the Dolphins dry,
No plant shall prooue vpon the sencelesse land,
The Temis shal turne, the Sunne shal lose his light
Ere I to thée become a faithlesse wight.

I neither am nor meane to bee,
None other than I seeme to thee.

The Authors Epilogue.

LO here the end of all my worke,
    behold the thréed I drew
Is wrought to cloth, accomplisht now,
    you sée this slender clew.
A péece (God wot) of little price,
    scarce woorth the Readers paine :
And in mine owne conceit
    a booke of barren verse and vaine.
I blush to let it out at large
    for Sages to peruse:
For that the common custome is,
    in bookes to gape for newes.

                                    And

And matter of importance great
  which either may delite
By pleasure, or with sad aduise
  the readers paynes requite.
But this of mine so maymed is,
  for lacke of learned stile
And stately stuffe, as sure I shall
  the readers hope beguile.
Who doth expect some rare report,
  of former ancient dædes:
Or new deuice but lately wrought,
  that breatheth yet and blædes.
But truely none of both in these,
  my verses is to finde:
My slender ship hath kept the shore,
  for feare of boystrous winde.
I bore my simple sayles but lowe
  I dreaded sodaine showers:
Which sundry times from hauty skies,
  the puisant ruler powers.
I durst not stir amid the streame,
  the chanel was too dæpe:
Which made me haue the more regard
  about the bankes to kæpe.
It is for mighty hulkes to dare,
  aduenture out so farre:
And barkes of biggest sise,
  and such as builded be for warre.

                I

I write but of familiar ſtuffe,
   becauſe my ſtile is lower
I feare to wade in weighty workes,
   or paſt my reach to rowe.
Which if I ſhould, the Reader might
   as boldly blame my quil:
As now I truſt he ſhal accept,
   my ſhew of great good wil.
Though diuers write with fuller phraſe,
   and farre more hawty ſtile:
And burniſh out their golden bookes
   with fine and learned file.
Yet meaner Muſes muſt not lurke
   but each in his degrè
That meaneth wel, and doth his beſt
   muſt wel regarded be,
Though Nilus for his bignes beare
   away the greateſt name:
Whoſe ſcuffold ſtream hath gaind ẏ gulfe
   of ſuch a laſting fame.
Yet muſt not leſſer lakes be loſt,
   nor had in vile account
That ſerue for vſe and eaſe of man
   though Nilus doe ſurmount.
Great Alexander mighty was
   and dreadful in the warre:
Yet thats no cauſe why Rome ſhould not
   of Cæſar boaſt as farre.

                         The

The Planets are the pride of heauen,
and chéefest lampes of light:
Yet other starres doe yelde a shew
and helpe to cléere the night.

Likewise though diuers write in verse
and doe exceeding wel:
The remnant must not be refusde,
because they doe excell.

Ill may we misse the slender shrubs
for all the princely Pine:
No more we scorne the baser drinkes
though most we way the wine.

Which makes me hope that though
my Muse doth yelde but slender sound:
And though my Culter scarcely cuts,
or breakes the marble ground.

Yet sithens that I meant with verse,
to féede the Readers eyes:
And to that purpose bent my braines
these fancies to deuise.

I trust he takes it wel in worth
and beares with what he findes.
And thereunto the Reader aye
the writers trauaile bindes.

Which if he doe I haue my hire,
who happy then but I?
That wrote this worke for grateful men,
to vewe with thankfull eye.

                                        And

And so I giue the congé now,
   with wish that this my booke
Be such as may thy sprites delight,
   that hapnest here to looke.
Ill were my fortune if in all
   this treatise as it standes:
There should be nothing worth the vew
   when so it comes to hand.
Roscarockes warrant shal suffise
   who likte the writing so
As did embolden me to let
   the leaues at large to goe.
If il succæde, the blame was his
   who might haue kept it backe:
And frendly tolde me that my booke
   his due deuise did lacke.
But as it is, loe there it goes,
   for euery one to vew:
The man that each ones humor pleasde,
   as yet I neuer knew.
Sufficeth if the courtly sort
   whose doome is dæpe in dæde:
Accompt it ought, with baser wits
   I care not how it spæde.
The courtier knowes what best becomes,
   in euery kind of case:
His nature is, what so he doth
   to decke with gallant grace,

                          The

The greatest clarkes in other artes,
  can hardly doe the leeke:
for learning sundry times is there
  where iudgement is to seeke.

The Authors excuse for writing these
  and other fancies, with promise of
    grauer matter hereafter.

Lordings allow my light and lewde deuise
And Ladies ye that are of greatest state
Beare with my bookes, imputing nought to vice
That I haue pende in youth, nor now of late,
My prime prouokt my hasty idle quil:
To write of loue, when I did meane no ill.

  Two things in cheefe did moue me thus to write
And made me deeme it none offence at all,
first *Ouids* workes bedeckt with deepe delight,
Whom we of Poets second best doe call,
I found him full of amours euery where:
Each leafe of loue the title eke did beare.

  Then next I liued in place among the moe,
Where fond affection bore the cheefest sway,
And where the blinded archer with his bow
Did glaunce at sundry gallants euery day
And being there although my minde were free:
Yet must I seeme loue wounded eke to be.

                              I

I sawe how some did séeke their owne mishap,
And hunted dayly to deuoure the hookes,
That beuty bayted, and were caught in trap,
Like wilfull wights that fed on womens lookes,
Who being once entangled in the line,
Did yelde themselues and were content to pine.

Some other minding least to follow loue,
By haunting where dame Uenus darlings dwelt,
By force were forst Cupidos coales to proue.
Whose burning brāds did make their minds to melt
So as they were compeld by méere mischaunce,
As others did, to follow on the daunce.

Some eke there were that groapt but after gaine
That fayad to frie and burne with blooming heate
Of raging loue and counterfetted paine,
When they (God wot) had slender cause to treate,
But all was done to make their Ladies déeme
How greatly they their beuties did estéeme.

And then (O gods) to vew their graeful chéeres,
And listen to their fonde lamenting cries,
To sée their chéekes déepe dented in with teares
That day and night powred out from painful eyes,
Would make a heart of marble melt for woe,
That sawe their plights, & did their sorowes know

And all for lacke of ruthe and due remorse
Their cruel Ladies bore so hard a hand,
And they (poore men) constraynd to loue perforce,
And fruitlesse cleane to sowe the barrain sand.

                                   That

That vnto me who pziuie was of all,
It was a death and grieued me to the gall.

Then foz my friends (as diuers loued me well)
Enuite I muſt ſome light deuiſe of loue,
And in the ſame my friends affection tell,
Whom nothing mought from beauties bar remoue
My pen muſt plead the ſillie Suters caſe,
I had my hire,ſo he mought purchaſe grace.

Some otherwhile when beautie bzed diſdaine,
And feature foztt a pzide in hawtie bzeſt,
So as my friend whs cauſeleſſe put to paine
And foz good will might purchace ſlender reſt :
Then muſt my quill to quarels flatly fall,
yet kéep the meane twixt ſwéete and ſower bzall.

Somtimes I muſt commed their beauties much
That neuer came where any beautie lay,
Againe ſomwhiles my mates would haue me tuch
The quicke,bicauſe they had recciued the nay:
And thus my pen,as change of matter grew,
Was foztt to grief, oz els foz grace to ſue,

Thus did I deale foz others pleaſure long
As who could well réfuſe to do the like)
And foz my ſelf ſomtimes would wzite among
As he that liues with men of war muſt ſtrike.
I would deuiſe a Sonet to a dame,
And all to make my ſullen humoz game.

So long I wzote,ſo oft my friends did ſue,
So many were the matters,as at laſt.

The

The whole vnto a hansome volume grewe,
Then to the presse they must in all the hast,
Mauger my beard, my mates would haue it so
Whom to resist it was in vaine you know.

These causes forst my harmeles hand to write,
And no desire I had to treate of ill
Who doth not know that youthfull heads delight
Sometimes to shewe the queintnes of their quil,
But pardon (Lordings) what is past and done
I purpose now a better race to runne.

I meane no more with loues deuise to deale,
I neuer wil to wanton Venus bowe,
From Cupids court to Pallas I appeale,
Iuno be iudge whom I doe honor now
Hie time it is for him to blow retreate:
And leaue to loue whom selfe rod now doth beate.

Wherfore, goe (wanton) trusse vp all your trash
Fancy farewel, to grauer gods I goe,
Then loue and Venus, cleane my hands I wash,
Of vayne desires that youth enrageth so
Vertue doth faire surmount such filthy vice
Amend my mates, or els you know the price.

Vtile consilium est sanas extinguere flammas,
Qui non est hodie, cras minus aptus erit.

FINIS.